Praise for *Extraordinary Grace*

Chapman and Fabry never disappoint. Enjoy this fresh look at the gift of grace and **you'll be thrilled anew at the redeeming miracle of unmerited favor.**

> ~**JERRY B. JENKINS**, novelist, biographer, and Owner, Christian Writers Guild

Who knew that Jesus' family tree could be so encouraging? For most of us, reading the genealogy of Matthew 1 is something we do once a year to get to the "good part" of the story. Gary Chapman and Chris Fabry show us how that long list of names belongs in the "good part" of the Good News of Jesus. For anyone who feels like you don't measure up, take time to read *Extraordinary Grace*. **There were some real rascals up in the limbs of Jesus' family tree. If there is room for them, there is room for you and me.** Read this book and then rejoice in the "extraordinary grace" that brought Jesus from heaven to earth. **Read it! Study it! Share it!**

> ~**DR. RAY PRITCHARD**, author, *An Anchor for the Soul,* and president, Keep Believing Ministries

EXTRAORDINARY GRACE

*How the Unlikely Lineage of Jesus
Reveals God's Amazing Love*

GARY CHAPMAN &
CHRIS FABRY

MOODY PUBLISHERS

CHICAGO

All Scripture quotations, unless otherwise indicated, are taken from the Holman Christian Standard Bible ®, Copyright © 1999, 2000, 2002, 2003 by Holman Bible Publishers. Used by permission. Holman Christian Standard Bible®, Holman CSB®, and HCSB® are federally registered trademarks of Holman Bible Publishers.

Scripture quotations marked NASB are taken from the New American Standard Bible® Copyright © 1960, 1962, 1963, 1968, 1971, 1972, 1973, 1975, 1977, 1995 by The Lockman Foundation. Used by permission. (www.Lockman.org)

Scripture quotations marked KJV are taken from the King James Version.

Scripture quotations marked NIV are taken from the *Holy Bible, New International Version* ®, NIV® Copyright © 1973, 1978, 1984, 2011 by Biblica, Inc.™ Used by permission of Zondervan. All rights reserved worldwide. www.zondervan.com. The "NIV" and "New International Version" are trademarks registered in the United States Patent and Trademark Office by Biblica, Inc.™

Interior design: Ragont Design
Cover design: Brock, Sharp & Associates / DBA Faceout Studio
Cover image: Getty image / 157775494
Author photos: Gary Chapman-P.S. Photography / Chris Fabry-Herb Wetzel

ISBN: 978-0-8024-1079-5

We hope you enjoy this book from Moody Publishers. Our goal is to provide high-quality, thought-provoking books and products that connect truth to your real needs and challenges. For more information on other books and products written and produced from a biblical perspective, go to www.moodypublishers.com or write to:

Moody Publishers
820 N. LaSalle Boulevard
Chicago, IL 60610

1 3 5 7 9 10 8 6 4 2

Printed in the United States of America

To

C. Donald Cole and Naomi Cole,

full of grace and truth

Grace isn't a little prayer you chant
before receiving a meal. It's a way to live.

D. L. MOODY

'Twas grace that brought me safe thus far . . .
And grace will lead me home.

JOHN NEWTON

CONTENTS

The historical record of Jesus Christ, the Son of David, the Son of Abraham

Abraham fathered Isaac,
Isaac fathered Jacob,
Jacob fathered Judah and his brothers,
Judah fathered Perez and Zerah by Tamar,
Perez fathered Hezron,
Hezron fathered Aram,
Aram fathered Amminadab,
Amminadab fathered Nahshon,
Nahshon fathered Salmon,
Salmon fathered Boaz by Rahab,
Boaz fathered Obed by Ruth,
Obed fathered Jesse,
and Jesse fathered King David.

Then David fathered Solomon by Uriah's wife,
Solomon fathered Rehoboam,
Rehoboam fathered Abijah,
Abijah fathered Asa,
Asa fathered Jehoshaphat,
Jehoshaphat fathered Joram,
Joram fathered Uzziah,

Uzziah fathered Jotham,
Jotham fathered Ahaz,
Ahaz fathered Hezekiah,
Hezekiah fathered Manasseh,
Manasseh fathered Amon,
Amon fathered Josiah,
and Josiah fathered Jechoniah and his brothers
at the time of the exile to Babylon.

Then after the exile to Babylon
Jechoniah fathered Shealtiel,
Shealtiel fathered Zerubbabel,
Zerubbabel fathered Abiud,
Abiud fathered Eliakim,
Eliakim fathered Azor,
Azor fathered Zadok,
Zadok fathered Achim,
Achim fathered Eliud,
Eliud fathered Eleazar,
Eleazar fathered Matthan,
Matthan fathered Jacob,
and Jacob fathered Joseph the husband of Mary,
who gave birth to Jesus who is called the Messiah.

Authors' Note

The stories you're about to read come directly from the Bible. We encourage you to read them in the original source. Our approach for this book is to look at the story with fresh eyes, imagining the struggles these real people endured. They had faults, foibles, sins, and triumphs, just like we do. As God used them, warts and all, so may He use us today.

Introduction

You can choose many things in life, but your lineage is not one of them. You can't choose your parents. Or your ancestors. You're stuck with what you get, good or bad or in-between.

Except for Jesus.

Ponder this fact: Jesus was the only person in history who chose His mother, father, grandmothers, and grandfathers all the way to the beginning of time.

So who did He choose? People who obeyed God and showed great faith? Sinless, perfect people who always did what was right?

Hardly. Those people didn't exist, of course.

What do you know of your family tree? You may have pictures on a wall or in faded photo albums. These wrinkled faces represent stories shared and passed down. Lore, lies, and truth mixed and matched. You see the eyes, you recognize a little of yourself in their smiles, but most never read between the lines. Most never know the heart of their ancestors.

The Bible contains this kind of record of the lineage of

Jesus. Men and women who bare their souls in the struggle to know God and follow Him in challenging times. The fascinating thing about these stories is that they reveal more than the foibles and follies of desperate human beings. They also record the heart of God. The lineage of Jesus is a litmus of the love, mercy, and longsuffering of the Almighty toward His people. Toward you.

This record includes good news for your heart: 1) God is not mad at you, 2) God wants to lavish His love and blessing on you and, 3) God wants you to reflect His grace to others.

Of course, you've heard this news before. Grace has a popular acrostic:

Grace = **G**od's **R**iches **A**t **C**hrist's **E**xpense.

Everyone's heard of grace. But not everyone understands it. Not everyone receives it. And even fewer learn to give it. *Do you?*

Have you received it? Are you living in light of it? Are you expressing God's grace to others?

This is a dangerous book because it's a mind-blowing, heart-altering concept. It's threatening to the religious establishment that wishes to keep people in line. This is one reason religious leaders were so threatened by Jesus.

God wants you to receive His grace, possess it, and extend

it. It's a process that will change you from the inside out. You were created to receive, experience, and extend that kind of love every day to your family and friends.

Even your enemies.

This is not an intellectual concept for the brain or simply an ethereal, spiritual theorem. Grace is not a mystical, impossible-to-apprehend idea. It's a practical, hands-on exercise that will help you live fully, from the heart, rather than from obligation or expectation.

What would your life look like if you knew, somewhere deep inside, you absolutely *knew* you were forgiven? Accepted? Deeply loved? Embraced? What if you knew someone was looking at you with wonder and awe? What if someone saw you as perfect?

Read that again. *Perfect.*

No blemish, no spots, no defects. No wrong motives. No sin. Perfect.

That "someone" is God Himself. And He is the One who provides the grace to make perfection a reality.

Most followers of Jesus don't live this way. We know we're not perfect. So we compensate by clenching our fists and trying to please God. By sheer willpower, we will get on God's good side. This lasts about a half hour on a good day.

So we live defeated. We lose at life because we cannot be good enough. We cannot please God and never will because He will always look over heaven's portal with His arms crossed, shaking His head.

The problem lies in the chasm that exists between God's demands and our ability. Only one person has ever been able to bridge the gap.

The message of this book is that there is an extraordinarily better way. Here it is: God's love stripped bare. Hanging on a cross. Paying the penalty. Offering forgiveness. Cutting a new path of freedom for you to walk. A path where mercy bids you leave your guilt and shame behind. A path with a hand on your shoulder to guide you.

Let this truth wash over you. God has chosen to give you extraordinary, extravagant, exceptional *grace*. John Newton, the old slave trader, had no reason to claim God's love. He called it "amazing." It crosses the border of the unthinkable. We don't deserve to be treated like this. But here it is. God's grace.

This is a study of God at work among ordinary people. Our travels will take us through a massively dysfunctional family tree. These are not stories for the faint of heart. We will chart seven major characters in the genealogy of Jesus.

Seven people who failed, fell, or chose badly, but God used them mightily. Their failure was not final. Their past did not exclude them from God's love. Their sin did not determine their destiny.

And neither does yours. No matter what you've done, where you've been, what bad thing has been done to you, or what bad things you have done, the grace of God and His extravagant love are available.

When God sent the Word made flesh to dwell among us, He gave us the perfect representation of this extraordinary grace. In fact, if you look at the hinge-point of history, you will see the Creator of the universe nailed to two beams of wood, hanging between the incomparable need of every human heart and the undying love of God. This cursed God/man reveals God's extraordinary grace.

Father, forgive them; for they know not what they do.

Perhaps you've been following Jesus for years, but you feel aimless. Perhaps you know about Jesus, but you have no idea what "abundant life" means. Maybe you're skeptical that God even exists.

Wherever you are, whatever your background, these stories cry out about the incomparable, unbelievable love of God. Anyone willing to abandon their efforts to please God through their own efforts can receive the righteousness of Jesus. And once you receive this grace, you can begin to live fully from its power, and you will draw from that well of forgiveness and extend that to others.

Dare to take God at His word. Dare to believe. And see what He will do in and through you by His extraordinary grace.

PART 1

RECEIVING GOD'S GRACE

I do not at all understand the mystery of grace—only that it meets us where we are but does not leave us where it found us.

Anne Lamott

Chapter 1

Hearing the Call of Grace

ABRAM

The story of Abram begins before he is born. God was at work in the world. He created everything we can see and can't see. He created the first man and woman and watched as they chose disobedience. He fashioned animal skins to cover them. Their choice had consequences. They were forced to leave God's presence.

And when people had walked so far from His plan, God spoke to Noah and had him build a boat. The ark was salvation for Noah and his family. Those outside perished. Those inside lived. And from that remnant, people and animals populated the earth. But people continued to walk away from God. They believed in themselves, not in Him, and built a tower to show *their strength. So God confused their language and scattered them.*

And it was to one of these scattered people, at just the right time, that God spoke clearly. God invaded the heart of a man named Abram with fantastic words and unbelievable promises.

Abram chose to believe.

God said He would bless Abram, He would make his name great, and He would bless the entire world through his descendants. Abram's job was to believe. Then, acting on that belief, he was to leave his relatives and his country for a place God would provide. And believing, he would leave and then possess God's promises.

Abram packed and left everything he knew because God had given a promise. These are the first steps of Abram. This is the call of grace.[1]

The journey of a thousand miles begins with a single step. The journey of grace begins with hearing its call. And grace is calling you. It may sound distant, like a train whistle across a barren landscape, but grace is calling every heart. And the grace we're talking about will not be thwarted. As

John Newton wrote, it will "lead us home."

Your responsibility is to listen to this whisper. You have to be *willing to hear.*

Which brings us to Abraham, known early on as Abram. Here was a man ready for the call of grace.

Fifteen chapters in Genesis tell us about Abraham's journey, God's covenant with him, the promises He made, and how you and I are affected by those promises today. He had moved with his father, Terah, and extended family to a place called Ur. They had carved out a pretty nice life. Abram had married a woman named Sarai. He hit the beauty jackpot with her, which was both a blessing and a curse. Her beauty would cause him to make some bad choices. Actually, it wasn't her beauty; it was Abram's fear. But we're getting ahead of ourselves.

After Terah died, Abram received a message from God.

Stop and consider that. Direct communication from the Almighty. Have you ever desired such a thing? Have you ever said, "If God would just tell me what to do, I would gladly do it"?

Really?

If God were to speak to you right now, part the clouds, His voice booming, would you listen? Would you obey immediately? Or would you question? Would you doubt it was really God—wonder if perhaps you were dreaming or if it might have been the spicy salsa during yesterday's dinner?

"Could You tell me that one more time, please? And let me get my recorder."

Here's the truth. You don't need a bass voice from the clouds. God has spoken—not the way you might desire, but He has spoken through His Word made flesh, through the Scriptures, through the lives of believers throughout the centuries. The question is not whether God will speak. He has. The question is, are you willing to listen? Will you *hear*?

Abram was willing. This is what God said:

Go out from your land, your relatives, and your father's house to the land that I will show you.

That's pretty straightforward. Leave everything you've known, all the people who know your language, your customs, your relatives clamoring to help raise your children—just pick up, pack, and go. Put your future, your family, your fortune, and your life as you know it completely in My hands.

Oh, and by the way, I'm not going to tell you where you're going. You don't get to know the specific destination. It could be a beautiful place; it could be a desert. You have one job.

Trust Me. You don't get a postcard picture of your final destination. But no matter where I send you, no matter where you go, you have Me. And this process of leaving will begin to change you on the inside. You will be forced to firmly put your affection on Me, not on an object or a destination or a feeling or even the knowledge of My will. This is not about you finding a decoder ring or reading between the lines of what I'm saying and counting every fifth letter for the secret message. I don't want you trusting your own holiness, some idol you can fashion with your hands, or something you can conjure up in your mind. You must want Me and no other. Period. This is faith. And those who put their faith in Me receive extraordinary grace.

At this point in the story we're not told of any response Abram had to God's voice. We can assume he was a little shocked to be receiving such communication, for in all of Scripture there is a fair amount of fear and trembling and falling to the ground when angels or God Himself speaks. It's a bit unnerving.

But this was not the end of the heavenly communique. God continued with the second half of His message. This is where it gets really good.

I will make you into a great nation, I will bless you, I will make your name great, and you will be a blessing. I will bless those who bless you, I will curse those who treat you with contempt, and all the peoples on earth will be blessed through you.

Wow. Let's process the message. You need to move. Now. And I'm going to bring you into a land I've chosen. And in the midst of this I will do extraordinary things in and through you. You will be blessed and you will bless others. (Which means that your life and the lives of those who come after you will be made wildly different because of your obedience.) And those who get in your way are in My way. In other words, I'm with you, Abram. You and I are a team. And I, Yahweh, the Lord, I'm the one doing this. You obey Me. Follow Me. That's your part in this plan.

Deep breath.

Okay, did you get all of that? God is for Abram. Frankly, I'm a little jealous. (I keep thinking how great it would be to hear directly from God.) I get that God is directing Abram, telling him what to do and where to go, and that the end of this story will be great blessing for Abram and those who come after him. We're still talking about him today, thousands of years later, so it's clear God was right. This man was abundantly, amazingly blessed.

But wait. Think about the question behind the story, lurking under the surface of the promises and blessings.

Why? Why Abram? Why did God give him the privilege of hearing this directive? Why did He choose to bless Abram and all his descendants? Why was God even thinking of this man? *What is man that You remember him?* A descendant of Abram would later pen that in Psalm 8.

The answer isn't that Abram was the special one God knew would follow perfectly, because he didn't. He made mistakes. Lots of them. He was flawed, fallible, and not a good example for the kids in Sunday school you want to teach to always be honest. In fact, all of the ancestors of Jesus were of similar make and model. They messed up their lives in a thousand ways.

Did God choose Abram because he was wealthy and God needed a lot of livestock? No, He owns it all. He didn't need Abram's wealth or beautiful wife. The only ability God needed from Abram is the same ability He desires from you: availability. And if you are not available, He will use stones or donkeys.

Why did God choose Abram?

The answer to this can only be found in the mysterious grace of God. His unmerited, undeserved, and unlimited favor was poured out on this man. Extraordinary grace.

To his credit, Abram obeyed, packed up, and at seventy-five began a journey that started with hearing God. He listened and followed. His belief affected his actions and he was given credit for his faith.

But do you think Abram struggled? As they were loading up his possessions (imagine the yard sale!) and saying goodbye to those left behind, do you think there were questions? Were there conversations in the tent at night with Sarai?

"Go over this one more time and tell me what He said. Are you sure about this, Abram?"

Perhaps Sarai had heard the message from a distance. Perhaps she had such great trust in Abram that she simply turned and began to pack without question.

Hearing the call of grace forces you to decide. Follow or stay? (And indecision is a decision.) But any struggle like this leads to questions. More questions than you had before God spoke. God will complicate your life when He whispers His grace, and this seems counterintuitive. Hearing from God should make things easier. Now you know what to do. In Abram's case, he knew specifically how to respond. But the voice of God will put such a radical call on your life that it will force you to wrestle with yourself, the people you love, and your stuff.

The followers of Jesus had the same experience. He brought so many more questions because they realized His call on their life was not superficial but subterranean. He didn't just want them to adhere to a list of rules and regulations like the religious leaders of the day. He didn't want daily devotions and showing up at a weekend service. He didn't want to make His followers better. He wanted to transform them through the process of grace—the same process Abram learned through hearing the voice of God.

Following the call of grace will become the seedbed of faith. And these questions are good, for the person with questions must learn to trust not themselves but in God's power and direction.

"Trust in the Lord with all your heart, and do not rely on your own understanding; think about Him in all your ways, and He will guide you on the right paths."

Abram lived that proverb. Abram embodied those words. And another of his offspring would pen them. Another man in the line of Jesus. Another flawed human being who was graciously used by God.

Grace will uproot you. Grace will relocate your heart. Grace will move you so far toward God that, in the end, you won't care how much the moving van costs. In fact, you may want to leave some of that stuff behind because it will weigh you down. Grace liberates and casts a vision for your life you could never predict. Grace changes you; it is a holy transfusion giving you the power and ability to pass the same grace on to others, for you can only give what you possess.

Abram heard. Abram responded. He believed. Not perfectly. Not without trying to take control, which we'll talk about next.

Are you ready for this kind of grace? Would you like transformation instead of a limited makeover? Listen for the whisper of grace in your life. He is drawing you to a thousand-mile journey of the heart.

Chapter 2

Laughing Because of Grace

ABRAHAM

*A*bram *heard the call of grace and believed. Then he acted. He took his wife, family, and possessions and headed for Canaan. "Are we there yet?" was the continual question of his own heart.*

God affirmed His promise at an oak tree at Moreh. Abram's "offspring" would inherit this land.

However (and there's always a however with Abram), a famine struck and Abram traveled to Egypt. The beauty of his wife and the fear in his heart overtook him. He told the Egyptians a half-truth that his wife was his sister. Sarai was taken into Pharaoh's palace and God plagued that house.

Pharaoh confronted Abram and asked why he didn't tell

the whole truth. Abram learned the lesson. Don't lie about your wife. Don't try to control the situation because you're afraid. God will take care of you.

Then it was back on the road. His wealth and possessions increased. But there was no heir, no son of the promise.

Years later, as if God did not know this, Abram informed the Almighty that He hadn't kept His bargain. God spoke again and said Abram would have a son. In fact, he wouldn't be able to count the number of people coming through his line.

Abram believed God.

Then Abram heard the voice of his wife. Fear rose up again. Sarai suggested that Hagar, her handmaiden, be the surrogate for God's promise. And Abram slept with Hagar and Ishmael was conceived.

Like a daisy in the field, Abram believed, he believed not. He believed, then he took control.

Much later, Abram, who was renamed Abraham (father of many) by God Himself, had another chance to trust God. He moved into an area where Abimelech ruled and he again said that his wife was his sister. God warned the king and Abimelech was furious with Abraham.

The pattern was set. Abraham was moved by his belief and trust in God, then he became weak and fell. But God's grace *brought forth the promised son, in spite of Abraham's failure. This is the grace of God at work.*[2]

You're seventy-five and you're starting over. You're seventy-five and you're building your own U-Haul, like Noah built his ark. You're seventy-five, without a child, and you've been told that you'll become a great nation.

You'll have many offspring, Abram. And one of those off-spring, way down the line, will be the promised Messiah, the fulfillment of God's plan set in motion from before the beginning of creation.

What a promise! What a future!

But there's a problem. You're seventy-five, for crying out loud. And you don't have any children. And your wife is—well, she's beautiful but barren. You see no children and you ask questions. How can this be? How will this happen?

We don't have a record of Abram saying, "Yeah, but . . ." We're told that Abram packed up, gathered up, and left. He believed and acted on that belief. He exhibited faith, a work of grace that began with God's message. He *believed* what God said.

Hearing is the first step of faith. Believing is the second step. Acting on that belief, moving out, is the third.

When he and his family reached the great tree of Moreh at Shechem, God spoke again. Want to know how far that was? About four hundred miles. And he didn't have a GPS or an app for his phone. That's a little farther than a trip from Chicago to Lexington, Kentucky. Or Atlanta to Jackson, Mississippi. And there wasn't a McDonald's in sight. And there were no interstate highways.

That's a long way to travel on foot. That's a big commitment. A lot of steps of faith. But remember, Abram didn't know how far he was going or how long it would take. He simply had God's word, His promises.

So he wound up at a tree near Moreh. God created a garden with a tree and created the first man and woman. Now he meets Abram at a tree, a sign and symbol of growth and beauty and life. There are many people already living in this fertile area, but God appears to Abram and says, "I will give this land to your offspring."

This must have made Abram at least cock his head in wonder. He probably saw the Canaanites in the land, the Canaanite children roaming the hillside, and pondered how this would become reality since he was already seventy-five and his wife was barren.

Maybe God is speaking metaphorically? Maybe God was really saying, "To others' offspring . . ."

No, the promise was clear. Abram would have offspring. Children. God was not only promising something to Abram, He was promising something to people who didn't yet exist. Grace to the unborn. Grace to Abram's family tree.

By extension, grace to you and me.

Abram built an altar to God there and moved again and built another altar and continued in the direction God led, toward the Negev.

And here the story turns dark. Because of a famine, Abram heads to Egypt and just as they're crossing the border, as an undocumented traveler, Abram's fear rises.

"I know what a beautiful woman you are," he says to Sarai.

Husbands, this is not a bad way to start a conversation with your wife. Pointing out her beauty is a good thing. I call it "words of affirmation." But the results of Abram's actions that followed were devastating.

"When the Egyptians see you," Abram continued, "they will say, 'This is his wife.' They will kill me but let you live.

Please say you're my sister so it will go well for me because of you, and my life will be spared on your account."

Abram was correct about Sarai's beauty and the reaction of the Egyptians, because when Pharaoh's officials saw her, they told their leader and Sarai was whisked away to the palace. She must have been gorgeous. Abram did well with this arrangement, procuring flocks, herds, and slaves. But the wheels fell off Pharaoh's household soon after because God inflicted diseases on the Egyptians. Pharaoh was no dummy; he put things together and confronted Abram about his lie, and the man had no excuse.

The long trip didn't seem to push Abram's fear button. But the prospect of the Egyptians did. Abram's fear caused him to act in his own ability to reason and connive. And it cost him and the others around him. Think of what it must have done to his relationship with Sarai. She saw his glaring weakness. No doubt Lot, Abram's nephew, also observed his actions.

The problem was not Abram's fear. Fear was a natural response to the situation. Instead of trusting God, however, Abram trusted in himself.

Fast-forward in Abram's life. God appears to him in a vision. Does He scold him for lying about his wife? Notice

God's words: "Do not be afraid, Abram. I am your shield; your reward will be very great."

God's grace will speak to your deepest need. God's grace will assess your weakness and meet you there. For Abram, his fear was overwhelming. His fear controlled him. So it makes sense that his response would be to control the situation and figure a way out.

Ever been there? Have you ever let the circumstance trump your trust in God?

Notice Abram's response. This is the first time his words are recorded in conversation with God.

"Lord God, what can You give me, since I am childless and the heir of my house is Eliezar of Damascus? . . . Look, You have given me no offspring, so a slave born in my house will be my heir."

Credit Abram for being honest—and concerned. He is operating by sight, not faith. He is trying to figure things out—*Lord, You said something back there about offspring, but I think You must have forgotten I need a son.* Abram now lets his fear move him from managing the situation to managing God's affairs.

Again, have you ever been there? Ever tried to manipulate circumstances? Ever tried to help God stay on your timetable? If so, you are thwarting the work He wants to accomplish, a work of grace.

From Abram's perspective, he was just reminding God of His promise about the baby, the offspring. He was helping God stay on track.

> Now the word of the Lord came to him: "This one will not be your heir; instead, one who comes from your own body will be your heir." He took him outside and said, "Look at the sky and count the stars, if you are able to count them." Then He said to him, "Your offspring will be that numerous."

Don't you love the way God answers this doubting man? He could have used some other word picture, livestock, Canaanite children, but instead He points Abram to the stars that He Himself crafted, too many to count—and stars beyond stars Abram couldn't even see.

God, in His infinite mercy, takes Abram aside and makes it as clear as He can without a biology lesson. You, Abram, will have a son. This was not a rebuke, but kindness. A merciful, grace-filled answer.

I know you're afraid. I know you don't understand. Let Me

tell you again. Listen carefully. You will have a son, and he will have children, and they will have children; and you're not going to believe the exponential power at work here.

God's amazing grace in action.

Here's the fascinating, faith-affirming aspect to the story. It is written that "Abram believed the Lord, and He credited it to him as righteousness."

Grace is ready to break through your fear. Grace is ready to break through your doubt. If you listen to God's voice and hear His call, you will believe, and that belief will be credited to you. Something God is doing in you will be credited to your account.

Do not miss this. This is the same message of grace that Jesus brings us. What is extended to Abram is the same grace we are given in the person of Christ.

There is no guarantee that you won't retreat and that fear won't return, because that's exactly what happened. This time, Sarai comes to Abram and thinks she has it figured out. If Abram will sleep with her handmaid, Hagar, maybe this will produce a son.

Between the lines, we can see Sarai's fear rising. Perhaps she felt insufficient for the task. Perhaps she felt it was her fault there was no heir. She's holding the promise of God back.

This was the perfect opportunity for Abram to lead. He could have said, "Sarai, I made that mistake before, giving in to my fear, but I'm not going to do that. I'm going to believe that God is able to bring a child from our union."

Abram doesn't say that. Instead of using the opportunity to be strong and affirm the plan of God and what he has been told (twice), he sleeps with Hagar. He's eighty-five and has no son until he becomes the father of Ishmael. This sets in motion long-lasting consequences.

Fourteen years later, when Abram was ninety-nine, God reaffirms what He said and reinforces the message with a name change, Abraham, the father of many nations. He also gives his wife a new name, Sarah, and names his son, who is yet to be born, Isaac.

The grace of God. The extraordinary, powerful grace of God that calls life from death. That brings children from withered wombs past childbearing years. And gives the strength to raise a son.

Abraham eventually moved into the territory of Abimelech and though he was fearful, this time he didn't give in but valiantly stood up for himself and . . . sigh. Sorry. Again, Abraham lied about Sarah and the cycle repeated. New name, old fear. And fear gave way to sin, and sin has consequences for everyone.

Genesis 21 reveals the fulfillment of God's promise.

> The Lord came to Sarah as He had said, and the Lord did for Sarah what He had promised. Sarah became pregnant and bore a son to Abraham in his old age, at the appointed time God had told him. Abraham named his son who was born to him—the one Sarah bore to him—Isaac. When his son Isaac was eight days old, Abraham circumcised him, as God had commanded him. Abraham was 100 years old when his son Isaac was born to him.
>
> Sarah said, "God has made me laugh, and everyone who hears will laugh with me." She also said, "Who would have told Abraham that Sarah would nurse children? Yet I have borne a son for him in his old age."

Fear leads to sin. Grace leads to blessing. Fear causes pain and hurt. Grace yields laughter.

Imagine the sight of that old woman with a newborn, the look on her face, the look on Abraham's face. The faces of the astonished people who simply couldn't believe what they were seeing. All because of grace. All because of the promise of God.

Grace received will change you. It transforms your outlook. It overcomes fear, no matter how many times it takes to learn the lesson. God's grace brings blessing to you and those around you. God's grace brings laughter and joy, and life from death.

The Promised One, who came through the line of Abraham, through King David; Jesus, the Word made flesh, came to us filled with "grace and truth." In Matthew's gospel, written to Jewish readers, the writer made sure everyone understood the unique family tree of Jesus. The Messiah's line had to come through King David. But Matthew tells his readers of the connection that extends all the way to the promise of blessing God gave Abraham.

In one dramatic scene with religious leaders recorded in John 8, Jesus clashes with these teachers who are at odds with

His message. They don't understand the work of God, the person of God, or the grace of God.

Jesus says, "If you continue in My word, you really are My disciples. You will know the truth, and the truth will set you free."

"We are descendants of Abraham," they answered Him, "and we have never been enslaved to anyone. How can You say, 'You will become free'?"

Jesus was offering them a different way, a different understanding of God. Their lives were filled with sin, but they couldn't see it. They feared the teaching of Jesus because it assaulted their I-am-of-God-if-I-follow-the-rules faith. They had a righteousness of their own doing but it didn't please God.

Jesus responded and said, "I assure you: Everyone who commits sin is a slave of sin. A slave does not remain in the household forever, but a son does remain forever. Therefore, if the Son sets you free, you really will be free. I know you are descendants of Abraham, but you are trying to kill Me because My word is not welcome among you. I speak what I have seen in the presence of the Father; therefore, you do what you have heard from your father."

The conversation spirals downward at this point because

Jesus is saying their father isn't Abraham or God, but the Devil. You can hear the wounded pride of the leaders. It's offensive—even blasphemous. Jesus is not just accusing them of being sinners; He's saying they're thwarting God's work, spurning God's truth and grace. They don't realize that the man they're speaking with created Abraham, created the universe.

Jesus puts them in their place and finally says,

"Your father Abraham was overjoyed that he would see My day; he saw it and rejoiced."

The Jews replied, "You aren't 50 years old yet, and You've seen Abraham?"

Jesus said to them, "I assure you: Before Abraham was, I am."

At that, they picked up stones to throw at Him. But Jesus was hidden and went out of the temple complex.

Abraham was promised an heir, Isaac, but there was also the promise of another who would deal with our sin. Without the sacrifice of Jesus, we would be without hope. But because of God's grace, we are free, no longer bound by sin.

God's grace called Abram, sustained Abraham, and gave him what was promised. You're ninety-nine and you're holding your son. Grace with skin on. Amazing, extraordinary grace.

Chapter 3

The Way of Disgrace, or, Lessons from a Prostitute

RAHAB

Rahab was an Amorite and her life was not pretty. She was a prostitute. This is not hidden from us. She gave herself to men for payment. Her home was built into the wall of the city of Jericho and was a popular place for men.

Two men from the Israelite camp visited her home. They were sent by their leader, Joshua, to spy on Jericho and bring back information. The king of the city heard about the unwanted visitors and sent a message to Rahab to expose the spies. Instead of obeying, Rahab hid the two men and lied to authorities, sending them to pursue men who hadn't fled.

Rahab went to the roof where the men were hidden and

had a conversation. She revealed what she knew about the Israelites, what she knew of God, how He had worked on their behalf, and how much fear there was in the land because of them. "For the Lord your God is God in heaven above and on earth below."

Rahab made a deal with the spies for her own life as well as her father, mother, and her extended family. She asked that their lives be spared, and the spies agreed to deal kindly and faithfully with her and her family. She had to display a scarlet cord from her window and, when the siege began, gather her family into the house.

She helped the spies escape and they gave their report to Joshua. The leader of Israel knew that God was confirming the land was theirs. As the Israelites crossed the Jordan with the Ark of the Covenant, Jericho shut its gates. For six days the Israelites circled the city. Then, on the seventh day, miraculously, the walls of Jericho fell and Rahab and her family were the only ones saved from destruction.

This prostitute, this sinful, foreign woman, is named in the lineage of the Messiah.[3]

She's in her thirties, maybe forties. She loves her family. But something is missing. Something deep inside is churning. There is a hole in her soul that no one can fill. Not even God.

Or so she thinks.

She comes to my counseling office with a sad smile, betraying the thought that she's out of place. She shouldn't be here. Why stir things up that have settled? People don't come to my office to chat. They come because they're desperate. They're out of answers. Out of hope.

I'll call her Julie. Her problem is her past. It's bubbling up again and she can't hold the tide back. She can't reconcile what she knows to be true about herself and what she knows about God. She feels dirty and ashamed.

Julie and Rahab have a lot in common. Rahab had a past. It was not a pleasant story. As we meet her in the book of Joshua, she has an unpleasant present. She had little hope of a future. She was a prime candidate for God's judgment. She was not one of the "chosen" or the "blessed." She was an Amorite. And she was a prostitute. Two strikes against her and a fastball low and inside called the Israelites who were churning through the Promised Land. She lived in a city about to be reduced to rubble, and everyone feared the worst.

Remember the Canaanites from Abraham's day? These

were people who lived in the land and no doubt had overrun it with an abundance of children. And there was Abraham, childless. But God made a promise to Abraham that He would give him this land and heirs. And now the family is back with a vengeance. The promise was true. And though it looks like judgment is coming, Grace is arriving in Jericho.

If you lined up every person in Jericho, not one Israelite would have said, "Red Rover, Red Rover, send Rahab right over." She was not one of the desirable people to save.

And Jericho was a city filled with fear. (Remember what fear caused Abraham to do?) The people of Jericho had heard about this horde, how they crossed the Jordan River on dry ground. God was doing miracles, one after another, leading them, guiding them, preparing the way. And Jericho was terrified. Their hearts were "melting with fear."

Rahab knew *about* God, but she did not *know* Him. She didn't understand He is a God of grace. Even then, even in the wipe-everything-out-as-you-go epoch, God's grace was evident. She bargained with the spies and told them their God was the supreme God.

"Now please swear to me by the Lord that you will also show kindness to my family, because I showed kindness to you. Give me a sure sign that you will spare the lives of my father, mother, brothers, sisters, and all who belong to them, and save us from death."

The two spies sent into the city made a deal with Rahab for her safety and that of her family. But she had no idea that she was about to receive much more than safety. More than just her life. God's grace had a plan. God's grace had a future and a hope for her.

People today face this same fear and misunderstanding. Some have been hurt by church people. Some suffer self-inflicted wounds. They believe God wants only to punish. They don't understand God's love. They also believe things are always going to be the way they are now.

Look at Rahab's life. It was one of great disappointment. As a child, she no doubt had that Jericho Dream, the white picket fence and the nice husband and the 2.5 children. A goat of her own. Whatever the dream, things didn't work out. She had become a prostitute, which in that day and culture meant . . . well, that she was a prostitute.

There's no nice way to say this. She welcomed men into her home and provided a service for payment. Money. Perhaps she bartered for food or an animal or utensils. What God had intended as an expression of love between husband and wife and a means to create children was simply her night job. Another chore in her hardscrabble life.

Each day was another exercise in futility, doing jobs around the home for her family, meals, gathering water, one sunset leaking into another sunrise and starting all over again.

She knew the desire of men but did not know the desire of God. Was there a stirring somewhere deep in her heart that she could have more? Was there a spark that gave her hope that she, too, could follow this pillar of fire and cloud that parted seas and decimated walled cities? Was there some particularly devastating event in her life that preceded the men of Israel slipping into town and finding her home at the edge of the wall?

We don't know all the backstory of Rahab's life, or the circumstances she found herself in when the spies arrived, but we do know this is the type of thing God loves to do. He loves to slip into town and talk with those on the edges. He loves to make Himself known to those who *know* they do not deserve His favor. Proverbs 25:2 says, "It is the glory of God to conceal a matter." He is an odd God, for He chooses people we would not. He hangs around sinners. He showcases His love to the most unlikely people in the most unlikely circumstances.

People like Rahab.

"Rahab the harlot." You can hear the disdain echoing through the centuries. She is pigeonholed—marked as a whore. Put in a category and dismissed. Called a name to keep her humanity and dignity from us. She is defined by what she has done, like a leper, someone unclean. A shepherd boy judged not worthy to be considered. Or a carpenter's son.

Can anything good come from Nazareth?

Think of the ways we do this today. People brand you for being a Christian. If you believe God created everything, you must be a rube, a simpleton, a flat-earther. You're unenlightened and unwelcome at the marketplace of ideas where your voice is desperately needed.

Sadly, Christians are guilty as well. We brand and segment and categorize, and in doing so, we exclude, we judge, we keep those people who need the grace of God away from us. A neighbor has a bumper sticker for a candidate we don't support, so we write him off. A child in the neighborhood exhibits repugnant behavior or simply doesn't wave as you pass. Someone smokes. Someone uses bad language at work. Has a tattoo you don't approve of. The list goes on.

It is endemic to the human condition that we would seek those like us, those who agree with our way of thinking, play our kind of music, paint their houses the colors we would paint them.

But this is not, thank God, the way of God or the way of grace.

Julie has this same problem. She doesn't see her dignity or worth after what she's been through, whatever brings her to my office. She doesn't measure her humanity by anything but the past that continues to hang over her like a cloud.

So what is the way of grace?

Centuries after Rahab has died, a man sits at a well in the midday sun, alone. He is tired and thirsty, and He simply wants refreshment and rest while His followers hurry for food.

A woman of ill standing in the town comes to the well. She is not a prostitute, but she might as well be. Because He is religious, because He is a holy man, He has every right to walk away or at least turn His back so He doesn't have to see her. He has the right and, some would say, the obligation to give her the silent treatment.

This is what we do. This is how we engage those around us, and we call it righteous indignation or holy living. Or we call it pity, and in our pity we expose our own hearts.

This is not the way of grace.

The way of disgrace defines a person by what they have done. The way of grace defines a person by who loves them.

The way of disgrace looks at the outside only.

The way of grace sees beyond the exterior to the heart.

The man engages her. He asks for something—a drink of water. And in doing so, He reaches out in scandalous grace. Scandalous on the face of it. Just speaking a word to her— why, the religious people in town would be incensed. Why would a respected teacher do such a thing?

Could part of the answer be that Jesus saw in this woman a reflection of someone from His own family tree? He could have said to her, you remind me of my great-great-great-great-, etc., grandmother. Her name was Rahab.

But He didn't say this, of course. He didn't make their meeting about Him; this was about her and her need. Her deepest need. A need she might have felt could never be met, and in this chance encounter at a well, as the bucket falls into the water, the stars of her life align in recognition that this is the man she has been looking for all her life. This is the love she has been searching for and has never found in the arms of anyone in Sychar.

We all have skeletons. People in the family tree we would rather skip or keep hidden from plain sight. Rascals and villains. Less-than-honorable folks on the relative rap sheet.

Rahab's problem was not so much the skeletons as the things she shoved in her own closet. The things she had done to make ends meet. The disdain she had brought on herself for being who she was.

She had every reason to want to run from God. She had every reason to fear the spies sent by the Israelites, and if not them, to fear the leaders of Jericho. But something drew her to these men, these people walking across the desert. Something drew her to the God who would lead a people miraculously through the wilderness.

Perhaps she saw she needed a miracle in her own life. Perhaps that need trumped the fear she felt with the others of the town. Though she had lived a life of shame and degradation, she abandoned herself in search of something. She submits to the mercy of those she has hidden. She puts her full faith and confidence in a people she does not know and a God she does not understand.

Until grace, unbidden, reaches into her life.

And this grace will have profound effects not only on her life, but those whose lives come after, who will look at this woman as one of God's prime examples of exactly what we are to know.

The author of Hebrews puts it this way, "By faith Rahab the prostitute received the spies in peace and didn't perish with those who disobeyed."

Many wonder if, in the telling of this story of Rahab's life, God condones lying. Did God honor Rahab for deceiving Jericho's king? No. There are many examples of things the Bible describes truthfully that God does not condone or suggest we follow as an example. This is one of the reasons you can trust Scripture. It doesn't sugarcoat the truth. And it doesn't dress up in politically correct speech what was evident to the people of that day.

"Rahab was a righteous woman with a few flaws." Not true.

"Rahab welcomed many people into her home, and it just so happened that she befriended two spies from Israel . . ."

No. Rahab was a prostitute. Period. There is no reason

God should favor someone of such low standing. Someone of such ill repute.

But this is the way of grace.

And this is the way God wants to work in your life, if you will let Him. God does not want you to simply know *about* Him. His goal for your life is not to get you to cower in fear of Him or of His people. His desire is to, by grace, draw you to Himself from whatever situation you're in and showcase His love and mercy through your life.

"But you don't understand! You don't know what I've done! Or what's been done to me."

We know this: Rahab was a prostitute. She sold herself. She was on the edge of society. And she lived at the edge of town, in a house built into the city wall of Jericho. She couldn't get any more on the outskirts of life. The biblical record never tells us she had a husband before the spies show up. Perhaps he had died and she turned to a life of prostitution to support herself and her family. Perhaps she was never married before this and she fell into prostitution.

There is much we don't know. But we do know this. God, in His grace, chose Rahab to be part of the lineage of Jesus, the Messiah. God, in His infinite mercy, decided that this despised and rejected person would be the wife of King David's great-great-grandfather, Salmon.

But let's not go to her vaunted state yet. Let's linger here in her shame. For at the heart level, Rahab was a needy woman. She is just like Julie. There is something about her past, something about life, at the very core of her that needs healing and no amount of success or positive thinking will satisfy this need. She cannot pull herself up by four steps and a positive-thinking podcast.

There is a scene in Shakespeare's *Macbeth* that perfectly illustrates Rahab's predicament. Lady Macbeth has encouraged her husband to kill King Duncan, thereby allowing her to be queen of Scotland. In a famous sleepwalking scene, she rubs at invisible bloodstains on her hands: "Here's the smell of the blood still. All the perfumes of Arabia will not sweeten this little hand. O, O, O!"[4] No matter how hard she scrubs, those stains haunt her and eventually push her over the brink.

What Rahab needed, and what Julie in my office needs, and what you and I need, is cleansing that goes to the soul level. We need the purifying grace of God to wash over us, to soak and scrub us in those places we can't reach, those spots on our soul that, no matter how hard we try, can't be made clean because of shame, because of past hurts, choices we've made, and choices others have made against us.

And this is the glorious news. This is the incredible, unimaginable offer of God. That the unholy, the defiled, can be made holy. Not because of anything we offer, but because of the goodness and the mercy of God Himself.

But we dare not try to manufacture this ourselves. We must allow God to work the way He will work, for this is the only way to true healing and wholeness. If we circumvent the process with our own effort, we'll miss the truth. We'll miss His grace.

Rahab did not become righteous and was not listed in the Hebrews Hall of Faith because she started a ministry to prostitutes. She wasn't affirmed and used by God because she cleaned up her act and led Torah studies or raised funds for her local crisis pregnancy center.

Rahab *believed.*

She believed that God existed. She believed He was powerful and was the only true God. She believed He was working in the descendants of Abraham and had unlimited power. And, at some level, she believed that same God had the power to change her life, as much as others might have thought it impossible.

To become whole, Julie must believe in this same way. She must believe what God thinks about her and not the voices that bring up her past sin. In the midst of her fear and uncertainty, she must welcome the spies. A small thing. Opening the door to the truth.

Truth and grace. When you believe God and open the door to these two spies and see the truth about yourself and the truth about God, you will then be able to discern the far-reaching effects His grace can have. Truth will lead you to repentance, and His grace will give you hope.

As a counselor I cannot change Julie's heart. I can ask questions and point her in a good direction, but I can't get her to see the truth unless she opens her life to the possibility that her past does not define her. Truth and grace make all the difference. When she does this, God can take her heart and transform it. He can remove the shame and silence the voices of the past and turn them into whispers of His grace.

The lie from the enemy is: *You don't deserve to be here. You are a wretched piece of humanity. You will be haunted by your past forever. You do not deserve to become God's child.*

The whisper of grace says, "Therefore, no condemnation now exists for those in Christ Jesus . . ." "Neither do I condemn you. . . . Go, and from now on do not sin anymore."

"Having been liberated from sin, you became enslaved to righteousness."

Rahab was a bad woman who met a holy God who didn't obliterate her. The walls of her heart came down. She was not only named in a list of faithful heroes, she was chosen to be in the bloodline of the Savior.

Don't let the shame of your past and the failure you've known in life keep you from allowing God to change you. Don't let the sin you're in enslave you any longer. You can have more than safety and redemption in your life. Like Rahab, you can know God fully and follow Him. The result was that this woman, so tainted by her past, was dramatically transformed. She married an Israelite prince, Salmon, and became the great-great-grandmother of King David.

Allow this God of amazing, unbelievable, extraordinary grace to tear down the walls of your heart. Allow the blood-red thread of the love of God through Jesus Christ to wash you and cleanse you and make you a new creation. Believe the truth about His grace. Just like the family that stayed in Rahab's house, if you are "in Christ," there is a different outcome possible for your life.

Therefore, if anyone is in Christ, he is a new creation; old things have passed away, and look, new things have come.

Chapter 4

Finagling Grace

TAMAR

Tamar is pregnant. Hear the whispers. Hear the conjecture about the father. Tamar is pregnant. This is scandalous. This is reason for punishment—even death!

But you must know the backstory of Tamar, a Gentile woman who married into a prestigious family with a long history of a relationship with God.

Tamar married Er, the oldest son of Judah, who was the fourth son of Jacob and Leah. But Er was a wicked man and God ended his life. Judah told the next son in line to "do his duty" with Tamar, but Onan did not, and God slew Onan as well. This left the last son, Shelah, to become Tamar's husband, but he was too young at the time. Judah promised this would *happen and Tamar went back to her father's house to mourn.*

But Judah did not keep his promise. And Tamar was left childless and alone. Abandoned.

Tamar is pregnant! Her belly is swollen with a child. What a disgrace!

When Judah heard his daughter-in-law was pregnant, he raged. He couldn't believe the scandalous, despicable way she had lived. In his righteous indignation, he condemned her to death by fire.

Tamar sent word to her father-in-law and confirmed the pregnancy. She also revealed that the man who was responsible owned the signet ring and staff that she sent with the note. They belonged to him.

"Judah, you are the father."

Imagine Judah's puzzled face. How could she accuse him of such a thing? He had never touched his daughter-in-law. In fact, the only person he had . . .

And then it came back. The temple prostitute by the road. He hadn't dreamed this might be Tamar. This brought Judah to his knees—not only his sin, but also the fact that he hadn't kept his promise to her. He had withheld his third son from becoming her husband.

"She is more righteous than I," Judah said.

Abandoned, heartbroken, cunning Tamar gave birth to twins.[5]

If you've ever seen "naked" furniture, you've seen knots in the pine and rough, unvarnished exteriors. The "natural" aspect of the carpenter's creation is appealing because many like to take such pieces home and "finish" them.

The people of the Bible are a lot like naked furniture. The knots and unsightly swirls are everywhere, in every heart, but the grace of God is apparent as well. This is one of the reasons the Bible stands above other holy books: it does not gloss over the struggles of those who try to follow God. It does not paint the followers of Jesus as perfect. Far from it. And you and I identify with those people and their struggles, and we see God working in them as He is working in us.

Such is the story of Tamar. Like Rahab, her story is not pretty, but she is one of the ancestors of Jesus.

Tamar was a Gentile, a non-Jewish person. A woman. Someone not considered "worthy" in her society. Like Rahab, she had two strikes against her before her story even begins.

But there's more. The furniture gets more gnarled and

ugly. If you've never read the Bible, what follows may shock you.

Tamar married into a Jewish family—a really famous and high-ranking Jewish family. Her husband, Er, was the oldest son of Judah. Judah was a son of Jacob, also known as "Israel," the grandson of Abraham. The pedigree here is enormous. The God of the universe has been working in this family and has made specific, far-reaching promises. This is important to remember. Though she is a Gentile, Tamar is a woman who knows much. Too much.

Tamar's father-in-law, Judah, had many brothers. One of those brothers was Joseph, and it was Judah's idea to sell him into slavery rather than kill him. His thought was, *Why kill him when we can make money from the deal?* Shrewd. Self-seeking. Pragmatic. Whatever situation was before him, he looked through the lens of, *What can I get out of this?*

During the time Joseph was in Egypt, Judah wandered off and found a wife, a Canaanite woman. A Gentile. She bore him three sons, Er, Onan, and Shelah. The Bible says that Judah "got a wife" or "took a wife" for Er whose name was Tamar. We can only imagine what her life was like. This wasn't a case of Er and Tamar falling in love and dating, discovering their love languages, going to premarital counseling, filling out a personality profile (which I would recommend to every couple, of course). Instead, in that culture, you "took" a wife.

Judah's proclivity, his personal style, if you will, was to deal. We might imagine him bartering with Tamar's father about the payment, the arrangement set forth for her hand in marriage. Whatever happened, Judah came away with a daughter-in-law for a son who was less than pleasing to God.

We are not told of the sins of Er, just that he "was wicked in the Lord's sight." With all of the wickedness around him, the bad choices that Judah and his brothers had made, the wickedness of the surrounding culture, this makes Er appear decadent squared. In fact, God was not just angry at Er. The man went past the line of God's patience and sinned so greatly that God "put him to death." God didn't take Er's life for some greater good, some noble sacrifice; He executed him because of his wickedness. He would not allow Er to be part of the lineage of Jesus.

The question that immediately surfaces is, are some people too bad for God to use? Too far gone? Are there irredeemable people on the planet God wants to zap?

Don't interpret God's actions against Er as anything but a graphic example of how seriously He takes sin. In fact, God did not spare His own Son a horrific death on the cross in order to pay the penalty you and I deserve. God made Him to be sin for us so that we might become the righteousness of God.

At the very least, this action by God shows He had a different plan than using Er as an ancestor of Jesus. It's clear Jesus is prophesied to be a descendant of the tribe of Judah, so He will have to come through this line. Since Er died before fathering a child, the opportunity will fall to his brothers, Onan or the young Shelah.

Judah goes to Onan, the next brother in line, and informs him that it's his duty to take Tamar as his wife and have children. But Onan is unwilling. We're not told why he doesn't want his brother's line to continue, but his refusal is clear. And speaking of naked furniture—Onan doesn't consummate the marriage but allows his seed to be spilled on the ground. This displeases God so much that He puts Onan to death.

Two husbands, two slayings by God, and in the process, the ancestral line seems to be hanging by a thread. Judah is watching his sons drop like flies. He tells Tamar that she will have to wait until the younger brother, Shelah, grows up in order for her to start her family. She returns to her father's house and mourns.

Grief will do strange things to the human heart. And so will hardship and abuse. One can only imagine, with the selfish ways that Er and Onan lived, what Tamar endured. Her response to Judah's instruction is to obey. She puts on her mourning clothes and waits.

But at night she plans. She weeps. The wound festers. Her life, which should have been a wonderful thing—with all of the blessings of God poured out on His people—becomes rubble. She is back where she started, back under the roof of her father. Alone. Instead of a houseful of children, something that signified wealth and blessing and prosperity in her day, she was childless. And she was separated from the family she had aligned with—the prosperous, blessed family of Israel.

What happens next reads like a bad romance novel. Tamar plots her revenge. She will get what she wants, what she deserves, and in the process, she will make others pay for the way they've treated her. Her conniving to get back into the line of Judah shows how far she's willing to go to return evil for evil. She was promised something and she will get it any way she can.

Her actions are the opposite of true faith. She takes control. She finagles. God's grace and mercy were available. Perhaps the deaths of Onan and Er were actually aspects of God's grace, showing Tamar He would care for her. God loves to reach out to the broken and bruised.

Have you ever taken control of the situation that wasn't working out the way you had planned? It happened with Abraham. Sarah too. And here is Tamar following in their footsteps.

Tamar stewed on the slights that had come her way by Judah's family. She stewed on the way God had let her down, had filled her life with pain. Time plus sin plus a wounded heart brought forth a devious plan.

Keep in mind that the thing that Tamar wants is also what God wants. He has promised that a Redeemer will come from this ancestral line. But Tamar's desire overwhelms and overcomes the narrative.

Years pass. The King James says, "In the process of time . . ." meaning much time passes and she's a forgotten woman. Shelah is now of age but when there's no mention of him becoming her husband, Tamar decides it's time to act.

She hears that Judah's wife has died, and after recovering from his grief he's headed for Timnah on business. Tamar is told, "Your father-in-law is on his way to Timnah to shear his sheep."

Tamar seizes the opportunity and takes off her widow's clothes and covers herself with a veil as a disguise. She heads toward the main road where she knows Judah will be traveling. You can feel the anger mixed with sadness mixed with indignation.

She has a right to be upset. But rather than dealing with her situation in a righteous way, rather than confronting Judah's slight, she takes matters into her own hands and shows what's really in her heart.

Judah, traveling through the land, his mind occupied with everything but his daughter-in-law's plight, sees what he thinks is a temple prostitute. He wanders from the path and engages her and just as he did for his son, Er, he "takes her."

> "Come, let me sleep with you," for he did not know that she was his daughter-in-law.
>
> She said, "What will you give me for sleeping with me?"

Does she disguise her voice? Does she even have to?

"I will send you a young goat from my flock," he replied.

But she said, "Only if you leave something with me until you send it."

"What should I give you?" he asked.

She answered, "Your signet ring, your cord, and the staff in your hand." So he gave them to her and slept with her, and she got pregnant by him.

And because she placed herself there by the road where she knew Judah would be and because she knew his bent, Tamar finally got what she was promised. She received what was rightfully hers, a child in the ancestral line of Judah. But she deceived him. With her craft and cunning and her sexuality, she connived.

And what are we to make of Judah? That he was propositioning a person he thought was a prostitute shows the state of his own heart, the spiritual state of the family.

If God is holy, He had every right to zap both Judah and Tamar and a few others. How could God possibly use these people? How could He use this story? Why would God use a messed-up family to be in the ancestral line of Jesus?

Because these are the people who perfectly showcase His grace. And if you have made a choice in your life that hangs over you like the veil over Tamar's face, know this: you can be forgiven. God's mercy is so great for those who acknowledge their sin, their fallen situation. If you cry out to Him for mercy, He will give it. Just like the paralyzed man who had no power even to come to Jesus and had to be carried, God will create in you a clean heart.

Tamar's situation becomes quite desperate because three months later, Judah is told she is pregnant and guilty of prostitution. (Judah had sent payment to the "temple prostitute," but no one knew who she was. They couldn't find her.) Judah is livid at the news and commands that Tamar be brought out and burned to death.

Compassion and concern do not run deep in this family.

As she was brought out, she sent Judah a message, along with his seal, cord, and staff. "I am pregnant by the man who owns these."

Imagine the look on Judah's face. He was caught in his own web of sexual sin. To his credit, he didn't retaliate. He didn't try to cover up his faults. He simply said, "She is more righteous than I, since I wouldn't give her to my son Shelah."

Finally, Judah sees the truth about himself. Twin sons are born: Perez and Zerah. Even in the womb, these two struggled, just like the rest of the family.

A Gentile woman seduced her father-in-law in order for him to keep a promise. She used sex to deceive him. She was abused and forgotten. Who do you know that falls into this category today?

Proverbs 30 lists three things that cause the earth to tremble. One of them is, "an unloved woman when she marries." This is Tamar. We can't be sure what happened in her life after the events unfolded. We simply aren't told. But her story speaks to us today, to men and women alike. Her life points us to the grace of God, for it is only there that we can find the true love our hearts long for.

We only find that kind of love in the grace of God.

PART 2

POSSESSING GOD'S GRACE

*Saving faith is an immediate relation
to Christ, accepting, receiving, resting upon
Him alone, for justification, sanctification,
and eternal life by virtue of God's grace.*

CHARLES SPURGEON

Chapter 5

The Application of Grace, or, We Wouldn't Have Psalm 51 without This Story

DAVID

Where to begin? How do you sum up a life like David's?

He had a willing heart. He had a heart for God. He had an available heart. He fought a giant using the tools of a sheepherder and didn't let fear consume him.

He had a melodious heart, skilled at music that soothed King Saul.

He had a shepherd's heart, caring for sheep until he was called to appear and was anointed as king of Israel.

He had a respectful heart. He had a chance to take King

Saul's life, but regarded God's choice of leadership and would not take it from him.

He had a loving heart. His friendship with Jonathan, his commitment to the man's son, Mephibosheth, shows his kindness and faithfulness.

But David did not have a guarded heart, as we see in the episode with Bathsheba. David looked down into the home of his warrior-friend, Uriah, and saw something that moved his heart away from God, away from his friend, away from truth and love and faithfulness, and toward his own desires. It was not the glance that snared him; it was the longing, yearning of a heart after that which was forbidden—Uriah's wife.

In a sense, this story of David is the mirror of Adam and Eve. They ate what was forbidden. And in the act of eating, in their disobedience, their eyes were opened and the consequences were disastrous. The ripple effect of David's sin cast a long shadow on everyone in Israel.

But God had a way of moving into David's heart. And the good news about David is the good news for you and me. David had a remorseful heart. And this is something God loves. God responds to those whose hearts are broken and contrite.[6]

Grace is often wrapped in pain and failure. It is received with joy and hope, but it isn't applied until some deep regret sets in. Failure is the soil where grace grows. Such is the case with the man in the chair, slumped like a child who has lost hope.

"I'm a failure," he says.

"Why do you say that?" the counselor replies.

"Because it's true. Everything I've done, everything I've tried to accomplish, it's over. I'll never be the man I was. I'll never be the man I want to be. And my children. What will they think of me? What will I leave for them as a legacy?"

This man had it all. A consummate leader. Powerful. He led men into battle; they put their lives in his hands; they bled for him; they didn't just look up to him, they followed him into the mouth of carnage. And they followed not out of fear or obligation, but hearts devoted to this passionate leader.

But now he has fallen, and not by an enemy's sword or arrow. And the wound he inflicted upon himself is deep and deadly. He can't see a way out of the pit. He has made mistakes, horrible mistakes. Mistakes that have etched his boyish face—the good-looking man who seemed destined for lasting greatness—with fear, worry, and despair. He is at the end of his abilities.

The end of yourself is a good place to be if you want to experience grace. But he needs more than knowledge: he needs "experiential" grace.

He can't begin to comprehend the loss he has endured. Damage brought about by his own choices. From the way he sits, the way he talks, it's clear he is broken. Life has drained from his eyes, as if the blood has slowly been drawn from him and his heart is pumping nothing but air.

"I'll never get back what I had. What I've squandered."

"Tell me, who are you?"

He looks up. This tower of a man reduced to rubble. "You know who I am."

"I know your name. I know your past, your reputation. The good you've done, and some of the bad. But I want to know who *you think* you are."

He rises from the chair, this muscular man who has rarely known defeat. It's not some enemy outnumbering his forces that has brought him low. It is the storm that rages inside, past the handsome, rugged exterior.

I see this a lot in my practice. Call it the effects of "the law." These are the rules doing their work. A man at the height of his career steps off the ledge and falls. A man can define himself by a fall from such a dizzying height. He can define himself by that failure. He looks at the residue around him, the splatter his life has left on others, and he believes this is who he really is, the sum of all his failures. He feels God defines him this way, too. God sees his failure as him. How could He not? If the Almighty sees and knows everything, surely this stain of sin stands out to Him. How could it not? It's so apparent even a blind man could see it. And God is holy, He can't overlook . . . this.

As human beings, we look at a person and judge by the things done by him and to him. The loss and the pain, the success and struggle. How can we not? When things are so plain, we judge.

Jeremiah, the weeping prophet wrote:

Even if you wash with lye
And use a great amount of soap,
the stain of your sin is still in front of Me.
This is the Lord God's declaration.
—Jeremiah 2:22

It's like a child covered in the chocolate bar he has stolen. The thief with the exploding dye all over his hands. God sees. Period. It's over.

Men and women who have walked with God through the centuries have seen themselves this way, too. This stain. Like a dog that has ruined a carpet. As if God taps His toe and points at the spot. Asks for an account. People still feel this way. They don't understand that the grace of God is available to everyone who asks.

"I'm finished," he continues.

"Are you? Have you considered that perhaps you're just getting started?"

He looks up.

"No, seriously," the counselor says. "What if this failure, this wrong you've done doesn't keep you from doing what you were made to do? What if it could actually propel you—"

"You don't understand. You don't know what I've done."

His strong hand reaches up to rub his neck, as if the pain goes to the bone and through it.

"So the promises of God end here . . . You're *that* powerful."

He glances away but retreats into himself, into the stain, his nose firmly planted in his failure.

"The Lion of Judah will come from your lineage. A king that will step onto your throne. God has promised this and you can't circumvent Him. You can't stop God from being true to who He is, true to His word."

A flicker of recognition. Something sparks inside. A flash of the eyes. And then, a story. It is always a story that changes a heart. This is all it takes to bring him low. And the story is this.

"There were two men," begins the counselor. "One had everything, flocks and herds, and the other had nothing but one little lamb that he dearly loved. He raised it with his children. It was part of the family, like a daughter to him. A traveler comes to the rich man's house. Instead of taking from his own flocks and herds, he snatches this little lamb from the poor man and prepares a succulent meal."

This is the means by which God breaks through the stony ground of the heart. The story wraps itself around the soul of the most powerful man in the kingdom and causes indignation, righteous anger, and a passion that rises like incense.

Then comes the realization that the story is not about someone "out there"; the story is about him—his stain, his sin—and he is undone.

He took what he did not own, could not lawfully possess, what he coveted, what he saw from a distance and desired. And when he experienced how good it was, when he possessed it, he could not let it go . . . so he killed to keep it.

In the story, the rich man received what he didn't own, possessed the bounty of the ewe, and then extended it to the traveler. And his actions affected everyone.

This leader, David, stole another man's wife. A man who had sworn allegiance to him, who had never withheld anything from his leader, was wronged. David was the rich man. Uriah was the poor man. The betrayal was David's adultery, which began with lust, and that lust brought forth cataclysm in Uriah's life.

Sin, when it is embraced, brings forth spiritual death. And though it is enticing and seems like it will bring what you want, it will cause you to receive something you never bargained for—it will extend through you to others and affect them.

"If I could only have that choice back. If I could only do it all over again," King David says softly.

"You can't." The counselor and prophet, Nathan, looks down at the broken man before him.

"I conquered armies. I felled a giant when I was this tall. Just with a sling and a stone. I eluded the king's murderous rage—I had so many victories. But I can't conquer what's in here. I can't defeat this enemy inside me. My soul is pierced, just like Goliath's skull. And the sin taunts me."

"You can't undo this. It is part of your story now. But this is not the end."

"How could it not be?" He spits the words.

"Tell me what you're saying to God. What's in your heart right now?" Nathan asks.

Tears streaming, his body shakes. Then he chokes it out in convulsions of emotion that have been roiling inside; he spews out in a long, flowing confession.

"I'm sorry. I'm so sorry for what I've done. To Uriah. To her, to Bathsheba. To put her in this position. To my country. To *Him*."

"Talk to Him. Tell Him what's there."

More emotional wails and racking sobs cry out of his body. He prays,

Have mercy, O God, have mercy on me. Not because I have pleased You or obeyed You, for I have not. Have mercy on me because of Your unfailing love. Because You are filled with compassion. Forgive me. Wipe this stain from my heart, from my mind, from my life. Wash me. O God, clean this filth from me because I am nothing but filthy before You.

O God, I know how far I have fallen. My sin plagues me, when I lie down, when I get up, every moment of every day.

You have every reason to judge me, to condemn me, because I have done evil in Your sight.

At my birth, when I was still in my mother's womb I was stained with this sin, and I continue in it now. And I have no hope of righteousness outside of You. No hope of forgiveness. No hope.

Cleanse me, wash me. If You don't, I won't be clean.

I want to hear again, to be joyful again, to experience life and health and gladness and Your goodness. Though my bones ache and my body feels crushed, I know You have the power to make me rejoice.

Turn away from my sin, don't look at it, don't see it, don't count it against me. Erase all of my wickedness and create inside of me a pure heart, a clean heart, O God, and renew in me a spirit of faithfulness to You. I want fierce loyalty to You to be part of my life again.

Restore within my very being the joy that comes from knowing Your forgiveness, Your salvation, and sustain me with a desire to follow You.

And let my life, my example, teach others who have fallen that there is hope, there is a way back to You. A way back to Your love and mercy so that I don't have to live with guilt for all my sin, the blood I've spilled, the wrong I've done.

Give me a voice again. Open my lips and I will speak of You. I will sing of Your goodness and mercy.

This is the way of grace. He does not know it yet, but even his confession is part of the grace act—a three-part play that starts in the heart and works itself out through a life. It is the same progression as the three-act sin play, but it has the opposite effect.

When a person is tempted, they are dragged away and enticed by their desires. The desire conceives and gives birth to sin. And sin gives birth to death. You see the downward progression. We receive the enticement, we embrace or possess it, and it winds up possessing us, producing death. This is the way of the Enemy of your soul. He wants to kill, steal, and destroy.

But the lover of your soul wants exactly the opposite. Instead of death, God wants to give life, abundant life, filled to overflowing.

By receiving grace, and possessing grace (meaning, living fully in light of it), you are empowered to extend grace. Belief in the work of Christ, His sinless sacrifice for you, allows you to receive the grace of God and begin living in its power, letting it take you from death to life. That life cannot help but spread to others. This is the work of grace. It cannot be contained.

David sits with his head in his hands. He has wept. He relived the enticement, the dragging away, and the ensuing loss of his firstborn son of Bathsheba. The demise of his friend Uriah at his own hand—after all, he had given the order to have him sent to the front line. When he thinks of Bathsheba, he sees his sin. He sees his indiscretion. He sees himself.

"What do I do?" the king says.

"You've already done it. You've already begun the process."

"Repentance?"

"Not just repentance. You must first believe God will hear you. He will accept your plea. Something inside has drawn you toward God instead of away from Him."

"My belief?"

"That's part of it, but at the very core of your actions is a move of God Himself inside you. With the story, with the revealing of the sin, God has been unbelievably kind to you."

"Kind?"

"Not to let you follow this path until you reach the end— until you reach the bottom. God has called you back Himself, called you to life—a new life. And your brokenness will lead you to something better. You cannot be whole until you are broken in this way. You cannot choose life until you see the ruin you've chosen."

"But what about her? What about the child that grows within her?"

"Do you believe God is able to keep His promises?"

"God is able to do anything. I don't disbelieve Him; I'm unsure of myself and my own place in His plan."

"When you trust in Him, you won't have to believe in yourself. He will accomplish it. He will work even through your own unbelief, through these choices to run toward destruction. And this grace God has given you, let it seep into every pore of your being."

He still does not understand.

We still do not understand.

But that is okay. This is the way of grace. This is its mystery.

"I have not come to call the righteous, but sinners to repentance."

No one is beyond the pale of God's love. And if you fail after you become His child, God is not through with you. He is ready for you to turn toward Him. God retained David as king because David was brokenhearted over what he had done.

God is ready to forgive, ready for relationship, ready to adopt you into His forever family. Restoration is waiting. New life is waiting. Receive His grace. Cry out for mercy. It is new every morning.

Chapter 6

Pursued by Desire,
Overtaken by Grace

BATHSHEBA

She looks at the splendor of the kingdom. She anticipates her son becoming king. She is an old woman now, close to the death of the man she has loved. The man whose choice changed everything.

As she rehearses the events of her life, the pain she has waded through like a bog, things she would not wish on an enemy, she hears a sound that brings it all back. Her breath catches as water is drawn. She closes her eyes and is transported by the splashing, back to that time of year, the very hour when she washed in her home.

The beginning of the chaos in the house of David began

with her bath. She knows this. She can feel the downward spiral pushing this family, this line that stretches to Abraham and beyond. She feels the weight of sin like the waves of anguish that washed her after the loss of her firstborn son.

Bathsheba, daughter of a warrior, wife of a warrior, then wife to a king. Wife to an adulterer. A murderer. How did it happen? And how can she escape the truth that still hangs over her?

David sinned in bringing her to the palace and taking her body. Her beauty led his heart astray. But can a woman be guilty of too much beauty? And then she became pregnant, and the king tried to cover his sin. David asked her husband to return from the front lines so he would sleep with her, but Uriah would not do it. He would not take solace in her arms while his men fought. Or, perhaps Uriah knew.

Whatever the case, David sent him to the front and Uriah was killed. And the baby grew. And the prophet came and told a story that tore David's heart. He wept and repented.

But his remorse did not save the child. This son of Bathsheba was born, but something went wrong, his life ebbed, and after a week, he was gone. And there were more tears for her, more pain, and the questions lingered. She had another son, Solomon, such a wise young man. But in the back of Bathsheba's mind is always the question.[7]

Is God mad at you? Is He punishing you for something you've done? Ever asked that question? If not, you probably will. Can your life go on after something bad has happened? After you have committed evil? If someone commits an evil act against you, is your life over? Are you always to be judged by that act?

Be honest: when you hear the name Bathsheba, what do you think? Your first thought is probably not, "That's the mother of the wisest king in history, King Solomon, the woman in the lineage of the Messiah!" Your first thought of Bathsheba is the seduction by David. Her pregnancy. The demise of her husband. Here is another sordid tale of sex, lust, passion, and murder.

David was the father of Solomon, whose mother, Bathsheba, had been Uriah's wife. The family tree of Jesus included liars, cheaters, adulterers, and murderers. David, known as a man after God's own heart, fell into gross sin. He took advantage of his position and power and committed a heinous act against Bathsheba and her husband, a man who remained loyal to him. It was an act against God Himself. He made disastrous, far-reaching mistakes.

But what was Bathsheba's part in this story? Can we see

the grace of God through her life?

Bathsheba is one of five women mentioned in the geneal-ogy of Jesus in the book of Matthew, chapter 1. She was a well-connected young woman from a military family. She was the granddaughter of one of David's military advisors, the daugh-ter of a warrior who was in the elite group known as "The Thirty." And she married another military man of renown, Uriah, so her life was filled with men who knew how to fight.

She was also beautiful. David was so smitten with her that his lust carried him away. Was she a victim? Was she somehow complicit with David?

The biblical narrative says David saw her and wanted her. He used his power and influence over her. He was a person of trust in Bathsheba's life, so she would have obeyed his sum-mons to the palace immediately. It was an honor to be invited there. But perhaps she was frightened. Did she think there was news from the front lines? She was probably anxious, but she was not fearful of the king. She respected David. She had heard stories of his triumph over Goliath since she was a girl. She'd heard of David's anointing by Samuel, the way Saul pursued David, and the way David would not dishonor the king or God. She was in awe of this mighty warrior and man of God. Her husband, Uriah, had no doubt related stories of the battles they had fought together, the valor of David and his followers, the loyalty and trust that had developed among this band of brothers. So when she was summoned to the king, she didn't hesitate.

We aren't told what kind of advances David made, or that Bathsheba resisted. The entire scene, their conversation, the illicit seduction isn't revealed. This is the stuff of romance novels. Did David force her? Did she resist? Did she at first raise an objection only to be overpowered by his strength and passion, or were his words enough? We're told only that David slept with her.

Some have accused Bathsheba of being immodest, that she was being indiscreet while completing a ceremonial washing/bathing. This is close to saying, "She deserved it." Perhaps she could have washed in an inner chamber, hidden from any possibility of being seen by someone standing on a rooftop and looking into her house. Others conjecture that Bathsheba was the seductress, that she purposely enticed David in order to work her way into the palace.

Whatever the truth, David is held responsible. No woman deserves to be treated as an object. When he saw her bathing, he made the choice to sin and he coveted what he did not have, and in one evening he decimated God's law.

This is the opposite of grace because it entices, entwines the heart, and leads a person away from God. Once embraced, sin leads to spiritual death and spreads pain and hurt to everyone involved. Grace, however, gives freedom from sin and this destructive process, and when embraced, leads to life and gives life to others.

When Bathsheba arrived, this man who had wives and concubines (which raises even more questions) took what he did not have. He coveted what was not his.

If David could have foreseen the far-reaching consequences of his sin, would he have chosen differently? The result of this moral failure in his life affected the child that was conceived, it affected Bathsheba, Uriah was killed, and David involved his own warrior-brothers in the murder. What did that do to the morale of the troops? David actually called Uriah back from the front in hope that Uriah would sleep with his wife and cover David's own sin, but Uriah would not. His loyalty to his men sealed his fate. Read the detailed account of what happened after this event and the extended familial fallout for David.

Yes, David was forgiven. David received mercy and grace. But the consequences of David's wrongs, not just the adultery and murder, but the misuse of his power and authority to gain what he didn't own, went far beyond affecting just David.

Bathsheba lost her husband and mourned. As she dealt with the grief, the child grew inside her, a constant reminder of what had been done. Nathan, the prophet, had told David, "The Lord has taken away your sin; you will not die. However, because you treated the Lord with such contempt in this matter, the son born to you will die." David's repentance brought forgiveness, but the consequences of his actions brought death.

If you think immorality only affects the person who commits it, think again. Pornography has devastating, negative effects on a heart, on relationships and family. Adultery doesn't just affect the two who are involved in the sexual act. Lives are destroyed for momentary passion.

Bathsheba must have felt, as the child grew and kicked, that at least she could nurture and love this little one. With all she had lost, with all that had been taken, surely God would allow her this small consolation. What would they name him? Would she be able to look at him years later and not feel shame and sadness?

She delivered the child, watched him suckle, and then saw him become ill. We're told David pleaded with God, wore sackcloth, fasted, and spent all night crying out for the child's life. On the seventh day, the prophet's words came true and the boy died.

Put in Bathsheba's situation, how would you respond to this loss? Would your grief turn to bitterness? Would you lash out at God? Scream at Him and ask why? Accuse Him of causing evil?

God could have caused the child to be stillborn. He could have stricken the child immediately after birth. But God allowed this child to live seven days. Why? We can't know the answer, but where the judgment and justice of God fall, look for the grace of God as well, for it is there.

How have you felt God's judgment in your life? Have you seen the effects of your own bad choices injure the people you love? How do you avoid wallowing in guilt, shame, anger, and bitterness?

Let's go back to the initial question of this chapter. Is God mad at you? Is He punishing you for something you did? Is God pouring out His anger on someone you love because of your mistake?

It's a human trait to question the goodness of God. In the garden, Eve was tempted with the twisted words of God's enemy. "Did God really say . . . ?" Once you question the goodness of God, once you let this thought trickle along the backwaters of the mind, you will wind up in a stagnant pool.

Grace is a choice. It began as a choice in the heart of God to extend love to errant people. Grace meets us at our deepest need: our failure. It enters our lives as it entered Bathsheba's life, at her most vulnerable moment. Great loss. Great sin. Would she choose to trust God, believe the truth about Him, and receive His grace? Would she, instead, struggle to understand the "why" and spiral into anger? This crucible for Bathsheba, as deep and difficult as it was, forced her to choose. As she watched David's repentance, would she believe the truth about God and receive His grace, surrender to Him, even in the midst of her questions?

No matter what the circumstances, no matter what the evidence in front of you, God is asking if you will believe Him rather than what you can figure out about your life. He does not promise to make all of life better or give you an understanding about why He has done what He has done. But He does offer His grace in the midst of the storm.

When Jesus' disciple Peter stepped out of the boat and

walked on the water toward Him, Peter was exercising great faith. But when the waves rose and he took his eyes off Jesus and looked at his circumstances, he began to sink.

The question God asked Bathsheba, the question Jesus asked Peter, is the same question being asked of you today. Will you believe? Will you trust your life to the grace of God?

"Then David comforted his wife Bathsheba, and he went to her and made love to her. She gave birth to a son, and they named him Solomon. The Lord loved him; and because the Lord loved him, he sent word through Nathan the prophet to name him Jedidiah" (NIV).

What a difference in the two stories. During their first encounter David lusted, and then he took what he wanted. Here, David comforts her and makes love to Bathsheba. The change in his heart caused him to act differently toward the woman he made his wife. This is the grace of God.

Bathsheba is part of the family tree of Jesus. She is the brokenhearted mother whose husband was killed, whose infant son died, whose second son would become the future king.

Bathsheba. David. Solomon. All ancestors of Jesus.

All evidence of the grace of God.

Chapter 7

Answering the Greatest Question

SOLOMON

Say the name Solomon and you have spoken of wisdom. Solomon's name is synonymous with wealth and power and splendor. He built the temple of God that was a marvel to the ancient world. His father was known as a warrior, but Solomon became renowned for his wisdom, his possessions, and the blessings of God.

Solomon is also known for excess. He had many wives and concubines. He ran toward women and their gods. Idolatry. This man knew wisdom and could discern. For two women who both said they were mother to a child, Solomon passed the judgment to cut the baby in half. The reaction of the two women uncovered the truth about their hearts and revealed the real mother.

Unfortunately, Solomon's heart remained divided, and the kingdom of Israel would fall to the same fate after his death. His own family members would fight against each other for control of the throne after his father, David, died. Chaos and strife rained down on the lot of them, as if the sins of others were being visited, along with the abundant blessings of God.

But early in the reign of this king, a conversation with God showed a different perspective of the man. Though Solomon would run toward excess, God would ask a penetrating question and Solomon would respond with amazing insight into the heart of God.[8]

Who are you?

Many people never answer that question. It's too hard. Instead, they answer a different one easier to quantify and wrap their life around. They answer:

"What do you do?"

I'm an accountant. I'm an engineer. I'm a musician. I'm a full-time mom. I sell cars or computers or insurance. I'm a pastor. This is what I do every day. This is who I am.

No, it's not who you are. What you do is never who you are. And you've seen this truth reflected in the lives of Old Testament saints, the lives of men and women in the lineage of Jesus. It's never about what you've done or what's been done to you, what potential you have or don't have. It's not about who you're related to or not related to. Lineage plays a part in the plan, of course, but it does not determine worth or value in God's sight.

Who you are is a much deeper question. It mines a different, subterranean stratum of the heart. What are you trusting in? What gives your life significance? What provides you with purpose and meaning? What drives you? Why do you do what you do the way you do it?

Who are you?

Perhaps you've spent years, even decades, defining yourself, seeing yourself in light of the choices you've made or the bad breaks you've experienced. You've searched for comfort, resting in some ability, some niche carved out in life. You've mixed all of this together—who you are, what you do, what you've done, accomplishments, failures—and you've settled into a life, like sediment in a riverbed, and you've become satisfied with where you are because this is the way it is and always will be. Don't fight it. Just grow accustomed to the feelings. And since each segment of life is vulnerable to this question, it makes sense to gauge your spiritual life this way.

Who are you spiritually?

I'm a Christian. I go to the church on the corner. I taught Sunday school for years. I read my Bible every day. I give to missions organizations. I help out in the soup kitchen once a month. I volunteer at the pregnancy center. I try to live a good life. I'm trying to sin less every year. I have a list of good things I'm hoping will outweigh the bad. I've grown accustomed to the sin in my life, but it's not hurting anybody.

This is not who you are as a believer. This is what you've done and what you're doing spiritually. This is how you quantify your relationship with God, but this is not who you are.

God is not looking for what you can offer Him. That may sound unspiritual and shocking because many believe God desires and needs what you're offering. And in the rest of your life, people want things and judge you by how well you live up to their expectations. Isn't God the same?

The really bad news is this: God wants more than you can offer. He wants perfection. And you are not perfect.

Now for the good news, and it's really good news. God wants you to "be" who you were created to be—everything you were created to be. And by living from "who you are," you are enabled to do everything you were created to do. He wants to do something deeper than change the surface of your life or cause you to gauge your walk with Him on a "sin meter" or an "accomplishment bar chart."

The way God works is through His extraordinary grace. The perfection He desires is something He gives you. Only His power will lead you home, lead you to His heart, and lead you to your true self, the person you were created to be. Grace will set you free from having to measure up, make up, or achieve.

Ephesians 2:8–9 makes it clear that you were brought into the family of God by God's grace. He has given you this gift. You didn't earn it. You couldn't buy it with a good life. It's something out of your price range, off the charts of your ability to pay. He accomplished it. You believe in what He says about you and your sin and place full faith and confidence in Jesus Christ and allow Him to transform you from your inner soul to your outer actions, by His grace.

You were not created to live "a good, moral life." You were created by God and redeemed by Christ in order to do good works that God Himself prepared in advance for you to do in order to bring Him glory. He created you and redeemed you for specific purposes, and your heart will be restless until you discover the freedom of following this grace-filled path. It is something you must choose to follow. Your heart will yearn for lesser things, a more quantifiable way. You will be drawn to pleasing God by doing things for Him, by trying to make Him happy, just like the people in your life, because this is how you feel happy.

Take this truth in. God was thinking of you even before you came to Him, even before you were born, and was planning things to weave into the tapestry of your life that you will accomplish. This is because His extraordinary grace has made you who you are. His extravagant grace has given you the virtue of His Son. He could not be happier with you. He sees you as perfect, clothed in the holiness of Jesus Himself. He did not plan things for you to do that will earn points with Him or that will make you "better" in His eyes. He has plans for you that come from who you are in Him; plans that will make you grow closer to Him.

So, I ask again. Who are you?

The question goes to your heart. This is at the center

of God's question to Adam in the garden. God was not just asking, "Where are you?" God knew very well where Adam was. He was asking, "Adam, who are you now? Do you know what has happened to our relationship?" To the blind man, Bartimaeus, Jesus asked the question, "What do you want Me to do for you?" In other words, what is in your heart, what is the longing deep inside that I can fill to meet the need of your soul and assuage your longing heart?

God is asking you this same question, in many forms, every day. What is your deepest need? What is your true longing?

God gave Solomon a great test by asking a penetrating question. You probably know of this great king of Israel. He was said to be the wisest man who ever lived. Read Proverbs and you'll see the ancient wisdom he possessed and imparted. His words ring true today in every sphere of life. But Solomon had an uphill battle in answering the question posed by God.

Solomon was the second son of David and Bathsheba. His older brother had died when he was seven days old. His mother and father's relationship began in adultery. This led David to, in effect, murder Bathsheba's husband, Uriah. David took Bathsheba as his wife and after a time of mourning,

Solomon was conceived and born into a kingly but quite dysfunctional family.

Solomon had intrafamily struggles, a legacy of a warring father, and a struggle with women—because he seemed to want as many wives as he could find. He followed his father's good advice, but still sacrificed and burned incense at the high places. He built his own house before he even started on building God's house. Much of Solomon's life looks like a heart divided.

In spite of all of this, God appeared to Solomon and said, "Ask. What should I give you?" Another translation says, "Ask what you wish Me to give you" (1 Kings 3:5 NASB).

This was not a blank check, it was a gut check. This was not God as genie, but God testing what was really in Solomon's heart. What he was really longing for. The question exposed Solomon like no other. It's interesting to note that this is not asked of Solomon in a waking moment but in a dream as God peers deeply into the life of this son of an adulterer, a son of a man after God's own heart, the son of a divided father.

Here's what we find in Solomon's heart:

And Solomon replied, "You have shown great and

faithful love to Your servant, my father David, because he walked before You in faithfulness, righteousness, and integrity. You have continued this great and faithful love for him by giving him a son to sit on his throne, as it is today.

"Lord my God, You have now made Your servant king in my father David's place. Yet I am just a youth with no experience in leadership. Your servant is among Your people You have chosen, a people too numerous to be numbered or counted. So give Your servant an obedient heart to judge Your people and to discern between good and evil. For who is able to judge this great people of Yours?"

Solomon's answer pleased God. In it, Solomon uncovered his greatest need, his inability. He was admitting he wasn't up to the task of leading the Israelites. He humbled himself, and God loves a humble heart. Solomon begins his answer understanding his relation to God. In essence he was saying, "You are God, and I am not. I am in need, and You are the only one who can enable me to accomplish what the nation needs."

When you come to God with this attitude, He will hear and answer.

After acknowledging his need, Solomon gives God his request. He was not timid. He didn't hold back. *You have not because you ask not.* Solomon could have asked for many things, but his request went below the surface to what he needed most. He asked for discernment, an ability to tell right from wrong.

Is that what you would have asked? What is the greatest need you have right now in life? Is it your finances? Would you have asked God for money to pay off your house? Perhaps something for the retirement nest egg? Would you have begged God for the salvation of a family member or friend? Maybe for healing for yourself or someone you love? Would you ask for the perfect spouse?

Solomon could have asked for anything under the sun, but he admitted he was deficient and asked for help. Down deep, underneath all of the striving and finagling, underneath the layers of family dysfunction and the addictions and the wives and concubines, Solomon's heart yearned for true wisdom. And God gave it, plus more.

This is God's grace poured out. This is God responding to a request from a willing heart.

So God said to him, "Because you have requested this and did not ask for long life or riches for yourself, or the death of your enemies, but you asked discernment for yourself to understand justice, I will therefore do what you have asked. I will give you a wise and understanding heart, so that there has never been anyone like you before and never will be again. In addition, I will give you what you did not ask for: both riches and honor, so that no man in any kingdom will be your equal during your entire life. If you walk in My ways and keep My statutes and commands just as your father David did, I will give you a long life." Then Solomon woke up and realized it had been a dream.

But God's grace was real. And He did what He said He would do. And He will do the same in your life.

No matter how far you've run from Him, no matter how much value you have placed in things or health or wealth, God is ready to welcome you and give wisdom for the tasks ahead. He is willing to extend His grace.

Sadly, when Solomon grew older, this wise man who was king of Israel ended up marrying hundreds of pagan women and bringing them into the land of Israel. He did not obey God. His heart was divided as the kingdom he passed to his descendants.

And yet, this is an ancestor of Jesus. This is the lineage of the grace of God.

Who are you? What is it you want from God?

He is offering His grace, right now. What's holding you back from receiving it?

PART 3

EXTENDING GOD'S GRACE

Oh, the love that drew salvation's plan! Oh, the grace that brought it down to man! Oh, the mighty gulf that God did span at Calvary!

WILLIAM R. NEWELL

Chapter 8

He Almost Missed Grace in a Manger

JOSEPH

He is a carpenter in Nazareth. A working man with rough hands and torn fingernails in an obscure town on the back side of Israel. Sweating at his workbench every day, scraping by, he sometimes hears the footsteps of Roman soldiers. He hears news from travelers to Jerusalem. The domination of the foreign army hangs over the land and the people. Often, he thinks of the Promised One, the Messiah. He longs for God's consolation, like the rest of Israel, but his workaday existence brings him back to the task at hand. Do the next thing. Keep working.

He has looked forward to marriage and starting a family.

He has worked so hard to be in a position to provide for a wife and the children he hopes will come along, if God blesses. His family has chosen a wife, and he has been patient, as patient as a man can be. He has heard many good things about his betrothed, the young woman, Mary. And he is a righteous man. A chaste man. He has lived by the laws of his people, of his God, though he knows he has not been perfect. Who can truly be holy, like God?

Then Joseph hears news that shatters his world. He hangs his head and sweat drops on the wood before him like tears. How can it be? How could she treat him this way? Mary is pregnant. He had heard she was such a wonderful young woman, would make a wonderful wife. Now, that dream is dead.

He is angry, he is incredulous, and then he is simply disappointed with the way life has turned on him. And in the turning, in the midst of the pain and hurt, he thinks of her. He imagines her shame and guilt because of this lack of discretion. He thinks of how he would want to be treated in such a situation, with some semblance of understanding and mercy. So he shoves his feelings aside as well as the voices of those who tell him she should be stoned. Instead, he will absorb the pain. He will go about this quietly, sparing her more pain and embarrassment. He will not ridicule or toss stones at her. He will treat her with honor and respect, though she doesn't deserve it.

Dog-tired and almost falling onto his bed, Joseph sleeps and as he does, an angel visits him. The being speaks fantastic words. As many angels have said over the centuries, this one tells him not to be afraid. He says he should not be afraid to take Mary as his wife because . . .

Joseph awakens. Can it be true? Mary, still a virgin, and the child within her conceived by God, the Holy Spirit? The baby is a boy. The baby's name is to be Yeshua, or Jesus, for He will save His people from their sins. The Promised One will be his stepson. God with us. Immanuel. God is presenting him with the opportunity and responsibility of fathering the Son of God.

Can it be? Can this possibly be happening? What will Joseph do? [9]

How do you know you've received the grace of God? You don't get a notice in the mail or confirmation by phone. God doesn't turn you bright orange or give you a halo. But there is a telltale sign that you have received grace and are walking in it.

When God invades, when His grace breaks through, subtle changes begin. You see the world differently. You live in gratitude for grace, not using your freedom as license to sin. Your world is illumined by truth, and God begins His slow, inexorable drawing of your heart toward Himself. The closer you get to God, the more change you see.

When grace takes hold, you no longer strive to earn God's favor. You know you possess it. You can rest in His love. As you rest, you see yourself differently. You no longer live to please only yourself. Your life looks outward and asks, "What is best for the other person?"

Pastor and author Chip Ingram has a quote he uses to describe true love. "Giving another person what they need the most when they deserve it the least at great personal cost."[10]

God's extraordinary grace was what we needed the most. It was given to us when we deserved it the least, for while we were still sinners, Christ died for us. It was given to us at great personal cost. It cost Jesus His life in order for us to receive this indescribable gift. He became sin who knew no sin so that we could be made righteous.

Grace is never free. It always costs someone.

Grace means you do not trust in your own understanding, in your own ability, or your own goodness. God accepts you and loves you and envelops you, welcomes you into His family, not because of anything you have done to earn the right, but because of His love toward you. This construct means God receives glory and you participate by receiving grace.

But grace does not end there. Grace is not a means to an end, but a beginning. Grace will spread from a forgiven heart.

The telltale sign that grace has dawned is that you will begin to give it to others as God has freely given it to you.

This brings us to the story of Joseph. Though he was not related by blood, he was chosen by God to be the earthly representation of a father to Jesus.

We don't know a lot about Joseph. Matthew's gospel declares he was a "righteous man." A carpenter by trade, he and Mary were betrothed until Joseph was told that Mary was pregnant.

Betrothal in the Jewish culture was different from engagement in ours. Betrothal was the signing of a contract between two sets of parents who had decided that their two children would marry each other. And once the contract was signed, it was considered binding. But the couple did not come together until they had a wedding ceremony. And that was often months and sometimes a year after the betrothal. And then they had the wedding ceremony and then the consummation of the marriage.

Mary and Joseph were betrothed. The contract had been signed by their parents. You don't get out of that contract without a divorce, and the purpose of that betrothal period is probation time to make sure that both families are still happy with this and to make sure that the couple lived in fidelity even though they had very little social contact.

When Joseph got word that Mary was pregnant, he knew he had no option. She had broken the contract. But the way he handled it shows you something of his character. It says that he did not want to expose her to public disgrace so he had in his mind, "I'll just go to the attorney. We'll do it behind closed doors, and we'll let it happen quietly."

I don't know about you, but if I'd been Joseph I don't think I'd respond in that way. If the woman had been unfaithful to me when we were committed to marriage, I don't think I'd be concerned about her disgrace. She disgraced me. I think I'd be pointing a finger and throwing stones. But Joseph didn't do that. Even in his mind, he didn't do that. He wanted to be humane.

This tells me Joseph loved Mary. He didn't want to disgrace her despite the fact that she had disgraced him. That's how he viewed the situation.

One can imagine, years later, Jesus meeting Pharisees and religious leaders who loved to use their adherence to the rules for their validation. The story His mother, Mary, told about Joseph was so different from these men. The woman caught in adultery cowered before these "righteous" men, but Jesus sent them away with a few words, and extended grace to her. Had He seen this kind of love in His earthly father's heart?

Did the boy Jesus ask His mother to tell the story again about His father, how he decided to "put her away quietly"? The story was told because it was central to the family history. Part of their family album. Joseph did not succumb to the pressure to show Mary how powerful he could be. That was not his way.

Why?

Joseph worked with his hands. No doubt he had gnarled fingers and broken fingernails. His skin was rough and his muscles tested by years of hard work. Perhaps he looked like the gruff, insensitive type—but his actions toward Mary show a heart of kindness and love in the face of great disappointment.

Though Joseph had the right to "make an example" of Mary, to have her stoned for high treason against his heart, against tradition he chose a different way, possibly at great cost to himself. People in the small town probably looked at him with pursed lips and shook their heads. How would he recover from such a betrayal?

Instead of disgracing her, he would absorb the pain. He would extend grace.

We don't know from the text if Mary explicitly told Joseph what had happened to her, if he found out and questioned her, if someone else in the family discovered it and with sadness told Joseph, perhaps as a prayer request. "I hate to be the one to tell you this, but I just heard . . ."

It seems plausible that Mary would have at least tried to explain the visitation from the angel Gabriel and the shocking news he delivered, the most shocking news of her life, that God Himself was coming to make Himself at home in her womb. Did Mary fear what Joseph might do with the news that she was pregnant? He would certainly know it was not his child since they had not been together physically.

But Mary had not made a mistake. She was simply going about her daily routine, the boring, everyday, hardscrabble life in first-century Nazareth. And then the grace of God came upon her, surprised her, astounded her. She had been waiting—the whole country had been waiting for hundreds of years for the Promised One, the Deliverer of Israel, the Messiah, the Christ. And now He was coming. Such joyous news, but so incomprehensible. Mary would deliver the Deliverer. She would birth the Great I AM. This news was too much to comprehend, so how could she ever hope to convey it to her fiancé? How could she get him to believe? To believe her?

One takeaway from this story is that it is not up to us to get someone to understand. Grace is not about convincing others to believe. This is something only God can do. We are to be faithful with the message of grace and the expression of grace. God takes care of the rest.

Grace is hard to believe. Grace, when it is given in its fullness, will upend your life. God's grace, when poured out in your heart, changes everything, as it did for Mary and Joseph.

Joseph's response is evidence that God was already at work in his heart. You cannot give this kind of grace if you haven't received it. It's difficult to love when you've never experienced such a thing. But to give grace when you've never received it is like trying to speak a foreign language without ever encountering it. It's drawing from a dry well. Impossible.

Did God choose Joseph because there was something good in him? Did God know the carpenter would be open to extending kindness and generosity to Mary? As we've seen throughout the stories of the people in the lineage of Jesus, each person had their own sins and struggles. And because Joseph was a member of the human race, he had problems. We don't know what they were. But his first response is to wash his hands of this problem. He wasn't going to injure Mary and her unborn child, but he wasn't going to take responsibility either. He was walking away from the problem. He was moving on with life.

God does not look for what you offer Him. Time and again we see this in the lives of saints. God uses our weakness and inability. God takes withered hands and blind eyes and gives glory to Himself. He takes some bread and a few fish from the hands of a child and turns it into a feast. He takes water in stone jars and turns it into the most delicious wine served at the wedding. He takes a man chained in a cave, the scourge of the town, and turns him into a clear-thinking evangelist.

> Brothers, consider your calling: Not many are wise from a human perspective, not many powerful, not many of noble birth. Instead, God has chosen what is foolish in the world to shame the wise, and God has chosen what is weak in the world to shame the strong. God has chosen what is insignificant and despised in the world—what is viewed as nothing—to bring to nothing what is viewed as something, so that no one can boast in His presence. But it is from Him that you are in Christ Jesus, who became God-given wisdom for us—our righteousness, sanctification, and redemption, in order that, as it is written: The one who boasts must boast in the Lord. (1 Corinthians 1:26–31)

This is what happened with Joseph. In his own strength and power, his own vision of the way the world was, he would have walked away from the assignment of being stepfather to the Prince of Peace. What a tragic mistake. Standing by his wife, looking at the newborn baby, conceived by the Holy Spirit, Joseph must have looked at the night sky in Bethlehem and whispered, "I almost missed this." When the wise men came bearing gifts for the King of Kings, when the shepherds tumbled into town telling what they had heard from the lips of angels, Joseph must have marveled at how thin a thread held him connected to the scene. He had nearly walked away.

Instead, the grace of God invaded, to the glory of God the Father. And the small bit of grace Joseph offered Mary opened floodgates to the fullness of grace God wanted to bring to his own heart.

It always does.

God does something wonderful in this story. He affirms the message He gave to Mary and includes Joseph in the grand design of His work in the world.

The birth of Jesus Christ came about this way: After His mother Mary had been engaged to Joseph, it was discovered before they came together that she was pregnant by the Holy Spirit. So her husband Joseph, being a righteous man, and not wanting to disgrace her publicly, decided to divorce her secretly.

But after he had considered these things, an angel of the Lord suddenly appeared to him in a dream, saying, "Joseph, son of David, don't be afraid to take Mary as your wife, because what has been conceived in her is by the Holy Spirit. She will give birth to a son, and you are to name Him Jesus, because He will save His people from their sins."

Now all this took place to fulfill what was spoken by the Lord through the prophet:

See, the virgin will become pregnant
and give birth to a son,
and they will name Him Immanuel,
which is translated "God is with us."

When Joseph got up from sleeping, he did as the Lord's angel had commanded him. He married her but did not know her intimately until she gave birth to a son. And he named Him Jesus. (Matthew 1:18–25)

Grace is not a feeling. Grace is an action. Grace is not an emotion. It is a decision. A choice. Grace is a lot like love wrapped in forgiveness with skin around it. Grace absorbs the pain of another's faults and keeps loving.

Grace is not some nebulous, undefined concept. You may not be able to see it, touch it, or put it under a microscope, but its effects are eternal. Grace changes everything. And nothing grace touches remains the same.

In order to extend grace, you must possess it. In order to possess it, you must receive it. And in order to receive it, you must see your overwhelming need for it. Without grace, God's unmerited favor, we are hopeless. With grace, there is nothing but hope and love.

The goal of grace is not to make you feel better. The goal is to make you more like Jesus, more like grace personified. Jesus was grace deployed. Knowing Jesus is knowing grace. Following Jesus is experiencing grace. Loving Jesus is giving grace.

Chapter 9

Grace Made Flesh

JESUS

Before Abraham. Before Adam. Before the world was fashioned. He was. Before time. In fact, He created time itself.

And the perfect plan of God, conceived before the foundation of the world, was set in motion with a word.

He spoke and it was created. He spoke and there was light. He spoke and waters formed and the dry land as well, and birds took wing and animals crawled on the face of the earth.

With a word, He called creation forth, and then, in Bethlehem, His cry broke the night. Creator of all came down the virgin's birth canal. Conceiver of the most ingenious plan of redemption in all of history was conceived by the Holy Spirit.

Full of grace and truth, He was Grace and Truth. The Word

made flesh. And the lineage of His family, these broken people with broken hearts and lives, would be mended by His wounds and stripes and blood.

Jesus, Son of God, son of Mary, fully divine, yet fully human, would speak and a dead man would rise. He would touch and blind men would see. Leprous skin would turn soft as a baby's. Lame, limp legs would dangle helplessly no more, restored to full strength and potential.

But the greatest miracle He came to perform would not be seen by human eyes, for the change He came to bring happened inside those who followed. The grip of sin, the hold of pride, the unforgiving heart was made new by God's infused holiness. He who knew no sin became sin so that you and I might receive His righteousness, His right-living.

All the prophets and patriarchs and men and women called by God before His birth looked forward to His coming. And all the followers since have anxiously awaited His return.

Do not wait. The Redeemer has come. The Messiah, the Promised One, God Himself has dwelt among us and will dwell with you. Today.

Amazing, unbelievable grace.[11]

As you can see through the lives we've studied through-out Scripture, grace was at work to them, in them, and through them. God wants the same for you. Because of His love and His extravagant mercy, He wants to extend His grace through your life to others. Ultimately, God wants to bring glory to the only being in the universe who deserves it—Himself. This is what grace is all about, the glory of God. Grace was God's ingenious plan to redeem His creation, to bring people back from rebellion, and to defeat the enemy of our souls. We'll be considering this interconnecting grace and basking in the stories for eternity.

This was not our idea. Grace is not something you and I could invent, because it exacts too much from the Giver. Our inclination is to base our goodness and worth on things we have done, not things God did. We quantify our good-ness, compare ourselves with others, make a checklist and feel good about our standing.

This is *faux* grace, a cheap knockoff that looks real but is an imitation. Faux grace nods at God's gift, then rolls up its sleeves and gets to the heavy lifting of working to please God, working to earn its way into the club.

Faux grace is our default because it's something we've constructed. It comes from our own spiritual intelligence and makes life fit into a neat box. I do good things, God rewards me and I'm happy. I do bad things, God is mad and I'm sad. I'll try to do good things so I can be happy.

The trouble is that hardship will come to your life, and you'll have to deal with bad things that cause you to feel God's perpetual anger. How you define grace will have a huge impact on how and why you live the way you do. If you live to please God in order to get Him to do things, you will, at some point, feel let down by God because He will only be as big and as holy as *you* can make Him.

God does not exist to make us feel better. God's grace is not bestowed to give us happiness or purpose or meaning. Purpose and meaning come from embracing God's grace and letting it work itself out in our lives, not the other way around.

We know from John 1 that,

In the beginning was the Word,
and the Word was with God,
and the Word was God.
He was with God in the beginning.
All things were created through Him,
and apart from Him not one thing was created
that has been created.

Life was in Him,
and that life was the light of men. . . .
The Word became flesh and took up residence among us.

The Word was Jesus. God's communication to us, His revelation of His essence came in human form, fully God/ fully man. But before the Word was made flesh, in the council of the Father, Son, and Holy Spirit, before time began, before anything was created, as difficult as it is to comprehend, Grace was the chosen means for redemption. Revelation 13:8 talks about this decision. The Lamb was "slain before the foundation of the world" (KJV). God's perfect plan, the one that would bring Him the most glory, was grace. He decided, before temptation ever entered the picture, before Adam's sin, to absorb the penalty Himself for all who believe.

Jesus was not only the Word of God made flesh; He was the Grace of God made flesh. And it pleased God to bruise Him, wound Him, and have Him pour out His life upon the cross, not because God is sadistic and cruel, but because of His love.

When God seemed silent for hundreds of years after the

prophets' voices were stilled, Grace moved out of heaven and into a manger. Grace donned rags. The night of God's silence was pierced by a baby's cry. The voice of God, not thundering, but vibrating an infant's vocal cords.

Grace walked barefoot to His father's shop and watched the man plane wood that would one day lift Him high. Grace learned a trade.

Grace stayed behind in the temple, listening and engaging the teachers in such a way that they marveled at His questions and wisdom. Grace grew in stature, and at just the right time walked into the water and was baptized.

Grace chose disciples, not for what they offered the kingdom, but for what the kingdom offered them. And by Grace they were sent into a hurting, hungry world and were used to turn it upside down for the glory of God.

Grace took the bread and fish of a little boy and fashioned a feast for thousands. Grace spoke and the water in the jars changed to choice wine.

When Grace came, He brought with Him abundant life. And all who receive it also receive, by extension, the mission of grace that extends to every tribe and nation and tongue.

Grace healed the paralyzed man on the mat and answered the prayers of his friends who let him down through the ceiling. Grace pulled little children to Himself rather than send them away, for this is the way of grace, to believe that the kingdom is like welcoming a little child.

Grace restored dignity to a sinful woman, forgave her, and deployed her to choose against sin and tell others about Him.

Grace confronted the religious leaders who thought they were righteous. Grace confronted the demon horde wreaking havoc in tormented souls. Grace calmed the storm and spoke peace to the wind and waves, and they obeyed.

Grace spoke in the darkness to a man who wanted to be born again but had no idea how. Grace wept at His friend's tomb and then brought him from death to life.

With every footstep, every conversation, every healing, the Word made flesh was on this mission of grace, and He would not be deterred by temptation by the Enemy or by a friend who misguidedly tried to steer Him away from that mission.

Resolute Grace, resolved to fulfill the demands of the law, kept moving, kept walking toward the inevitable destination, the place where the story was leading—toward Jerusalem, toward death.

It was God's extraordinary grace that propelled Jesus to

the garden. Grace sweating drops of blood, pleading, begging, and then abandoning Himself again to complete surrender.

Grace arrested.

Grace imprisoned.

Grace flogged and spat upon.

Grace torn and bloodied and bruised.

Grace with a crown of thorns shoved onto His head.

Grace beaten and pulled before unrighteous judges.

Grace stripped naked and condemned.

The question brought by skeptics of this message is why God would allow suffering. Why would God allow sin? These are not the greatest questions. The question of the ages is this: Why would God allow the holy, righteous Word of God to suffer and die? Why would God plan the horrific death of the only One who did not deserve it?

This is God's hidden, unbelievable plan, to lift up grace in order to give life. Here is the cost of sin, the devastation it brings, the price that must be paid, and the answer to our guilt and shame and death.

For God loved the world in this way: He gave His One and Only Son, so that everyone who believes in Him will not perish but have eternal life. For God did not send His Son into the world that He might condemn the world, but that the world might be saved through Him. Anyone who believes in Him is not condemned, but anyone who does not believe is already condemned, because he has not believed in the name of the One and Only Son of God.

Grace bore the rugged cross and walked up Skull Hill. Grace welcomed the soldier's nails.

Grace was lifted up and embraced the ultimate punishment that did not come from any leader or human government or religious sect, but from God Himself. On the cross God poured out His wrath, and Jesus drank that bitter cup for you and me.

Jesus knew no imperfection, no impurity, no sinful thought or action. He never acted in His own self-interest. This perfect man who had no sin *became* sin for us so that we might become righteous in God's sight.

Look at Grace struggling for breath, pushing Himself up to gain a little air in His lungs. Grace bleeding from rich wounds. Grace crying out to His Father, experiencing judgment. Grace, framed by angry clouds, hanging His head, saying, "I thirst."

Even in agony, at the point of death, Grace extends itself.

"Father, forgive them, because they do not know what they are doing," Jesus said.

The embodiment of Grace—Jesus, the Messiah, King of Kings—humbled Himself and let go of what was rightfully His to die on a cross.

Grace made Himself nothing. Grace became a slave. Grace emptied Himself of everything but love and poured Himself out as an offering.

The grace of God extended to Abraham and Tamar and Joseph and Rahab and David and Bathsheba and Solomon, and every human being who has ever lived, this grace of God is ready to invade and forgive and work. This is the only way to a relationship with God. This was His plan for our redemption. To choose any other way or add to it spurns God's perfect sacrifice.

The effect of this grace is that you will be compelled, not to please God with a holy life, but to allow the holy life of Jesus to live in and through you. You don't have to grasp what you can from life, but with open hands you can give and with open arms receive those who need grace.

When you receive this grace, when you live in its reality, you extend it from a reconciled, forgiven heart. And you become an agent of grace, not repulsed by sinners, but welcoming them to this reconciling task you were given. You are an ambassador of Grace, compelled by this extravagant, extraordinary compassion.

You not only become a heavenly envoy, you also participate in the grand design, the story that began before the world was created, the reason this grace was extended.

> Therefore God exalted him to the highest place
> and gave him the name that is above every name,
> that at the name of Jesus every knee should bow,
>   in heaven and on earth and under the earth,
> and every tongue acknowledge that Jesus Christ is Lord,
>   to the glory of God the Father. (NIV)

When you receive this grace, live in light of it, and extend it to others, you participate in giving glory to God the Father.

If all of this is true, if this extravagant love has been lavished on us, why do the followers of Jesus sometimes fall short? Why are our lives characterized by judgment, anger, revenge, counting wrongs against others, and lack of forgiveness? Why are we so unlike Jesus?

When you have been graced, you extend it. When your sins are great and they have been forgiven, you want to forgive those who wrong you. As Jesus said to Simon when the "sinful" woman used her tears to wet His feet and anointed Him with oil, "But the one who is forgiven little, loves little."

Our problem, followers of Jesus who appear angry and upset with "sinners," is that we see ourselves as being "forgiven little." We do not see our own truckload of faults. We forget how desperate we are, how much we need this grace. We would never say it, but our belief is that we're a little dirty here and there; we've had problems, but a simple dusting of forgiveness and a sprinkle of blood will suffice. But those people over there, the ones who are really bad, they need a bath. They're *really* sinful. Murderers and adulterers and idolaters and the like. We, like the religious leaders of Jesus' day, have not seen how needy we really are.

Truth leads us to grace. When we realize our helplessness and lack of virtue, grace helps us see ourselves and others in a new light. We believe the truth about the gospel, that God Himself dealt with sin totally and irrevocably on the cross. Therefore, we can be forgiven. We can be in right standing with God because of His perfect sacrifice. We receive forgiveness and then extend it to others.

Now, as we move out into a world filled with sinners, both believers and unbelievers, it is this tension between truth and grace that will tip us toward an all-embracing love that never sees the truth or an all-condemning truth that never communicates love. If we're out of balance here, those around us will either experience our judgment or a squishy, emotional love that feels good but has no effect.

Think of it like this: When Nathan the prophet confronted David with the story of the lamb slaughtered by the wealthy landowner, this was truth wrapped in grace. The story touched all the cylinders of David's heart. When he saw *himself* in the story, it hit him much more deeply than simply being told he was a sinner. This is the power of a good story. This is the powerful love of God mixed with the truth of our sin and wrapped in grace.

Grace is love in action. God's grace was embodied in Jesus as He lived a sinless life and died in your place and mine. Now, Jesus calls us to die to ourselves and move out into a world in desperate need of this kind of love. God's extraordinary grace is divine love in motion toward you so that you can give that kind of love to others.

This grace in our lives is a process. It is a new realization each day of how much we need it and how much others do as well. Grace is not in a hurry. It isn't rushed or harried. You simply rest in it. And as you rest, the peace of God will flow through your life.

Look at the amount of time God was willing to invest in this plan that was fashioned from eternity past. Are you willing to let grace work in you like this? Are you willing to invest this kind of grace in the lives of those you love? If you are forcing people to change, this is not grace. Grace requires you to absorb pain.

Some time ago I was visiting a prison in Louisiana. It was known as the worst prison in the entire state. The men incarcerated there are in for life. There were more murders and sexual assaults inside that prison than in any other in the state—until a Christian warden showed up and began to share Jesus. And one by one by one, those men began to become followers of Jesus.

When I arrived, half the population of 5,000 inmates were already believers. They had four churches inside the razor wire. Chapels built by Christian people. And the pastors of those four churches were inmates. And the people who led the music, the people who sang in the churches, were all inmates. And they had reached out into that community to share the good news of Jesus. And every Sunday, those chapels were filled.

New Orleans Seminary teaches classes there for the men who want to be pastors and learn how to work and walk with God. And I thought, "What a trophy of God's grace."

You would think that when you get in prison for life, that would be the end of the road. But not for these men. When those men realized the truth about themselves and received forgiveness, God's grace moved in and began to change them. They began walking in the light of that grace. And what happened? They gave it to others.

They've turned their lives over to Christ and now they're spreading the message of reconciliation in a community of 5,000.

They'll never get out of prison. Those men are there for life. But that's all right because God didn't promise to take away the consequences of our actions; He promised to forgive us and give us His blamelessness. They're winning people to Christ. And when people like me come in from the outside, we get to take the story of God's grace outside and tell other people that whatever you've done, whatever has happened in your past, you're not beyond the forgiveness of God. You're not beyond the grace of God. God has a plan and God wants to use you wherever you are.

They're in prison for life. But Jesus Christ has given them life abundant.

This is the extraordinary grace of God.

You've seen the difference grace will make in your life. Have you received that grace? This is where it begins. "Jehovah will save" is the meaning of the name *Yeshua*, the man we call Jesus. Receiving grace is not about going to church or doing good things; it doesn't come because your parents were Christians. It's a choice you make. God has done His part. He has paid your debt. And His grace is calling you. He is ready and willing and able to forgive because of the perfect sacrifice of Jesus.

Cry out to Him. Confess your sin to Him. Tell Him you believe the truth about yourself, that there is no way you can earn His favor. And then, by faith, receive the gift of grace He's offering.

"I know I've broken Your law, but I thank You that Christ paid my penalty. I want to come into Your family. I want to be forgiven. I want to live my life with You."

That's where it starts, and if you've never done that, call on God and He will answer.

Second, if you are a believer in Jesus and you're following Him, do you believe what God has said about you? Or do you think your past excludes you from His full love? You could not have done anything worse than the people whose lives we've studied. These were big-time sinners, but because of His grace, He brought them into His family and commended His love to them. Do you believe this? Then live in light of that truth today.

Third, a challenge to you. Have you let Satan use your past to keep you from following God? That's one of his tactics. He will say, "God could never use you. Look at what you've done." He condemns. He's called the Great Accuser. He wants you to live under the guilt of what you've done. Don't listen to that voice. If you've confessed your sin to God and you've turned to Him, God has forgiven you and God doesn't see your sin when He looks at you. He sees you as clean because you've come to Him and let Him forgive your sin. Don't let Satan use that against you. Believe what God says.

Finally, if you've received the grace of God, how are you doing with extending it? Do the people in your life compliment you on the grace you give, the forgiveness you offer? Do others feel love from you or condemnation? Would they characterize you as angry and bitter? If you're struggling to extend grace, let the truth of God's Word wash over you. Through this book you've been reminded of what you received in Christ, the righteousness that can only come from Him. And that He loves you not for how good you've been or will be. Don't run out right now and make a list of all the people you need to extend grace to. Don't try to rustle up the will to extend it. Instead, accept the love God has shown you, praise Him for that forgiveness and mercy, thank Him for His longsuffering. When you truly accept this amazing grace of God and allow it to embrace you, those around you will feel a difference in your attitude and actions toward them.

A PRAYER

O God of Abraham, Isaac, and Jacob, O God of all comfort, wisdom, and mercy, empower me now to accept the grace You have lavished on my heart. Open my eyes anew to the wondrous love You commended to me in Christ. Help me get a glimpse of Your holiness so that I might see the depth of my sin and repent. Like Abraham, help me to hear Your call and believe. Tear down the walls of my heart, my pride, my self-sufficiency, and show me how You fulfill my greatest need. Deliver me from my efforts to control and short-circuit the things You're teaching me in the pain of my life. Like David, give me a broken and contrite heart that seeks You above all else.

I believe, Lord, that You have the power to forgive and restore me, no matter what I've done in the past. Would You give me wisdom to walk forward and follow You closely? Would You help me view my past the way You view it? Help me make the most of every opportunity, every relationship, every decision I make. I do not want to miss anything Your grace has for me. Help me now to receive the love You're offering, to walk in light of that love and forgiveness and acceptance, and enable me to spread that same love to those in my life who are in desperate need of it. Make me more like Your Son, O God, for my good, for the sake of Your kingdom, and for Your glory.

I pray this with a grateful heart for Your grace.

In the name of Jesus, Amen.

The *Extraordinary Grace* Study

CHAPTER 1
HEARING THE CALL OF GRACE—ABRAM

QUESTION TO PONDER: If you could have God audibly speak to you right now as He did to Abraham, what would you want to hear? What question would you want Him to answer?

Read Genesis 11:26–12:9.

With the information you have about Abram before God spoke, how difficult do you think it would have been to obey God's directions?

How do you relate to this in your own life? Has there been a time when you knew what God wanted you to do but found it difficult to follow Him?

What specific things did God promise Abram in Genesis 12:1–3?

Genesis 12:9 says that Abram's journey to the Negev progressed in "stages." What does this mean to you today regarding your own journey?

Go back to the question to ponder. Has your perspective changed after looking at Abram's response and God's promises? If so, how?

Abram's life is the pattern for the modern believer in Jesus. He heard the call of grace. He believed God. He responded to the call by obeying, by acting on that call. How have you heard the call of grace and responded?

CHAPTER 2
LAUGHING BECAUSE OF GRACE—ABRAHAM

QUESTION TO PONDER: Have you ever had the experience of starting over? Describe this time of your life and the questions and feelings you went through.

In Genesis 18, we see that God meets Abraham at the oaks of Mamre. What is the significance of God meeting him at a tree? What other "trees" do we see in Scripture, and why do you think this is a significant place?

Earlier Abraham's fear button was pushed by the Egyptians. What is your fear button, and how is it pushed?

What comfort do you get from God saying to Abraham, "Do not be afraid . . . "? Do you think God wants to speak to your deepest need through His grace?

Have you ever tried to manipulate circumstances? Ever tried to help God stay on your timetable? Has that effort thwarted God's work of grace in your life?

Fear leads to adversity. Grace leads to blessing. Fear causes pain and hurt. Grace yields laughter.

Read John 8:31–59. Those talking with Jesus bring up Abraham. How did Jesus use Abraham's life to present the truth about Himself? How did Jesus compare Himself with Abraham?

On the surface this seems like a heated argument at best, but how is Jesus loving these people who do not believe in Him? (He could have not engaged with them at all.)

Spend some time identifying the fears you have and ways you have "controlled." Confess your fear to God and give Him control over those areas of your life.

CHAPTER 3
THE WAY OF DISGRACE, OR,
LESSONS FROM A PROSTITUTE—RAHAB

QUESTION TO PONDER: What "past" do you have that makes you identify with Rahab? Is there anything you've done that makes you feel like you are disqualified from God loving you?

Read Joshua 2.

Put yourself in the place of someone inside Jericho. What would be going through your mind and why?

Compare and contrast the fear that Rahab had with the fear of Abraham. How did the two handle their fear?

Rahab lived an immoral life. Does it surprise you that God would spare her? Why or why not?

Is there a Rahab in your life, someone you think would never respond to God or be a candidate for God's grace? From this story, how can you effectively communicate God's love to this person?

What was Rahab's deepest need, and how did God meet that need?

How were others around Rahab affected by the grace she received?

Why do you think the story of Rahab is preserved for us today?

The walls of Jericho fell, but even more miraculous, the walls of our hearts can fall, and we can allow the grace of God to forgive and cleanse. Have you experienced this? Spend some time thanking God for His extraordinary grace.

CHAPTER 4
FINAGLING GRACE—TAMAR

QUESTION TO PONDER: Revenge is a common theme in film and fiction. How have you battled revenge in your life? Have you felt like getting back at someone recently? Are there some people too far gone for God to change?

Read Genesis 38.

As Tamar watched God eliminate her first and second husbands, what do you think went through her mind?

Put yourself in her place, in this arranged marriage, in this influential family. How would you have felt?

After Onan died and Tamar went into mourning, what do you think was happening in her heart?

Have you ever been promised something that didn't come to pass? How did this affect you and the other person?

When Tamar is discovered to be pregnant, Judah is ready to pass judgment. But Tamar's planning and cunning prevents this. What do we learn from Judah's admission in Genesis 38:26?

What was the deepest longing of Tamar's heart?

What is the deepest longing of your heart, and how do you think God wants to meet you there?

CHAPTER 5
THE APPLICATION OF GRACE, OR, WE WOULDN'T HAVE PSALM 51 WITHOUT THIS STORY—DAVID

QUESTION TO PONDER: Have you ever been surprised by the fall of a respected believer? How did this affect your relationship with the person and your view of God?

Read 2 Samuel 11.

Identify the underlying reasons for David's immorality with Bathsheba. Describe the lengths to which he tried to cover it up.

Read the account of Nathan's visit with David. Why do you think God sent the prophet?

Give three reasons why you think God used a story to convict David.

Have you ever been convicted of sin through unconventional means?

Read Psalm 51. How can you tell David is not just a man who is sorry he was caught but is a man filled with repentance?

Do you think David felt the forgiveness of God in his life? Why or why not?

David's story doesn't end with his failures. He isn't disqualified from life. Yes, there are dire consequences, but God shows His love and compassion in forgiving David. Have you ever experienced this kind of sorrow and mercy?

CHAPTER 6
PURSUED BY DESIRE, OVERTAKEN BY GRACE
—BATHSHEBA

QUESTION TO PONDER: Is there something you've done or failed to do that you feel God is punishing you for? What are the similarities of the story of Bathsheba to the modern-day issues of sexual immorality?

Read 2 Samuel 12:15–24.

The death of a child rips hearts apart and can tear relationships. In this account of losing an infant, we only see the perspective of David. What do you think Bathsheba is going through?

Compare and contrast the affair with Bathsheba, their first encounter, to what happened at this point in their relationship.

If "grace is a choice," how does this story of David and Bath-sheba exhibit that truth?

If you've asked God to forgive you of a wrong you committed in the past but still feel God is mad at you, have you really allowed yourself to receive grace?

Name some of the ways that you might be able to move to the next step in your relationship with God and receive His mercy.

CHAPTER 7
ANSWERING THE GREATEST QUESTION
—SOLOMON

QUESTION TO PONDER: What comes to mind immediately when you read this question: If God said, "Ask for whatever you want Me to give you," how would you respond?

Read 1 Kings 3:5–9.

Break down Solomon's answer to God's question. What did Solomon proclaim, and what did he ask?

How did God respond to Solomon in 1 Kings 3:10–15?

Why do you think God was so generous with Solomon?

Do you think God wants to be generous with you, or is His blessing only for other people?

Looking at the totality of his life, Solomon made many mistakes. Like his father, his heart was led astray. In spite of this, God gave grace. What does this say to you about the grace available to your life?

How has God changed the desires of your heart over time? Compare how you would have answered the first question in this study earlier in your life with how you would answer it today.

CHAPTER 8
HE ALMOST MISSED GRACE IN A MANGER
—JOSEPH

QUESTION TO PONDER: Have you ever made a decision, big or small, when you almost missed something really good? Or, have you made a decision and chosen a path that led you away from something good?

Read Matthew 1:18–25.

Joseph had decided what he was going to do in this situation. Why do you think God went to these extraordinary lengths to change his mind?

How do you think Joseph's actions toward Mary affected Jesus? As the boy heard this story told later, how do you think it influenced Him?

How did Joseph respond to God? Do you see parallels between how Joseph acted and the responses of others we have studied?

"Grace is not about convincing others to believe." Do you agree with this statement? How does this influence the way you interact with others about spiritual things?

The telltale sign that grace has invaded your life is when you want to give it to others. Have you seen that kind of grace at work in you?

Have you ever had a chance to "stick it" to someone and held back? How did that feel to absorb the pain they had inflicted instead of lashing out?

If Jesus was grace deployed, how might God want to deploy His grace through you?

CHAPTER 9
GRACE MADE FLESH—JESUS

QUESTION TO PONDER: If an outsider were to look at your life and judge all Christians by the grace you give, what would they observe? Give specific examples of the positive and negative.

In John 1 we read that Jesus was the Word made flesh. Jesus was God's perfect communication to a needy world. What does it mean to you that He was "Grace made flesh"?

Read John 3:1–21. As you read, focus on the theme of the grace of God.

How does this passage detail God's extraordinary grace?

Why do you think Christians can live with so little grace to give to others?

Walk through the final prayer on pages 145–146. How do you see the characters we have studied reflected in this prayer?

Would you add anything to the prayer?

Pray the prayer slowly, from the heart, emphasizing the parts that mean the most to you today.

NOTES

1. To read this part of Abram's life, see Genesis 11:26–12:9.

2. Abraham's stories from this chapter can be found in Genesis 12:10–20; chapters 15–16; and 18:1–15.

3. To read about Rahab, read Joshua chapters 2 and 6.

4. *Macbeth*, ed. Philip Weller, Shakespeare Navigators, 5.1.50–52. www.shakespeare-navigators.com/macbeth/T51.html.

5. Tamar's story is found in Genesis 38.

6. For David's story of sin and repentance, see 2 Samuel 11:1–12:15; Psalm 51.

7. Read more on Bathsheba in 2 Samuel 12:15–25.

8. Solomon's story of asking God for wisdom is found in 1 Kings 3:1–15.

9. For more about Joseph's life and the birth of Jesus, see Matthew 1:18–25.

10. Chip Ingram, *Living on the Edge*: Notes & Reflections, "How to Experience Authentic Community," 1. r12online.livingontheedge.org/pdf/r12_session4.pdf.

11. To read more about God's purpose in sending Jesus, read John 1:1–18 and 3:1–21.

THE WAY HOME

THE WAY

HOME

A German Childhood,
An American Life

ERNESTINE BRADLEY

Pantheon Books, New York

The photographs on pages 7, 75, 139, and 225 are
from the author's personal collection.

Library of Congress Cataloging-in-Publication Data

Bradley, Ernestine, [date]
The way home : a German childhood, an American life /
Ernestine Bradley.
p.   cm.
ISBN 0-375-42279-X
1. Bradley, Ernestine, 1935–   2. Bradley, Bill, 1943– —Family.
3. Legislators' spouses—United States—Biography.   4. United
States—Biography.   5. Germany—History—1933–1945.
6. Germany—History—1945–1955.   I. Title.

CT275.B59375A3 2005   382.73'092—dc22   [B]   2004053418

www.pantheonbooks.com

Printed in the United States of America
First Edition
2   4   6   8   9   7   5   3   1

For all my grandchildren
Tim, Julianna, Michael, Isabella
and
all who are still twinkles
in the eyes of
God

My wife, above all, was a child of the defeat.

—Bill Bradley, *Time Present, Time Past*

One may be born with the potential for a prodigious memory, but one is not born with a disposition to recollect; this comes only with changes and separations in life—separations from people, from places, from events and situations, especially if they have been of great significance, have been deeply hated or loved. . . . Discontinuity and nostalgia are most profound if, in growing up, we leave or lose the place where we were born and spent our childhood, if we become expatriates or exiles; if the place, or the life, we were brought up in is changed beyond recognition or destroyed.

—Oliver Sacks, *An Anthropologist on Mars*

CONTENTS

PREAMBLE

*Memories, to me, are like illuminated islands floating
in an ocean of darkness. They offer scenes, not a continuous story.
The story emerges as the islands begin to form a pattern.*

The impetus to write this memoir grew out of events that occurred while my husband, Bill Bradley, was campaigning for the Democratic presidential nomination in 2000. I thought I knew pretty well who I was and what had made me the person I was. Then an archivist in Germany, where I was born, put information on the Web site of the Passau town archives that related to my parents and me and raised questions about my identity. He suggested that I was a *Hochstapler*, someone presenting herself with a better pedigree than she was entitled to: "Irrespective of what Mrs. Bradley and *Der Spiegel*"—a highly respected German newsmagazine—"obstinately insist upon," he stated, "Mrs. Bradley's father was not an air-force officer but a hairdresser." This cavalier assertion upset me enough that I needed to go back to my roots, to gain access to documents not previously available, and to reconsider how I became who I think I am.

I was thrown back on my family history, and began to think again about being born in Germany during the Nazi regime and growing up there in the postwar period, about coming to this country at the age of twenty-one and embracing life in the United States, with all its promise, and about accepting my uprootedness as a permanent part of my psychological and emotional makeup—an uprootedness that creates an exhilarating sense of freedom, coupled with a sense of loss and sometimes deep disorientation.

When the 2000 presidential campaign started, I thought of myself as a person fully grown, with no problems of "identity." Many years earlier, I had discovered and explored my past, and I was proud of my intellectual honesty. Only now do I see that the truths I'd discovered were intellectual, not emotional. I had never been homesick. I had never needed roots, because the mobility that comes with freedom was too important to me. I had discounted what it meant to grow up, as so many German children of that era did, without a father (they were all in the war). I had discounted what it meant to grow up with a mother too young to focus on a child and too preoccupied with her illnesses. I had glorified a childhood spent roaming the streets of Passau unsupervised. We had our little gang; we were all *Gassenkinder* ("street urchins"). We stole apples in orchards when they were only half ripe; we swam in rivers we were told to stay out of. We had lots of fun, even as we heard on the radio that a war was going on and as I watched my mother track the path of the German Army with multicolored pins on a huge map in our living room.

During the campaign, another subject was highlighted that I should also address immediately: was my father a Nazi? By "Nazi," did the press mean a member of the Nazi Party, or did they simply mean a person who lived in Nazi Germany? No, my father, Sepp Misslbeck, the air-force officer, was not a member of the party. My mother's first husband, the hairdresser (or at least the son of the owner of a hair salon in Passau), and the man ascribed to me by the town archivist as my father, did join the party in 1937 and during the war served in the army as a clerk.

Like so many native Germans of my generation, I have been haunted by the question of how I, as an adult, would have behaved during the Nazi regime. It is easy to think of oneself as honorable, brave, regime-defiant; it is tempting to condemn those who stood by, silent, ashamed, inactive; it is perhaps only slightly more self-righteous to single out the active, ferocious, and fanatical Nazis and, even more insidious, the opportunistic denouncers who spied on neighbors and turned in loved ones. How intimidating was group pressure to conform? How intimidating was the possibility of being denounced? What excuses were invented to serve the cult of obedience and the demand to place the national good above personal interests? How could mothers whose sons were killed at the front speak of *stolze Trauer* ("proud mourning")? Proud to have sacrificed what they presumably loved most? (When my maternal grandmother heard that her son had been killed on the Eastern Front, she was not proud. She went to bed and never got up again. It took her three years to die.)

Once the regime was in power, there were the legions of denouncers, the *Hauswart* and the *Blockwart,* spies in each building and on each block, collecting information on the visitors people had in their homes, on where people went or came from, on their tone of voice, judging with how much fervor (if at all) they gave the "Heil Hitler" salute as they passed. Children were charged to observe their parents and inform on them. Did their parents listen to forbidden radio stations, receive visitors with whom they whispered? Along with the thugs came the support of the intelligentsia, the university professors and their students, civic and church leaders, the judges and the civil service. Why was there so little resistance to the Nazi regime? Because in the absence of a democratic tradition many were drawn to Hitler's promise of strong leadership, a dream inspired by the political impotence that had haunted the German imagination for more than a century; because most Germans agreed with Hitler's invectives against the "peace dictated from above," the *Friedensdiktat* of the Versailles Peace Treaty, which they found unfair; because much of the politically organized opposition and leadership of the socialists and communists had been murdered during the tumultuous years of the Weimar Republic, and those still active fled once Hitler was appointed chancellor (while they still could, that is); because the system was firmly established by the time it became apparent that it should be opposed; because the indoctrination into obedience, absorbed over generations, made the thought of opposition nearly impossible; because the terrible odds against the Weimar Republic had not converted many to democracy; because anti-Semitism offered a streamlined answer to all problems; because . . . because . . .

Obedience and group mentality are two branches of the same tree, and they produced horrible blossoms in all the social institutions of Germany, from family structure and the educational system to bureaucratic and military hierarchies. How damaging was an educational system that demanded unquestioned obedience—a system instituted long before the Nazis, yes, but used by them with chilling effectiveness? Even on the smallest and most private scales, the pressures to conform showed their power. My mother could not tolerate it when my younger sister, Monika, wanted to wear a skirt that was too short, a hat that was too flashy. "What would the neighbors think if you went out like that?" she would exclaim, appealing to deeply inculcated community standards, of which she totally approved. (Monika, instead of giving in to my mother's "conventional" taste, would stay home.) I curtsied until I left home at age eighteen. One of the liberating aspects of coming to this country was that I did not have to shake hands all the time. When I returned to Germany for a visit, it completely slipped my mind that one is invariably supposed to shake hands when greeting someone. My mother apologized in front of me to her friends: in my time away from home, she said, I had forgotten my manners.

PASSAU

M emory is often stored at such depths that it eludes the conscious mind. The French philosopher Jean-François Lyotard speaks of the "unforgettable forgotten." What have I, as an adult, forgotten that is yet indelibly, "unforgettably" inscribed in my bones, in my gestures, and that breaks out in unexpected moments from deep within?

I was born in Passau, which is now on the Austrian border, in 1935. Passau is a city of three rivers—*die Dreiflüsse-Stadt*. It is mentioned in the *Nibelungenlied*, the German epic poem written around 1200, but its origins date back roughly fifteen hundred years. Here I spent the first ten years of my life. The picturesque old town, the Altstadt, with its Italianate buildings, is set on hills high above the confluence of the Danube, Inn, and Ilz rivers. It also sits on top of formidable walls, constructed over centuries to defy the periodic floods, and its heart is laced with tunnels, steep steps, and narrow alleys—a child's dream landscape, where you could play hide-and-seek all day long. (During the war there were practically no vehicles in the streets.) Street names like Hennengasse (Hens' Alley) and Löwengrube (Lions' Den) suggested a magical past, and the high, narrow buildings created canyons that promised protection.

The Danube was, for us kids, the least interesting of Passau's

Me as an infant, with my Tante Betty, probably around December 1935.

rivers. It had a harbor, or perhaps it was just a long, extended boat-landing, where ships coming down from Regensburg or up from Vienna docked. The dockworkers would yell at us and chase us away, but there was nothing to do there anyway, except watch the loading and unloading. In former times (so we were told), boats would come from as far away as Budapest and the Black Sea. It all sounded very mysterious: I had no idea why those boats no longer arrived. In the 1980s, my nephew, who was then a student at the University of Passau, invited me to ride out into the countryside. Not far from town, he stopped before a huge boulder overgrown with ivy. You had to push the ivy aside to see a plaque commemorating an *Aussenlager;* it was a subsidiary of the Mauthausen concentration camp, which itself was located about eighty miles down the Danube from Passau. This subcamp was small—it never contained more than a hundred people—but what went on there? When I asked my mother about the camp many years later, she gave me the usual answer: she did not know.

Not even that the area was closed off and nobody was allowed to go near it? Well, yes, that of course one knew, since one was not allowed to go there.

What do you think was going on there? One didn't know, precisely because one was not allowed to go near the place. And nobody ever really went? Not to her knowledge. Could you venture a guess? Perhaps they built secret things. Who built them? Prisoners. What kind of prisoners? Prisoners, political prisoners, those who opposed the regime. And what about the Jews? She did not know.

The Inn River was my river, perhaps because we lived in the Innstadt, the section of town wedged between the Inn River and the Mariahilfsberg, a mountain rising behind the river. Overlooking the Innstadt, perched on top of the mountain, was a famous pilgrims' church, Mariahilf, which gave the mountain its name. It was an attractive building, the outside walls washed in a Baroque yellow, with white accents and carved stone masonry surrounding the windows and doors. Leading up to it on one side of the mountain, opposite the roadway where in winter we went sleigh-riding, was a covered passage with perhaps three hundred wide stone steps, where pilgrims would ascend, saying prayers on each step. When there was a drought or some other calamity, long processions of farmers came from miles around to appeal to Mary, Mother of God, praying, *"Maria, hilf!,"* carrying banners and fingering the beads of their rosaries as they walked. I watched them from a window of our apartment as they walked by, making their way up to the church, barefoot all the way.

My "Tante Betty" (not an actual relative but a person I loved dearly) had a grandson, Gerhardi, with Down syndrome. On several occasions she prayed an entire rosary on each of the steps leading to the church at the top of the mountain and would have to spend the night on the steps, because she could not finish all her prayers in one day. Only much later, after her death, did I realize that Gerhardi had been a prime target for the euthanasia program the Nazis launched in 1939, and that her prayers had a very specific purpose. Gerhardi survived because in August 1941 Bishop Galen of Münster preached a single sermon against the euthanasia program, and the killings were stopped—at least officially. How often have I wondered what would have happened if Bishop Galen or someone of similar authority had spoken out against the deportation of the Jews, who were neighbors, German citizens. Most Germans were opposed to the euthanasia program, since it was directed against members of their own families, and the bishop knew he spoke for the majority when he condemned it. The Jews, a minority, had no such advocates. Even so, in 1943, when the gentile wives of Jewish men who had been sent to the camps staged a weeklong protest in Berlin at the Rosenstrasse—

under constant threat of being shot at—they were successful: the men were released. How often would the Nazis have caved in when faced with convincing public protest?

In late spring, the Inn River would swell with snowmelt from the Alps and often carried *Hochwasser* ("high water"). The floodings of Passau occur regularly; there are high-water marks on the outside of many houses, and inside, damp cavernous hallways lead from ground floors to the safe upper floors. Sometimes when you walked across the Inn Bridge, you were drenched by the spray and you could feel the bridge swerve. It was exciting. Several months after one particular *Hochwasser,* there appeared a gravel island in the river, toward the Innstadt side and separated from the Innstadt by a deep and fast current. It was early summer. I was eight years old, and our little gang decided to jump from the bridge into the river and swim to the new island. The Inn is a swift river at all times. A little downstream, past where the Inn emptied into the Danube, a ferry went back and forth on a cable, and the river was so strong that it once tore the ferry from the cable. Rumor had it that people drowned. We jumped; we swam; we landed on the gravel island a long way downstream from the bridge. Neighbors, acquaintances, somebody must have told my mother. Obviously, she was very angry with me and took me to "Opapa," her husband's father, who flourished his cane and said he would thrash me with it if I ever jumped again. The threat of a beating did not scare me, and I could not understand why everybody got so upset about something that had been so much fun— but I never jumped into the Inn again.

Opapa's son, my mother's husband, was Baumeister Max, the proprietor—or the son of the proprietor—of the hair salon where she worked. (In Bavaria it is customary to refer to a person by his or her last name first, followed by the given name, a custom that may be a vestige of the importance attached to family identity rather than to the individual. The name of my mother's first husband forever rings in this reverse sequence in my ears, and I will keep it that way.) Baumeister Max loved my mother, and with enormous gallantry had married her after she became pregnant with me by the man she was in love with but felt she could not marry. She often told me, with a slight bitterness in her voice, that a week after I was born she was picked up from the lying-in hospital—elegantly, by taxicab—and went right back to work at the Baumeister salon; as the owner's wife, she felt this was expected of her. So, upon coming home from the hospital, I was immediately given into day-and-night care with Tante Betty. Tante Betty became the most important person in Passau for me. It was she who invented my nickname, Wuschi, and she tied a string to my cradle with the other end attached to her foot, so that when I cried during the night she did not have to get out of bed but simply rocked me back to sleep by pulling the string with her foot.

Tante Betty was married to "Uncle Avril," who had a huge dark-red nose that had been frozen during World War I. I don't know why he was only called by his last name, the French word for "April." For me, the name has an interesting historical resonance: I assume that one of his French ancestors stayed behind in Bavaria after the Napoleonic Wars at the beginning of the nineteenth century. They lived in a large apartment on the second floor of one of those houses with dark and enormous ground floors constructed of huge stone slabs. Tante Betty had a net shopping bag suspended on a rope from the second-floor banister so that when she brought home groceries she did not have to carry them upstairs but pulled them up on the rope. Tante Betty and her husband rented out rooms to young boys from the country who went to the Passau *Gymnasium*. She would cook for them and make their beds, and during the war, when the *Gymnasium* students came back from their weekends in the country they would always bring food. I remember Tante Betty's big dining-living room. (Was it really that big, or did it just seem so to the little girl I was?) Over the table hung a lamp made of dark-green fringed silk, which could be raised and lowered on a cord. Even after I was a little older and had been taken away from Tante Betty, I visited her as often as I could. In those remembered scenes, the students sit around the table, she supervises their homework, and she sews; she must have taken sewing in. I am just old enough to crouch on a chair and bend over the table to paint or draw. I am busy, like the big boys around the table, and Uncle Avril sits on the sofa and reads a paper in semi-obscurity, because the light of the lamp over the table does not reach into the corners of the room. These scenes around the table—I see them as if they were a painting, the green lamp shade, the bright light on the table with the people congregated around it, and the uncle in the shaded background. Does his newspaper catch a glimmer of the light and reflect it on his face? Is this how it was? Is this how it could have been? Is this how I wish it had been? This scene is the only memory I have of an intimate, tranquil domesticity during my early childhood.

My mother took me away from Tante Betty when I was about a year and a half, old enough to be entrusted to a young woman from the Arbeitsdienst ("Workers' Service"), or, more precisely, the Reichsarbeitsdienst, a Nazi-invented organization requiring young people to do what we might today call community service, such as draining swamps, working on farms, or, for girls especially, working in households. My mother's pride would never have allowed her to admit it, but I know she was jealous of Tante Betty. She often told me that, when she ran over to Tante Betty's apartment during a break in her work routine, Tante Betty would invariably say that I was asleep and could not be disturbed. My mother at that time was nineteen years old and no match for Tante Betty. But she could and did take me away from her. From that time on, a succession of girls from the Arbeitsdienst would, every afternoon, put me in a stroller and take me to my mother at the hair salon. When my mother was free, she took me to a café around the corner for ice cream and a *Torte*. These scenes I know from photographs. But I also remember, unaided by photographs, that I waited for the times when my mother was too busy to attend to me, because then I could insist on being taken to see Tante Betty. I had little fits, yelling in the stroller or stomping my feet on the sidewalk, and there was no girl in the Arbeitsdienst who did not want to get rid of such a difficult child and leave me with the adult whose name I so demandingly screamed.

Once the war started, the girls from the Arbeitsdienst petered out. I started going to nursery school, which was close to where Opapa and Omama Baumeister lived. Here Lina, their longtime housekeeper and cook, took me under her wing, and I felt empowered enough to be not very nice to my mother. The earliest sign of rebellion I remember dates back to my high chair days in the Baumeister apartment. Lunch in Germany is a much heavier affair than in this country, and so it was in the Baumeister family. On this particular occasion Lina had fixed me *Griesbrei*, a soft and sweet kind of porridge made of matzoh meal and served with raspberry syrup. It's a favorite of children, and I assume Lina thought I didn't have enough teeth yet to chew on something harder. I decided I didn't want the *Griesbrei*, so Lina fixed me scrambled eggs. I didn't want those, either. (My mother, years later, as we reminisced about Passau, would insist that I looked at her as I asserted myself with another "No!" This I don't remember, but it makes sense.) Lina then heated and cut up some soft little sausages (*Weisswurst*) for me, with kind words of encouragement, since she did not want me to go hungry, but she did not understand that there was a major power struggle going on. I rejected the sausages, too. At that point, my mother tried to pull me out of the high chair to spank me, but Opapa intervened: under no circumstances should she touch that sweet, lovely child! Was I in triumph? I must have been, for the scene is still so vivid in my mind that I see the kitchen in full color with all its furniture, a glass door into the dark hallway, and on the other side of the hallway the door to the living room, where I sat a few years later on the windowsill to watch the beginning of the campaign against Poland.

Opapa spoiled me in accordance with his tastes. He was a great lover of horses—the Rottal, not far from Passau, was great horse country—and when I was four years old, he bought me a pony. There are photographs of me sitting on the pony, and I remember the stable where Opapa would take me to feed it. It must have been a good pony, because it never frightened me when I combed it with a rough brush, but I don't remember its name. I had the pony into the early months of the war; when all the horses were confiscated, my pony replaced a horse in a circus.

After I was in kindergarten, I did not see Tante Betty very often, but I missed her. And I lied so that she would feel for me. In this scene, my mother is walking with a girlfriend in one of the parks along the Inn River and holding me by the hand. I see Tante Betty coming toward us; I run to her, hide my face in her skirts, and cry, "Tante Betty, Tante Betty, my mother always beats me so!" (*"Meine Mutti schlägt mich immer so!"*) My mother is incensed, Tante Betty only too willing to believe me; and their discussion turns into a dispute as to whether or not I am telling the truth. My mother, in her sense of insulted dignity, never asked herself why I loved Tante Betty so much, why I would be lying, or why I could feel so antagonistic toward her. I did not dislike her because she neglected me, but because she had taken me away from Tante Betty.

Another instance of my challenging my mother also stems from around that time. It must have been in the early months of the war, because Baumeister Max was already gone, yet I was still small enough to ride horsey on the back of a casual friend of hers—he, too, already dressed in a grayish-green uniform. Possibly I had just picked up a new word and wanted to test it out on him when I said, "You know, Uncle Fred"—he was not my uncle, just as Tante Betty was not my aunt—"sometimes my mother can be a real bitch." (*"Manchmal kann meine Mutti ein rechtes Mistvieh sein."*) I was so proud when I used that word, it made me feel so grown up.

Did my mother really want me for herself? She was so young, she had so much living to do, she wanted not a secure life but an exciting life, and though I was her "special" child, I was also in the way. She did not know what to do with me, except possess me and display me, and she mistook that for love. By the time I was five, I had had more experimental hairdos—including a Shirley Temple poodle cut—than I have had over the last thirty years. I felt, as Bavarians say, like a *trainierter Affe* ("a trained monkey"). My older daughter, Stephanie, who is a clinical psychologist, thinks my mother saw me as a narcissistic extension of herself, a "self-object." This would explain what became ever more explicit over the years: even though she was extremely possessive of me, I also had to fit precisely into the image she had constructed of herself and her relation to me. Never was she able to see me as an individual in my own right, a little person who needed to be nurtured and given space to grow.

My mother adored her own mother. Did she tell me so in order to set an example? I did not adore my mother's mother. She was too pious for me, and too *wehleidig* ("woebegone"—this is an English word to which I have no emotional connection; any combination of other letters would elicit the same nonresponse; the German word, for me, is loaded with self-pity, with being excessively lachrymose). She longed for Alsace-Lorraine, where she had grown up and been happy, and she remained embedded in the values and lifestyle of the late nineteenth century. She wore long skirts and a hairdo that recalled late-Victorian ladies—a bun on top of her head with the hair loosely arranged around it. When I think of her, I never see her walking straight—she always wobbles from side to side like a penguin. I thought she was an old woman, whereas in fact she had merely given up. I hated it when, in my grandfather's garden in Ingolstadt, she would pee on the plants instead of going to the (admittedly uncomfortable) outhouse, but today I think she was re-enacting some arcane ritual from her childhood on the farm in Lorraine.

I tried to battle her, too. When she came to Passau to visit us, there was not enough closet space, so she hung her clothes over the railing of my crib. I did not like to sleep surrounded by them, and I did not like their smell. One day we had company; at the time, it was considered polite to show the guests, particularly on a first visit, through one's house. My grandmother did not want these guests to see her clothes draped on my crib, so she bundled them together on the mattress and covered them with my blanket. I was livid. I screamed and yelled and had a fit, but the clothes stayed under the cover. A few days later, after my grandmother had departed, my mother remarked that a child, even one small enough to sleep in a crib, should not behave this way; if she, as a child, had dared to have such a fit, she said, her mother would have slapped her with a loose flick of her wrist and the back of her hand. Despite this warning that I deserved a slap, my mother never struck me.

I did have a moment of triumph over my grandmother. It occurred early in the summer of 1939, right before the beginning of the war, when I was not quite four years old. My mother, my grandmother, and I were vacationing in the Bavarian Alps. At an inn, they served blood sausage (*Blutwurst*), congealed blood with thick chunks of lard in it. I refused to eat it. My grandmother insisted that what is served on the table must be eaten; you must not return precious food and let it go to waste. Perhaps she was also embarrassed in front of the waitress, to be seen with such a spoiled child. She insisted and I had to eat; I wanted to cry but could not. My mother sat by, immobile, totally quiet, and let her mother take charge. Was she just watching to see how this struggle would end, or did she defer to her mother? I remember a traumatic moment, when my own Stephanie was about two and a half years old. It was wintertime, after Christmas, and we had come from Atlanta to visit in Ingolstadt. It had snowed overnight, and the next morning the ground was white. My mother wanted to take Stephanie on a sleigh ride, but Stephanie had never seen snow and did not want to step on it. She was dancing on her tiptoes, trying to keep her feet in the air, so as not to touch the snow. Of course it did not work. In panic, she started to cry. I wanted to pick her up. My mother grabbed her and put her forcefully down on the sled. On the sled, Stephanie cried all the more. I stood by, paralyzed. Maybe this was how my mother felt when my grandmother made me eat the blood sausage. However, I was over a year older at the time than Stephanie was in Ingolstadt, and I fought back: I managed to vomit the sausage up and was proud of it. I felt vindicated when my grandmother felt bad.

A few weeks later—I had just turned four—on September 1, 1939, Germany started World War II by invading Poland. I have two distinct memories from that time. The first is Mobilization Day. It was a Sunday in August. Baumeister Max loved to go fishing. A little upstream on the River Ilz, the third of the three rivers that give Passau its distinctive charm—and not far from where, later, the *Aussenlager* would be constructed—there was a big fishing pond. At one time the river used to drive a mill, and the area, wooded and grassy and with a restaurant, was called the Oberilzmühl (the Upper Ilz Mill). You could swim there and fish, drink a beer, have a picnic. We spread a blanket on the grass, like so many around us, and Baumeister Max went fishing. Did I splash in the water? Did I drink a *Limonade*? I know I licked yellow *Brausepulver* (a powder that, poured into water, made a soft drink) and it tickled in my nose. Everybody seemed to be listening to the radio. Was the loud voice on the radio Hitler's? Then there was a big commotion and we all went home earlier than anticipated.

My mother and Baumeister Max had come on bicycles. He must have taken his fishing rods apart and tied them to the center bar of his bike. He also had a reed basket, specially woven for small children, with leg protection, hooked to the handlebars. Sitting in that little basket as we bicycled home, I looked directly into his face, and he into mine. He had brown eyes and dark hair; I thought of him as "mine," and, balanced on that bicycle, I felt good. This is the last image I have of him. I don't know whether I ever saw him again. He must have left for the war soon afterward, and if I saw him again later on I don't remember it. But he had left his imprint on me. It is amazing to me that as an adult woman I was never attracted to blond, Germanic-looking men but always to the ones with dark hair. There are no photographs of Baumeister Max that might have influenced my memories of him. My mother must have destroyed them—as if by eliminating the photographs she could eliminate that part of her past, and a sliver of my past, too. Except for that one clear image of him that afternoon at the Oberilzmühl, I have no impressions of the man who, for the first few years of my life, was "my father." I don't even know whether I called him Vati—I must have—but he has shaped my predilection for a certain type of man.

And then I remember images of the event that started World War II: the campaign against Poland, the *Polenfeldzug*. I remember being in Opapa and Omama Baumeister's large ground-floor apartment, which overlooked the avenue where the soldiers "going to war" marched by. The windows had wide sills and no screens, and someone (my mother?) put a cushion on the sill and sat me on it so that I would be comfortable as I watched column after column of soldiers march past. The people in the street threw flowers at them, or ran up to them and pinned them with little wreaths and more flowers. Everybody in the street seemed full of good cheer, and the people leaning out the windows were waving. Not long afterward, the Einsatzgruppen in Poland started their work, with deportations and the initially awkward and "inefficient" mass executions. How many of the soldiers marching by—caring husbands and devoted fathers—would soon take part in killing children the age of their own, women like their wives, older people like their parents? (Until quite recently, the German Army denied complicity in the crimes of the SS and the Einsatzgruppen, but newly accessible documentation shows otherwise.)

With the beginning of the war, the escape routes for German Jews shut down. Those who lived in or managed to flee to surrounding countries had fewer and fewer places to hide, particularly as the German armies advanced and the conquered territories bowed, more or less voluntarily, to German demands. I sat on my pillow and waved with a bunch of flowers someone had pushed into my hand.

The political noises, the marches and songs, the devastations of the Kristallnacht—all of these I now know only from pictures, reports, readings, even though I was alive when they happened. I do remember one of the barbers in my mother's hair salon; he had slicked-back dark hair and very long fingernails, and that impressed me. His name was Wenzel, and he always fussed over me. One day he was gone, and I missed him; my mother explained that he was Czech and that it was better for him to be gone. Who else was gone because it was "better" for him or her? There was a big department store in Passau called the Grenzlandkaufhaus. Only in the late 1950s did I know enough to ask my mother who the owners of the Grenzlandkaufhaus had been, and she said that they had been Jews.

And what happened to them? She did not know, but they left early. Early in relation to what? Before the war started. Had she known them? A little bit, as a customer in the store, and they were always so nice. When she started working in the Baumeister salon, investing every penny she made in what she thought would be her trousseau, they would always put a little extra in the packages sent to her—a pair of gloves, a scarf. My mother wanted to be sure that I knew she was fair, not prejudiced, when she spoke about Jews.

Did the owners of the Grenzlandkaufhaus have to sell their business for a pittance? She did not know that, either, but wasn't it good that they were able to leave?

But they were Germans. Why should they leave? Would she like to leave Germany, just like that, with a pittance for what she had worked all her life to accomplish?

Many years later, when I visited her with Rita Jacobs, an American friend of mine who had lost members of her family in the Holocaust, my mother spoke to her about the horror of "what Hitler did to the Jews." She was so ashamed that she cried. I think Rita's presence had somehow made what was usually safely abstract, impersonal, distanced, into a palpable reality my mother found hard to endure.

In trying to remember the past, I simultaneously and constantly doubt the "truth" of what I remember. I am caught in the cage of my memories and cannot get outside it. I call the scenes at the Oberilzmühl and on the windowsill watching the soldiers "true" memories because they are not reproductions of photographs. So often we remember photographs when we think we remember original scenes. Photographs can distort memory and etch impressions in our minds of events we don't actually remember at all, but they may be the only reality we have. I still see myself, as a nine-year-old, in such a photograph, shot from behind, braids dangling and shoulders hunched, as I push my brother's baby carriage over cobblestones. In another picture I hold him like a doll; I am stiff and awkward, just as I was when I held the doll I never liked—a coveted *Schildkrtenpuppe* made of stiff, unwieldy plastic so that it was difficult to dress or undress or to hug, and I could never snuggle with it because it poked me. But I have no independent memory of these scenes.

Yet even "true" memories distort, impose a new reality, adjust themselves to a person's needs. My memory of Baumeister Max, as I sat opposite him on that bicycle seat, feels true to me, but I don't know what he really looked like or who he was. There are memories elicited by images or by the gestures of strangers, and there is the unexpected, overwhelming invasion of past events called forth by sensory experiences—a melody, a smell in unfamiliar surroundings—that can make you happy, or move you to tears.

Why was my mother so young when I was born? This is a highly charged story, full of passion and pain, and it is the story my mother and father had so much wanted to write together. They never did, but the way in which their deep bondedness played out is a romantic and stirring drama for those who are inclined to see love as they did.

My mother, Erna Keller, grew up in Ingolstadt on the Danube, about 120 miles west of Passau. The Kellers had been expelled from Lorraine right after World War I, and my maternal grandmother, though she was a German, considered herself a refugee. My mother was thus imprinted early with a sense of not belonging. I see her whole life as a struggle to combat that sense, to be admitted. Because she was a girl, her parents never considered letting her pursue the high-school track that led to university studies or a career in business. This was not a question of money, since the public schools did not charge tuition and the Catholic schools charged very little. It was a decision based on gender. When she was fourteen, she had reached the age when in Germany you start an apprenticeship for a trade. Just then, the Depression hit, and unemployment rose rapidly. Hitler's demagoguery found a desperate and receptive audience. When I hear people speak about the Great Depression in this country, I cannot help thinking about the last years of the disintegrating Weimar Republic, when unemployment rose to about 50 percent. Despite America's populist demagogues, the institution of democracy here was never endangered. Europe, by contrast, was overwhelmed by totalitarian regimes that gained the upper hand in their fight against communism and the Soviet Union, which was trying to export its successful revolution of 1917.

By 1930, when my mother left school for an apprenticeship, Italy had long been fascist and Hungary, after a communist stint, was a dictatorship. Within three years, Hitler would assume power in Germany, and Spain prepared for the civil war that lasted from 1936 to 1939, ending with the victory of Franco's Falange over the communists. What options did my mother, as a fourteen-year-old, have? While she was still at school, she would stop at a hair salon in Ingolstadt after classes and pitch in, washing the proprietor's laundry and the customers' towels, just so she would be assured of a position. After she finished school, she was accepted at the salon as an apprentice without salary.

When she told her family that she had succeeded in finding a position in this hair salon, her mother cried, humiliated to think that her daughter had to wash "the dirty bozos' heads" (*die Grindköpfe*). I think my mother chose to become a hairdresser because young *Friseusen* (female hairdressers) looked so chic and fancy in the movies of the Weimar Republic. In those movies, they always had enough cash to help a forlorn lover or rescue a friend in need, and my mother adopted these role models. She had a great zest for living: she liked the movies; she liked to dance; she liked to sing. Just listening to her, I learned a great number of songs from the Weimar period—a time before I was born. She sang the songs in their popular adaptations, so that the opening lines of *Warte, warte nur ein Weilchen* ("wait, wait just a little while") were followed not by a promise of happiness—"*bald kommt auch das Glück zu dir*"—but by the sinister promise of Harmann, a mass murderer of women who with his cute little axe would make hashed meat out of you: "*bald kommt Harmann auch zu dir, und mit dem süssen Hackebeilchen macht er Hackfleisch dann aus dir.*" And as she sang, she would dance along to the happy rhythm of an American import, the fox trot. Or she would sway in slow steps to *Schöner Gigolo, armer Gigolo*, a text that for me voices the despair and cynicism of the Weimar Republic, but wrapped in an enchanting melody.

During the Nazi period, I learned other songs from my mother, listening to her imitating Rosita Serrano or the deep-voiced Zara Leander, watching her dancing and singing along with Marika Rökk, and I was desperate to learn to whistle so I could chime in as she whistled along with Ilse Werner. And I was proud when, as a six year old, I understood the subtext of the verses she intoned with a full heart as she waltzed to *Es geht alles vorüber, es geht alles vorbei*—a song which promises that as everything passes, December will be followed by May; in the popular version of this wartime favorite, the play on the words *Mai* and *Ei* had each December followed by a (rationed) egg: *Auf jeden Dezember folgt wieder ein Ei*. (The Nazi marching songs we learned later, in school; to my mother's credit, she never sang those.)

Her relations with her father were strained, primarily (as she would repeat throughout her life) because he had not allowed her to finish the high-school track that would have qualified her for university studies. Only her brother, my Uncle Fritz, was allowed to follow this track. How often did she tell us that in the midst of the Depression, with her first tips as an apprentice hairdresser, she bought herself a big piece of sausage (no one in our family has had much interest in sweets and cakes), sat down at the dining-room table, invited her sisters to share it with her, and did not offer any to my grandfather, who was also there. (I don't believe my grandfather depended on her sausage, but he must have been hurt.) Had she really meant to go to the university, in the Germany of the early 1930s? Or was she merely jealous that some of her girlfriends, who were not as smart as she but whose parents let them continue studying, did not have to find apprenticeship positions? One of my great disappointments was that when she was widowed, at the age of only fifty-eight, she did not pursue what she had always claimed was her dream, and what she had allegedly sacrificed to her marriage: a wider and deeper education. For many years after my father's death, she volunteered in an orphanage, took long walks, had her friends in to coffee, and preferred embroidery and crocheting to reading. "I am too tired," she would say, and she meant not only physical exhaustion but mental fatigue. I, who had grown up hearing her frequently expressed regrets over this missed opportunity, and who empathized with her as my own education advanced, could not understand that it was more important for her to keep her dream intact than to test it against reality. I was haughty enough to be disappointed.

My father, Sepp Misslbeck, was born in 1912. He came from an old, established family in Ingolstadt, where, emerging from the guild system, his father, and before him his grandfather, had a *Drechslerei*, a lathe-turner's craft shop, which produced, as we used to say, anything that was round and made of wood: lamp stands, legs for chairs, wooden plates, bowls, spindles for banisters, even picture frames and beautiful boxes made of many woods. Seppi, my brother, now has some of these objects on display at his tool-and-dye company in Ingolstadt—they look like museum pieces.

My father was the youngest of six children, the only son after five girls. The children came fast; the oldest one, my Tante Anny, was only ten years older than my father. In 1916, in the middle of World War I and with their father away in the army, their mother died in the hospital after an appendix operation, at age thirty-nine. My father was four years old at the time, and he developed legendary temper tantrums. I think it was his way of showing his grief and protesting that he was deprived of motherly care. I cannot conceive that there were any cuddling adults around in the middle of the war to console a child on the loss of his mother or the absence of his father. Tante Anny herself would have needed love and consolation, yet she had to manage, if only temporarily, the household and five younger siblings.

My father's tempers, his raging against circumstances, never abated over his lifetime. When I first became acquainted with him and his outbursts I was not scared, because the tantrums never lasted long, blew over like thunderstorms. Today, sometimes when I see people really angry and screaming I smile inwardly; they remind me of my father, and that is a source of comfort, not a threat.

With six young children to take care of, my grandfather had to remarry. One of his wife's sisters had a fiancé who was killed in the war. He married her: his sister-in-law became his wife, and the children's aunt their stepmother, whom they called "Muttl." She had one child with my grandfather. After she had raised her sister's six children, her own son was killed in World War II.

For my father, pursuit of the higher-education track was equally out of the question, and again it was not for financial reasons. The thinking was that what was good for the father certainly was good enough for the son, and that one day he would succeed his father in the woodworking business. And so he was apprenticed in his father's trade. On his eighteenth birthday, when he reached majority, he informed his father that he had been accepted into the Munich-based Landespolizei. The Lapo, as they abbreviated it, was a Bavarian State Police organization. In its paramilitary organization it circumvented the Versailles Peace Treaty, which stipulated that Germany's army could not exceed a hundred thousand men. What must my grandfather have felt when his son refused to continue the Misslbeck tradition, packed up, and left for Munich?

For a number of years, my father came home to Ingolstadt on weekends to help in the *Drechslerei* and to see his former school buddies at a local sports club. My mother, independent and wanting to mingle with other young people, had also joined that sports club. There they met, and fell immediately in love. It was a vehement and intense passion, and it lasted a lifetime.

My father must have seen in my mother the incarnation of a larger, perhaps even exotic life. He came from a small-town, petit-bourgeois family; he had the urge to see the world, to experience more than what Ingolstadt had to offer. My mother's unconventional spontaneity must have enchanted him, as did her lively looks, which her mother allowed her to enhance with ribbons and laces and bows rather than rein in with a wet hairbrush and pins and collarless blouses. (When she was invited to visit my father's family for the first time, his father also took a liking to her, indicated by his offering her to drink from his beer stein; this made my father's five sisters, who had never had such a treat, furious with envy—not a very auspicious beginning!) My father must also have been taken with my mother's mother herself, the Victorian lady in long skirts and starched ruffles. She insisted that her daughters had not "boyfriends" but "young men" who were "suitors"; and suitors were "received," with tea and cookies. Even at the height of inflation, she would serve two different courses of meat, or one of fish and one of meat, and in a region where pork and beef were the common, homegrown staples, she would search for fowl and venison and mutton and invite the young men to Sunday dinners. In summer, she would walk into town with parasol and lace gloves.

My father became the dominant influence in my mother's life. She finished her apprenticeship in 1933, the year Hitler came to power, and my father, imbued with the idea that one should go out and see the world, found her a position as *erste Kraft* (principal hairdresser) in the Baumeister hair salon in Passau. My mother took great pleasure in telling us often how the Baumeisters were shocked to see that the *erste Kraft* was such a young girl, and how proud she was to show them that she knew her trade. During the summer, my father and his friends would canoe 120 miles down the Danube and visit "Ernche" as she worked and saved for a trousseau. Meanwhile, my father rose slowly through the ranks of the Lapo. Since he had not taken the high-school exams that would have allowed him to pursue a higher civil-service career, he spent his earnings on private tutors so that he could eventually take the exams and obtain the *Abitur,* along with the students who had spent their advanced-track school years getting ready for it. He helped his father in Ingolstadt on weekends and studied every night, hardly able to keep awake without cigarettes and coffee. I still wonder how he had the time and energy to produce a child!

In the fall of 1934, my mother moved back to Ingolstadt. Apparently Baumeister Max in Passau was in love with her, and she felt awkward. She and my father were reunited, and she became pregnant. (There is a well-known Ingolstadt writer, Marieluise Fleisser, a onetime friend of Bertolt Brecht, who wrote a play, *The Pioneers of Ingolstadt,* about young people and their calamities. Of course, one of the girls gets pregnant. It is a trite story for those watching a play, but it was not trite for my mother.) She was barely eighteen; my father was twenty-two. It was now December 1934 or January 1935. What should she do? She knew she could not tell my father that she was pregnant, since he would then marry her, and she did not want to ruin his career by forcing that decision on him. (Lapo-men were not permitted to get married until age twenty-seven.) She knew that he wanted to pass his examinations, travel, and see the world. And she knew, further, that she could not go back home, since her mother's desire for bourgeois respectability would not allow an illegitimate child in the family. My mother herself had been brought up with these values, and subscribed to them; she would have seen herself and her child as social outcasts.

There were stories and songs about just this situation, and my mother later taught them to me. I wonder what went through her mind when she sang to me, her love child, *"Mariechen sass weinend im Garten, im Grase lag schlummernd ihr Kind . . ."* ("Little Marie sat in the garden, crying, her child slumbering in the grass . . ."), a lullaby that ended in the refrain: *"Nein, nein, wir wollen leben, wir beide du und ich, / Deinem Vater sei vergeben, wie glücklich machst du mich"* ("No, no, we want to live, the two of us, you and I, / May your father be forgiven, how happy you make me"). She must have been desperate in a way I cannot even begin to imagine. At one point in her later life, she wanted to tell me about the predicament she was then in, but I did not engage. Perhaps I did not want the burden of knowing, since it involved me. It seemed clear to my mother that she had only one choice: She decided to marry Baumeister Max, a few months before I was born. I had a legal father, and she had a broken heart.

When she told her mother and the rest of her family, who knew and loved "Bebs," as they called my father, that she was marrying Baumeister, nobody could understand it, and her mother more or less threw her out. These are the words my mother always remembered and quoted her mother as saying: "If you don't like this wonderful young man anymore, you are a bad person and there is no place for you in this house." I'm not sure this was true; perhaps my mother made it up to highlight how lonely and forsaken she had been.

Until an assistant to the archivist in Passau sent me the documents, I had always assumed that my mother and Baumeister Max were married in January 1935, and I had marveled at how quickly she acted. But the documents tell me that they were married in June. There must have been gossip. Did "friends" assume that my mother had come back to Passau because of this pregnancy? My mother says she never told anybody who the father of her child was except Baumeister Max, who knew my father from his earlier visits in the canoe. I remember my mother pointing out to people that I had Opapa Baumeister's blue eyes; she felt she had to account for my blue eyes, since nobody else in the Baumeister family had them.

What I could never understand as an adult (before that I did not think about it) was that there seemed to be no one in my mother's family—not her mother, her brother, her three sisters, even her father—who could count. And couldn't they see? I resembled my father, a fact that my mother, for all the years in Passau, was anxious to hide. Was it simply more convenient for all concerned to act as if they believed my mother's story, that she had fallen out of love with Bebs? And all along, my father continued to visit my mother's mother in Ingolstadt, since she loved him so much. He heard that Ernche now had a little girl, and he, too, could have counted the months from conception to delivery. My mother must have felt abandoned, betrayed.

My mother had precisely four years—from my birth in August 1935 to the beginning of World War II in September 1939—to live the high life of the mistress of a hair salon. She and Baumeister Max had a fancy bright-red sports car; my mother learned to drive and was quite elegant by the standards of the time. She had this little girl who looked like the lover she had once had and still yearned for, and Baumeister Max adored my mother and her flamboyant ways. But my mother also had tuberculosis, which she thought she had contracted back in the days of her apprenticeship in Ingolstadt, when she had to fix the hair of a person who had died of TB, for display in the funeral hall. Or perhaps she had contracted it when she did the washing for the hair salon's family in Ingolstadt, outdoors in icy winter weather. She also thought that the foggy climate of Passau had brought the latent disease into the open, and then sometimes she thought that the profound sadness over the loss of her Bebs was the cause.

I started first grade in Ulm, roughly 160 miles up the Danube from Passau. On the first day of classes, and to sweeten the impression of school, children are presented with *Schultüten*, gay, multicolored cardboard containers in the shape of gigantic ice cream cones, filled with fruit and candy and pens and colored pencils. I received my *Schultüte* in Ulm where I lived with my mother's sister Emma and Emma's family, because my mother was for several months in a sanatorium. In the documents from the Passau archives, I found that, previously, she had also stayed, with me, in Bad Reichenhall, a mountain spa for pulmonary diseases. (These documents, which I received a few months after the end of the 2000 presidential campaign, gave me an eerie sense of what a police state must be like. There were records of the movements of my mother, myself, and Baumeister Max, of our addresses and changes of address, all with pertinent dates.) I liked being in Ulm. My cousin Inge was two years older than I, my cousin Günter just my age. I brought my *Schildkrötenpuppe*, the large stiff plastic doll that I never played with but needed as a status symbol. Yet, big as it was, Inge's was bigger and even more unwieldy.

I was six when I lived in Ulm. My granddaughter Julianna is that age now, and she has just started first grade. She likes to read a lot and makes a nest in her bed. But she does not, as I used to at that age, play house with sheets and blankets draped over table-tops to protect her and provide an enclosed, private space. Sometimes when she spends the night with me, and before she falls asleep, she wants to talk about her mom, my daughter Stephanie.

I lie next to her (what an enormous pleasure!), and we talk about Mommy and about ballet and school, and then she falls asleep. Did Tante Emma ever sit with me? Was I lonesome for my *Mutti?* Did I even want to talk about her? None of this do I remember, but I firmly believe that all these unrecognized and often contradictory emotions fell deep into the well of my being and have been simmering there ever since, erupting on occasion in unexpected ways.

Tante Emma gave me the biggest treat of my young life: she allowed me to design a dress for myself! The material was dark-blue crêpe de chine, and the only limit to my artistic inventions was the amount of material—just enough for a modest dress for the smallest member in the family. I still see that dress; it had a pleated skirt, long sleeves, and a white collar. My mother had excellent taste, but I was never allowed to decide for myself what I wanted to wear; she decided for me. Once, when I was perhaps five years old, she had enough of the same material to have a matching skirt and bolero jacket made for both of us. When the two of us walked through town dressed in identical outfits, we must have looked like incongruous twins. A soldier on furlough tried to pick up my mother, with me in tow. My mother, though never reluctant to accept a compliment, told him to behave himself—"Can't you see I am with my daughter?"—whereupon the soldier turned to me and asked, "Is this really your mother?" "Oh no," I said, in the familiar spirit of rebellion, "this is just Erna." Did he believe me?

A few months after I started school in Ulm, my mother was well enough to leave the sanatorium and go back to work, and I returned from Ulm to Passau. It was apparently important to keep *die deutsche Frau* in good spirits without any men around, and therefore hairdressers had an important function. I started to roam around Passau and hang out with schoolmates and friends. There were hardly any cars, and few people (the men were at war

and the women at work), so we kids had the town almost to ourselves. Passau had three or four movie houses, and since I was
small, I could sneak in without having to pay; I saw and remember a lot of the UFA movies of the Nazi period. (UFA is the
acronym for "Universum-Film AG," until 1945 the largest enter-
prise of the German film industry.) When I was an adult in this
country, I eventually found out how I could have seen Shirley
Temple movies in Germany in 1942. Apparently, since Goebbels,
too, liked American movies, the cultural imports continued deep
into the war. I had unsupervised freedom, no obligations, just
fun, and was old enough to enjoy it. This was the most glorious
time of my childhood. In Ulm, I also met my real father for the
first time.

My father and my mother each had a brother. When Hitler invaded Russia in the summer of 1941, both of these brothers fought on the Eastern Front, though not together. Both were killed in the early part of the invasion, in the fall of 1941, within one week of each other. Should I be thankful that neither of them was in the SS or with the Einsatzgruppen, which followed close upon the advancing armies and "cleansed" the conquered Polish and Russian territories of all "ethnic impurities"? Should I be thankful that they died while the German armies were still too busy advancing and could not yet be delegated to assist the SS or the Einsatzgruppen? Would my uncles have followed the orders of their superiors, or would they have refused to obey and been executed or simply sent to serve in penal battalions, which was another way of assuring death?

By the time of the invasion, my father, Sepp Misslbeck, had long completed his examinations, the Lapo had been absorbed into the military, and he had joined the air force. He was a first lieutenant, stationed in France, but not as a pilot: he was in the ground-supply units and an aide-de-camp. Since it was still early in the war, he was given a few days' furlough to attend the funeral services for his brother in Ingolstadt. The funeral services for my mother's brother were also in Ingolstadt, and they were coincidentally on the same day. My mother came from Passau, my father from France. My father went to see my mother's mother, who had been so fond of him, to give her his condolences. All the Keller sisters were also assembled. Bebs wanted to know whether "Ernstl" (his name for her) would be coming, too. Yes, she would.

At what time would her train arrive from Passau? They told him, and he went to meet her. They met in the street, seeing each other from a distance and walking toward each other. If I were to make a film of this scene, I would present it in slow motion, having them approach each other as if in a dream. They had not seen each other in seven years. How intimate or formal were their first words? He told her he knew she had a child. "How is your little girl?" he asked. And she said, "It is not *my* little girl, it is *our* little girl."

Perhaps she had waited for this moment for seven years. My father shook her so hard that her beautiful fancy hat fell to the ground. I still cry when I visualize this scene—their meeting in the road, his utter surprise, her vindication. He in a blue air-force uniform, she in her elegant clothes. How they both had changed in those seven years!

The next day they took a train together to Ulm, to see me. My cousin Günter and I were playing house in the dining room, under the table, when the doorbell rang. I remember someone calling out, "Wuschilein, your mother is here." How did I sense that this moment was special? I still see the light falling from the open kitchen door into the dark hallway, and there, in the entrance door, is my mother, in her dark-blue high-crowned hat with a decoration of white satin ribbons, and behind her a man in a blue uniform and a white scarf. Then I am introduced to him and told to call him Uncle Bebs.

Soon thereafter the gossip must have started. I was not so much aware of the gossip as of the tension. My mother had three sisters, my father had five. Apparently, my father and my mother started to make up immediately for the seven missed years, and not all of their sisters approved of the renewed liaison. They still did not have eyes; they still did not care to count. One of my father's sisters, in particular, found it a disgrace that their good-looking, blond, blue-eyed, athletic bachelor brother should get involved with a married and "diseased" woman. In Nazi Germany, with its cult of health, TB brought you close to the brink of being considered a candidate for *lebensunwertes Leben* ("life unworthy of living") and dealt with accordingly. As my father urged my mother to get a divorce, the sisters started to plot, writing to Baumeister Max to inform him of his wife's private life.

Just as she had told Max why she needed to marry him, she now told him, soon after she had met my father again, that she needed to divorce him. Was he given a furlough so that they could see each other for this discussion, or did she write to him? I don't know. I only know, from my mother, that Baumeister Max stood by her, as always. He implored her to wait until the end of the war. Either of them—he or my father—could be killed at any moment; this was not the time to make such a far-reaching decision. He even went on a furlough to see one of the sisters in Ingolstadt—a commotion I sensed but did not understand—and told her to mind her own business and leave his wife alone.

It appears that for all the important scenes in my childhood I have kept a clear and detailed memory of the external surroundings. Sometimes I think this must have been a way of shifting my attention from what was being said, creating a counterweight to often unbearable news. (It still happens today, so that I sometimes cannot recall the most crucial conversations in my adult life, either.) This is how, as a child, I experienced one of the most important conversations in my life:

My mother tells me about my "real father" as she puts me to bed. She sits on the bed, next to where I lie, as she talks to me. At that time, the summer of 1942, since there was no man in the house, she had me sleep in her bedroom, in one of the double beds, which were pushed together. I hear everything she says, but my eyes dart around the room and fasten on objects.

The sun is still shining outside and casts a strong shadow on the wall—a shadow that slowly moves as the sun goes down. It takes my mother a long time to talk to me, and when she is done, the room is almost dark. Essentially, she tells me, a seven-year-old, the story of her life, or, rather, of my conception; of how I was truly a love child and a loved child, how she was trying to protect my father by not marrying him, how my father loves me so much that we should now all become a family together. Do I think of Baumeister Max as she tells me this? Do I cry for him? I don't remember. I think I was too overwhelmed, too diminished by what I heard. This is when I began to think that I had ruined my mother's life, that she had sacrificed herself not for my father but for me when she married someone she did not love. I didn't understand that she couldn't bring herself to go home pregnant and unwed. All I heard was that she did it because of me. I was a special child, completely aside from the fact that I was sweet, smart, and so on. She told me that she and my father would get married as soon as possible, but that it might take a while. And she asked me not to tell anybody about this.

If the knowledge of my parents' lives and my role led me to feel guilty about my mother's sacrifices, even about her TB, it was nothing compared with the injunction not to speak about it. I could not even go to Tante Betty—above all, not to her! Secrecy began to envelop me in its peculiar aura: I was "special"—not better than my friends but outside their ordinary family constellations, different. That long talk in the gradually darkening bedroom created a need in me to keep to myself, to censor my words and ultimately my thoughts. I felt I no longer belonged; I had been cast out; the firm, thoughtlessly accepted ground on which I had based my existence, taken for granted like the air we breathe, had suddenly vanished. Who was I now?

In Passau I could still handle this burden. I had created my own world, populated it with my friends, and appropriated the streets and alleys for myself. I believe (I want to believe, even today) that the freedom of Passau in that crucial period of my life provided me with the self-reliance and skills to go on, despite inner turmoil, pain, and loss of trust. I have a friend who, in a critical situation, likes to say, "It is what it is." I learned very early in life that nothing is what it appears to be. Baumeister Max and I may not have developed a particularly intimate relationship, but I had still considered him my father, and when you are seven years old your father is a major part of your universe. In that darkening room it dawned on me that you should never trust anybody or anything. And now nobody could trust me, either, since I had a secret. I was not who people thought I was. On that evening my world became unhinged, even though the fissures did not show immediately.

The tremors of that revelation reverberate to this day: Reality is never what it appears to be; there is always something hidden that may pounce on you unexpectedly. Don't ever feel secure or safe. Protect, cover yourself; don't leave yourself open and vulnerable. Only years later, when I met my husband, Bill—and then with unconscious inner reluctance—did I begin to give up this defensive posture.

I had tried to keep an emotional balance of justice in my little life with little lies: I had told Tante Betty that my mother beat me; I had told the soldier she was "just Erna." Lying had been a weapon in my battles with my mother. That weapon was now shattered, since I myself had become a lie. Is a secret also a lie? It is a living lie, constantly reaffirmed, hence worse than a one-time lie. I developed, out of this inchoate sense of my universe gone askew, a habit of mind that later served me well in academe, in analyzing literary documents: I learned that there are always further and deeper layers of meaning to be discovered, silences that conceal information, words that hide rather than reveal. I am not surprised when someone's behavior seems unexpected, out of character, shocking to those who still believe they stand on firm ground.

And yet I, too, believe, need to believe, because without believing your soul dies. As an adult, I constructed a refuge for myself in a home-baked philosophy made up of ideas that responded to my needs. I borrowed from the existentialists, embracing the Heideggerian *Geworfensein*—the condition into which I was thrown—and I appropriated as my own what I had been handed. I convinced myself that ultimately I would find strength and identity in this acceptance. I walked a narrow, precarious path that demanded constant vigilance lest I fall into cynicism and callousness or into depression and despair. I accepted the condition that one could never, in this life, arrive at a firm position that allowed one to relax and simply "be," but that to be human in the fullest sense of the word, in all faculties and emotions and sensations, one must have the courage to live with inconsistencies, to live without a grounding.

Where does that leave happiness? The pursuit of happiness is so important in this country that it is anchored in the Declaration of Independence. How easy it is to forget about the *pursuit* and believe we are entitled to the thing itself, to happiness pure and simple. What do we pursue, anyway, when we pursue happiness? The definition is open, and not necessarily based on the insipid hedonism of a materialistic world. To me, "happiness" does not indicate a state of resolutions accomplished but the embracing of a jagged identity, open and alive to growth and new insights, to pain as well as joy. It consists of constantly expanding self-knowledge, of the desire to know who you are and the imperative not to lie to yourself or others. That was the "philosophy" I came to over many years. As a child I did not know that I needed a philosophy to cope, but the seed had been planted. As I grew, the seed sprouted into a plant, a flower, a bush, a tree. It is now a beautiful tree, and I can sit in its shade, reflect, and feel at home.

My mother saw my self-affirming lies (when I still told lies) and, later on, all challenges to her authority as "betrayals." For example, she felt "betrayed" when I told our dressmaker that my mother had never knitted a dress for me. I remember how angry she was on the way home, how she went to the closet the minute we walked into the apartment and showed me the dress, and made me wear it—a knitted wool dress on a hot summer day—the next time we went to the dressmaker. Today, I know that loyalty was a dominant value in her life, since as a young woman she herself had felt betrayed. But who in our relationship had betrayed whom? Hadn't I, too, been betrayed? In later years, I saw a profound irony and paradoxical logic at work: the very person who had betrayed my childhood trust in the solidity of my life saw me as a betrayer.

How close a relationship must my mother, in her own mind, have had with me, that a lie or a challenge (for example, what I should eat or wear) could become a personal betrayal? Were these the symptoms of a narcissistic extension, as my daughter Stephanie has called it? Just as my mother dressed us alike, she may have thought that we should think alike, and that if I thought like her I could never betray her. As far as I was concerned, the story of her sacrifice bound me to her through enormous guilt. At first I did not feel the weight of this bond; I simply became an obedient child. Only in my teens did I begin to feel its burden, and it took me a long time to break it. She, of course, saw my breaking away as the ultimate act of betrayal.

What role had she construed for me once my father was back in the picture? I remember a few times when my father and my mother would meet somewhere for a few hurried hours, or a day or two. On these occasions my mother brought me along. Their meetings would be arranged on the shortest notice and in the face of tremendous obstacles, since the war was raging and practically no soldiers were granted special leaves. Apparently it was easier to find reasons for a quick trip to Germany from France than it would have been from the Eastern Front. But why did a child have to witness the passion of a reunited couple? Did my mother want to impress on my father that he now had a child? Did she want us to become acquainted? Did she want me to get a sense of what "true love" was like? These are gaps I cannot fill.

Once, we met him in Munich, in the apartment of friends. It was a bright moonlit night, and my mother was in a panic because she was sure the city would be bombed, so the three of us spent the night with blankets wrapped around us in the woods. On one such occasion, my father tried to reach out to me, establish a personal bond. What did he, a bachelor in the military, know about little girls? He challenged me to a *Mutprobe,* a test of courage. I had to stand straight and let my body, all stiff, fall backward. His hands would be somewhere near the ground, to catch me. I was afraid; I crumbled; I did not pass the test.

Yet another time, we were visiting my mother's parents in Ingolstadt, and my mother gave me the choice of going off with her and Bebs or of remaining with my grandparents. I chose to stay, because I had set up a "store"—my grandmother's ironing board was the counter—and I was selling the contents of our suitcase. Below the store I had set up a house, the backs of chairs as walls, sheets as roofs, cushions as furniture. My parents could not compete with that.

And there was another rendezvous I remember, this time in Würzburg. For me, Würzburg is no longer simply a city with a bishop's seat and a beautiful bishop's palace with enormous, breathtaking paintings by Tiepolo. It is also a city that sent its Jewish population to the camps. Robert Gellately's *The Gestapo and German Society* has a cover photograph of men well dressed in jackets, overcoats, and hats and carrying shoulder bags with tin cups attached them. (You wonder what they were told, what they were allowed to bring.) The back cover explains: "It was forbidden to photograph the deportation of the Jews from Germany.

This picture, probably taken, for reasons unknown, by a member of the Gestapo or SS, shows one of the 1942 deportations from Würzburg to Lublin and Theresienstadt (now Terezin). On the right, townsfolk can be seen silently watching the orderly procession of Jews, many of whom had hitherto been accepted members of long standing in the community." Was it here—or in Berlin, as my mother maintained—that my father gave his ration card to an elderly Jewish couple? I wonder what he knew about the deportations, how he knew that the Jewish couple needed the extra ration cards more than non-Jews did.

I have often thought if I were a filmmaker making a film about this period, I would include the rattle of the cattle cars taking human beings to their deaths as uninterrupted white noise, grating on the viewers' nerves, jarring beyond endurance yet never letting up. For the three of us taking long walks through the vineyards surrounding Würzburg, the rhythmic click of wheels on tracks was inaudible. I did not like these interminable walks, with the two adults talking only to each other, stopping to embrace and kiss. I would look away, embarrassed. I single out Würzburg. Yet Würzburg is not the only city from which those trains left.

It must have been from the spring of 1943 on, after the defeat of the German Army at Stalingrad, that aspects of the war began to impinge on the lives even of second- and third-graders in Passau. Trains full of wounded soldiers, moaning and delirious, stopped in Passau, perhaps for a change of hospital personnel, perhaps for provisions. There could not have been enough personnel in the train station, because we children, entire classes, were sent to help feed the wounded and give them something to drink when they were incapable of doing that for themselves. Our teachers, mostly older women, were there to show us how to do it. I remember the enormous bandages and how, once, I helped a soldier drink, one in a row of many lined up on the floor of the platform. How could I have helped him lift his head? Did I hurt him? His entire head was one big ball of white gauze, with an opening for nose and mouth—but none for his eyes. Why were we children not horrified when we saw these mutilated, bandaged bundles of men? Or were we so traumatized that we immediately repressed what we saw? (Yet this scene has stayed with me my entire life.) Maybe because we were in a group and our participation was expected, we executed the tasks as if they were normal. I am not sure how often we did this. I just know that the tea we passed around was chamomile. During the school year we had collected chamomile blossoms. We were supposed to dry them at home and on specified dates bring them back to class, ready to be used. We dried the blossoms on newspapers, under our beds, and they made the room smell fresh, but to this day I cannot abide chamomile.

The soldiers who were too sick to be sent farther on had to be hospitalized in Passau. There was not enough hospital space, so our school buildings were converted into hospitals. We no longer had classrooms, and our classes were distributed among the restaurants and inns in the neighborhood. Where soldiers and nurses and leftover civilians congregated to drink and smoke at night, we sat in the morning, enveloped in cold, stale bar smells, and tried to pay attention. We felt very grown up.

Those large restaurant tables remained part of my education. Later, when we moved to Ingolstadt, we students again sat in a regular school building, but with kitchen tables as our desks. We were supposed to keep our books and pencils in the silverware drawers in these desks, so that the tops always looked neat and clean. I could open one of these drawers and, with my head bent, pretend I was deeply involved in listening to the teacher. In this way I found time to read Karl May, who wrote adventure stories about the American frontier. At home, I never had time. In class, I opened the drawer, put the book in, and slid into a thinker pose of holding my forehead in the palm of my hand. Once, I was so carried away with the story of Winnetou and Old Shatterhand that I did not hear the teacher approach. I closed the drawer too late. He made me open it and without saying a word, removed the book and took it home with him, to return it after three days. I continued my private reading periods in other classes, but not in his.

When I came to this country and sat in a classroom for the first time, I could not believe how small the chairs, with attached desks, were. You could barely put even one elbow on the surface of the little protruding table. You had to balance your books and notebooks on your lap, even put them on the floor. How could you take notes? How could you work with open books and notebooks if you did not have space to handle them properly? You sit on this little chair, an island unto yourself; you cannot just grab your neighbor's eraser if you forgot your own, because she sits too far away, and you surely cannot copy what she has written. I was an adult when I found myself in such a classroom for the first time, and I managed, but it felt strange.

My mother went through with her divorce in October 1943. I am sure it was not just Baumeister Max who felt she was making a huge mistake and should have waited until the end of the war. When I consider this shadow man in my life, whose existence was so vague to me that I remember only one scene with him clearly, I nevertheless think of him with great respect. He must have been a generous person, and of course completely in love with my mother. He stood by her throughout her calamities and hardships and was always there when she needed him. What if my father were killed, before he and my mother could be married? I assume that Baumeister Max's thinking was that if he, Max, were killed, my mother would at least be entitled to whatever widow's pension there was.

Even after she was divorced, my mother continued to work in the Baumeister salon, though not every day. She began to suffer excruciating migraine headaches. There was no medication for them. She would take a wide belt and wrap it tightly around her head to contain the throbbing; she would not get dressed; she would write letters to my father and wait every day for mail from him. The mail delivery was no longer reliable, and sometimes she did not get a letter for several days; she would pace around the apartment, disheveled, half crazed.

I did most of the food shopping, which meant standing in long lines. Most of the food was ersatz—substitute honey and substitute marmalade and substitute coffee—but I did not know the difference. I also stood in line for ration cards. Sometimes people tried to take advantage of my being so young, elbowing me back to the end of the line, complaining that I should not be treated like an adult; sometimes store owners tried cheating on the amount they gave me for the ration clippings. But I was sassy, and that helped.

And then my mother discovered that she was pregnant. How could she bear the thought that my father might be killed and that this second child of theirs was also under the threat of being born out of wedlock? The story of my parents' marriage is the stuff of family myth. For my parents it was supposed to be a highlight in the book they never wrote. My father often told the story of how, after several petitions, he was denied permission to marry my mother. (This explains why it took them relatively long—five months—after my mother's divorce to get married.) In Nazi terms, she was not marriageable material for an air-force officer, since she was divorced and had had TB. So, finally, my father caught an airplane to Berlin, went to the Luftwaffenministerium, the Air Force Ministry, and screamed and yelled his way through a succession of antechambers, to the consternation and admiration of any number of upper- and lower-echelon secretaries, all of whom would have loved to be loved by such a good-looking and passionate Bavarian who was risking everything for this undesirable woman. It was never clear—perhaps my father himself did not know—how far up the ladder he had to scream to get permission to marry my mother, but he came away with it. The decisive factor was undoubtedly my mother's pregnancy: if she was healthy enough to present "our Führer" with yet another child for his ambitious enterprises, then surely she was marriageable. In March 1944, six weeks before my brother was born, they were married in Munich. It was a hurried affair, with Muttl, my father's stepmother, and another friend as witnesses. I stayed in Passau, because the constant aerial bombings made Munich a dangerous place to be.

Did I know she was pregnant? She was so skinny that she didn't look it. During the preceding winter, she had still been working at the salon, and I used to pick her up in the evenings. On the way home, we would stop at her doctor's, where she went to get some shots. Those shots were mysterious to me; she would say only that they helped her. She developed carbuncles on her arms and needed surgery; the scars never disappeared. Carbuncles and furuncles became a very prominent condition in Germany during and after the war. I have two carbuncle scars on the nape of my neck; my father had his on his arm. Though medical dictionaries trace them to infection, popular belief at the time connected them to malnutrition. I also heard other mysterious medical terms, such as "hunger edema" or "atrophy of the muscles," and was impressed by people who had "water on the leg," which meant, for example, that if you pressed on their ankles the indentations would persist, because the water in the ankle had been displaced. I felt very grown up, picking my mother up after work. When we walked home together, she would walk in the street and I, next to her, up on the sidewalk; that made me several inches taller, almost as tall as she was. I began to think that men brought nothing but trouble, ill-health, and complications to women—that to fall in love was foolish, and that I would never let it happen to me.

Once my only brother, Seppi, was born, my childhood ended. I now had a living doll, whether I wanted one or not. I could still be out and about, but with a baby carriage in tow you cannot sneak into movies, you cannot climb fences, you cannot play cops-and-robbers all over town. My friends became bored with me, or, rather, with my tagalong. I visited Tante Betty more frequently.

Passau had no major industries, so there were few air raids. They came only toward the end of the war, when the trains arriving from the East were overcrowded with wounded soldiers and hospital personnel (and on occasion with some refugees lucky enough to get on a train), and the train station burst with commotion. For most of the people living in the Innstadt, the closest air-raid shelter was about ten minutes away—a huge, former commercial wine cellar blasted into the side of a mountain. Dark, cold, and very damp, it smelled of wine gone sour, and of the stale sweat of anxious people. The big steel door opening into the cave had to be closed after the air raids were under way, though the shelter guard tried to keep it open as long as possible. The cave's ventilation system had not been built for several hundred people. I don't remember how long these air raids lasted—hours? Did we ever stay there overnight? I only remember the smell. There were rows and rows of wooden benches, only very dim light, and little space for the suitcases people dragged along, but which had to be left outside. Seppi, an infant during the last year of the war, immediately developed asthma. When the sirens howled, we would race to the mountain shelter, my mother pushing the baby carriage with my brother in it, his mattress resting on the ever-increasing pile of letters my father sent to her from France nearly every day and which meant more to her than clothes or blankets. I was too young to carry a suitcase, so my mother filled my doll carriage with clothes and other essentials; each of us pushed a carriage as we ran. Once, the shelter guard argued with my mother, since he felt that sheltering a doll carriage was an unnecessary luxury—*der Fratz* ("the brat") didn't need it. He did not understand how clever my mother was. Everybody should have pushed a carriage instead of lugging those heavy suitcases.

The first American I ever saw in my life was the pilot of an airplane. He dived so low that I could see his face in the cockpit, and he shot at people still running to the shelter. Where was my mother? I remember that I threw myself on the ground, and that all around me soil exploded into the air. I was stunned, but not enough not to regret that now my coat was all dirty. For a long time afterward, I was convinced that the pilot had deliberately spared me—that he had looked at me, a child, and did not want to kill me. (Later, I learned that these fighter planes, Thunderbolts, had four machine guns attached under each wing; they could not have been targeted very precisely.)

My father's letters to my mother became another part of the family myth. In later years, my mother would occasionally bring them out and my father would read them aloud to her and tell her under what conditions he had written this one or that one, and then they would embrace and kiss. I don't remember whether my brother and my sister were there at such times. I remember only that, then in my teens, I would leave the room, embarrassed, disdainful at this overt display of romance.

In the last few years of her life, before her stroke, my mother destroyed most of the letters. This she revealed to me on one of my visits to her in Ingolstadt. She had already gone through several thick folders of them, and I just nodded when she told me. She read a few every day, she said, and then she shredded them. She showed me a letter whose first page my father had decorated with garlands drawn in red and green pencil. I was very moved, but it was my younger daughter, Theresa Anne, who implored her grandmother to stop destroying the letters. There was still one big folder left, from December 1944 to April 1945. My mother may have told us that she was destroying them because she wanted someone to tell her not to, wanted someone to say that they were precious to all of us, to the next generation. But even as an adult, I could not bring myself to say that. I told myself that they were too private, that I did not want to pry. Was that really the reason? Perhaps I did not have the detachment necessary to read them with love. Who would ever again read them? Who of my children—or grandchildren—could even decipher the tiny, idiosyncratic handwriting in a foreign language, on tissue-thin airmail paper? I think my mother was pleased when Theresa Anne asked her to stop destroying them. She did stop, and I have the letters now. Perhaps one day my brother's children in Germany will want them.

I do not remember seeing my father from the time he and my mother were married and my brother was born, in the spring of 1944, until after the end of the war. Yet even in the midst of disintegrating front lines he managed to meet with my mother, for in the fall of 1944 she became pregnant one more time. With a small baby and again pregnant, she was allowed extra milk rations, but never enough for my brother and me and herself—or, rather, for the baby she was carrying *unter ihrem Herzen* ("under her heart"), as the German saying went. She was good friends with the owner of a dairy store, a Herr Edenhofer, and he told her that if she could come early in the day, before most of the other customers, he would give her yet more extra milk. Well, my mother could not get there early in the day; she was weak and needed to rest. That left me to pick up the milk. I did not like Edenhofer, who had once reprimanded me for my dirty fingernails, and would not enter his store; but he knew why I avoided it, and to my great humiliation he would not let up. Whenever he saw me in the streets, he would tease me, shouting across the street for all to hear, asking whether my fingernails were now clean. This was the man I had to face early every morning. I hated it, and squirmed when I had to say "Thank you" for the extra milk. But I also hated having to get dressed and make my way from the Innstadt, across the river, past the hair salon, almost to the other side of town, to the Danube, where Edenhofer had his shop. Then I had to come all the way back and get to school, which started at eight o'clock in some restaurant or other.

The first time I had to go, I took my time getting ready. Surely my mother would understand that I could not be late for school and would go for the milk herself. I had braids; they needed to be unbraided, and my hair needed to be brushed, then braided again; that took a while. My mother lost patience, or perhaps she understood what I was trying to do. She sent me off with my hair unkempt and added insult to injury by making me wear a little white leather cap, with tassels and embroidery, that my father had sent me from France—as if that would hide my disheveled braids! And because I took too long to get dressed, she made me wear my *Trainingsanzug*, a dark-blue sweat suit. I looked ridiculous! I was furious! I knew I would meet my school-bound classmates on the way, looking like a clown. I pretended not to see them and took off the cap, then rebraided my hair as I walked. I lost this power struggle with my mother because I had thought that if I was late to school she would feel guilty. I miscalculated. She did not feel guilty. She thought I was smart enough to make up those fifteen or twenty minutes of lateness. (In fact, nobody cared whether I caught up on the knowledge dispensed in those first few minutes; what mattered to the teacher was that I was not punctual, not a reliable *deutsches Mädel*.)

In late fall of 1944 and the winter of 1945, the refugees from the East started to arrive. I was not sure what "the East" meant or how far "the East" extended; some refugees were Germans fleeing up the Danube, some came from Czechoslovakia, and there were many Ukrainians. Only much later did I realize that these Ukrainians must have been pro-Nazi, or in any event anticommunists, and had good reason to get out of the way of the advancing Soviet Army. Members of the Nazi Party went from house to house and apartment to apartment to assess the space and allot rooms to the refugees. An entire family was put in a room one floor below us. The rooms were partitioned with blankets or sheets; the smallness of the sectioned-off parts reminded me of the enclosures I had built when I played house, and since I liked tightly enclosed spaces

I thought these people must, too. Our spacious apartment was requisitioned; my mother, brother, and I lived in the bedroom; all the other rooms were occupied by refugees; the kitchen and toilet were shared with ever-changing groups of people who passed through on the way to elsewhere. There were women who smoked pipes; I was deeply impressed. They arrived in double and triple layers of clothes, their only possessions being what they wore on their bodies. Suitcases, bundles, knapsacks were often lost, abandoned, stolen in the surging waves of westward transports, and sometimes a child, too, disappeared. The women moaned and grunted to themselves in our large kitchen when they prepared food I had never smelled before, and when they spoke to each other they sounded as if they were singing. I would hear the women talking with my mother in broken German about fleeing the Russians, about rapes (I had no idea what "rape" was but did not dare ask my mother, since I judged from the way they spoke about it that it had to be something horrible), about mutilated and burnt bodies. One horrifying story—I understood the words but could not comprehend the magnitude of the event—had to do with a farmer whose intestines were wrapped around a tree while he was still alive and who was then forced to watch his wife being raped. I learned new words, such as *Nahkampf* ("hand-to-hand combat"), and I remember the hushed, awed voice in which a friend of my mother's told her that her husband had earned a *Nahkampfspange* in hand-to-hand combat with a Russian soldier. I learned the word *eingekesselt* ("enclosed on all sides"), absorbed the hopelessness associated with *Kesselschlachten* ("battles in which the enemy had you surrounded"), and the hope invested in *Wunderwaffen,* the "miracle" weapons: V-I and V-II rockets launched from Germany to England. I heard about skirmishes and battles, villages and towns destroyed. I heard about the horror of bombed cities and, most poignantly, about a woman who carried the charred body of her child in her suitcase and refused to part with it. I could not understand how *Phosphorbomben* functioned: if a person caught on fire jumped into a river, the flames flared up again as soon as the person surfaced. I learned that the best way to move about the streets after such an air raid was on roller skates, since the metal did not catch fire. Passau had been spared these horrors, and so I could afford to think that going on roller skates was a neat way to do your errands. All this I heard the women talk about, but I never heard them talk about the concentration camps, or, later, the death marches.

As the Russians took Vienna in mid-April 1945 and moved up the Danube, there was mounting anxiety about who would arrive in Passau first: the Russians or the Americans. We did not know that Germany had already been divided at the Yalta Conference in February 1945 and that there would be regions first occupied by the Americans that would later be handed over to the Russians. The Russians were dreaded; the Americans were said to be nice to children.

In early 1945, the concentration camps were being evacuated, and the prisoners who were still alive were sent on death marches deeper into Germany to avoid liberation by the advancing Allies. I never found anybody who said he or she knew, much less saw, the prisoners on those marches. Yet they covered Germany like a spiderweb. I saw the wounded soldiers; later on, I saw the soldiers who had been taken prisoner of war by the Americans; I saw the refugees coming through; but I, too, never saw concentration camp prisoners. Yet Mauthausen, the camp closest to Passau, received transports from other camps, especially Sachsenhausen, Auschwitz, and Gross-Rosen, into the spring of 1945, and Dachau, about a hundred miles from Passau, sent its prisoners on a death march to Tegernsee, in the Bavarian Alps. Though the advancing Soviet Army had liberated the camps in the East, these prisoners were not liberated until early May 1945.

As the Russians advanced, my mother began to urge me to

study languages, and again she regretted vehemently that she had been deprived of an advanced education. How handy a knowledge of languages would have been right then! If you could speak the language of the enemy, you could perhaps talk yourself out of an impending calamity, perhaps save your life and the lives of your family, perhaps get food, perhaps not be raped. I still hear her imploring me to learn many languages so as not to be undone by these eventualities. I would later follow her advice in high school, by then motivated no longer by her fears. After the end of the war, Germany was for a time completely sealed off from contact with the larger world. Learning other languages gave me a sense that there was a world "out there" and that one day I could see it; when that day came I wanted to be ready for it.

Toward the end of the war, my mother had a close brush with the authorities. She had been to a movie with a girlfriend, and when the *Wochenschau*—the weekly newsreel from the front—came on, she whispered to her girlfriend something like, "What madness, what a madman!" She was overheard and denounced. I still cannot fathom what pleasure denouncers get from denouncing. Even in Nazi Germany, denunciations were not required; there were no quotas. A denouncer acted out of his or her own free will. How much individual misery and suffering could have been avoided, even during the apogee of Nazi rule, if people had minded only their own business! A high-ranking party member (party members rarely fought at the front; they kept the home country "supervised"), a *Brigadeführer* who was a customer at the hair salon and liked my mother, heard that night in his headquarters that the next morning she would be taken in for interrogation and worse. I still remember the subdued commotion at the front door, and my mother telling me she had a medical emergency and must see a doctor immediately—at 1:00 a.m.! The doctor wrote her a predated certificate stating that she was pregnant (which she was). When the Gestapo came the next morning, she showed them the certificate, which protected her as a *deutsche Frau* and incipient mother: she was ready to have yet another child for Hitler and the war effort.

My mother was so scared of what might happen once "the enemy" arrived that she decided not to stay in Passau. When she gave birth to my brother, she had met, at the lying-in hospital, a woman who came from farm country. She now thought we would be safer and not have to worry about food in the countryside. It must have been April 1945 when a friend of my mother's managed to get us to Reding, in the Rottal, about twenty-five miles from Passau. We had a room in a farmhouse, which my mother paid for with silverware, china, and a fur coat, and we were not especially welcome. I remember the *Lederknödel* ("leather dumplings"—*Lederknödel* being a play on the word *Leberknödel*, "liver dumplings," which conjured up a very different reality) that served as food: dumplings made of water and flour and salt, so tough they were almost impossible to digest. They were meant to give the stomach enough to do so that one would not get hungry. Pocking, a military airport, was close to Reding, and from there, on a dusty country road in early May, I saw the American troops walking toward us.

What had I expected? Goose-stepping, marching? How often had I seen German soldiers in Passau? I don't know, but I must have seen them in circumstances that led me to expect soldiers to march upright, singing, the tips of their rifles pointing to the sky. I had seen German soldiers shipped back wounded, bandaged beyond recognition, moaning, lying on stretchers, unable to move. And most recently I had seen stray German soldiers walking

alone, or perhaps two and three in a group, trying to look inconspicuous, with the insignias on their uniforms cut off. But the
cloth of the uniforms had bleached, and the fabric underneath the
removed insignias had a different, fresher color. If you were an
expert on insignias and medals and their placements on uniforms,
you could tell what rank they had held, what feats of bravery they
had accomplished. (In the early postwar period, many sold their
medals for food and cigarettes.)

The American soldiers fell into none of the categories I knew.
They were walking several abreast, tired, in no hurry, and with no
apparent victors' euphoria. They had these strange, open cars—
these jeeps—driving alongside them and sometimes among them
on the road. These soldiers wore high, laced boots with their pants
tucked in, blouson-style, billowing over the top of the boots. They
were not only tired, they were dusty. Their rifles were slung casually over their shoulders, butts up, and occasionally they talked to
each other. They all seemed to move in slow motion, and it was
hard to see them as conquerors—except that the columns were
endless. I don't know how long we stood in the doorway of the
farmhouse and watched, the white bedsheet as a peace sign waving
above our heads, but it seemed the columns would never end. This
is how defeat felt to me then: there were no fires, no conflagrations,
no apocalypse (as there was in the cities), but we were overrun by
an indifferent mechanism of enormous magnitude—not hostile,
not frightening, simply indifferent. And this is the image of victory
that has always stayed with me: tired and dusty and totally unglam-
orous but overwhelming, endless, powerful. Ultimately, victory
and defeat were conjoined in grayness, dust, and exhaustion.

Little did I know then that defeat would be a recurrent pattern
in my life—yet it always retained an ambivalent quality, was
never an ultimate down-and-out. Defeat was always balanced by
a life-enhancing energy that would often lead me to success and
even triumph. As the soldiers walked by, defeat signaled the end

of horror; it promised freedom and gave hope. Defeat meant not to be broken down but to be built up. Defeat of an inhuman system contained the germs of a new, better life.

As evening fell, the soldiers stopped and were assigned to houses to spend the night. Farmers hoped that their white sheets, the flags of surrender, would save them. Save them from what? From rape and torture, which were not in the cards anyway—but it did not save them from having to evacuate their houses. As the rooms were requisitioned, they were also searched for concealed weapons. One young officer entered our room. My mother stood by the window, seven months pregnant with Monika, Seppi sitting on her left arm, I by her side. Under the blanket that she had wrapped around my brother, she held a small mother-of-pearl-inlaid pistol that my father must have given her. The officer inspected the room and then motioned for us to leave. At that moment, my mother removed the blanket, revealing the pistol pointed in his direction. He could not know that it was not cocked, but he must have understood that she did not want to kill him, since he did not seem afraid. Yet he did not get my mother's point: she had hoped that in exchange for the pistol he would let us keep our room. He took the pistol away from her, but in exchange he searched his pockets and came up with an unopened pack of cigarettes and a few loose ones to give her.

That night we slept in a hayloft. We climbed over suitcases and bundles and blankets that staked out people's "territories," and my mother pushed us into a spot in a corner where nobody would step over us. It was extremely crowded and noisy. The next morning I heard for the first time the word *Amischlampen* ("sluts who sleep with American soldiers"). Some younger women had apparently found their way into the beds of the *Amis* and came back with chocolate, cigarettes, and chewing gum. The women were despised, but their goods were coveted.

Life, at least for me, did not change much after the *Amis*

arrived. I felt I had to help earn our keep and show our goodwill toward the farmers who were sheltering us. Farmers are not shy about putting kids to work: I helped in the kitchen and in the stables. Sometimes I spread washing carefully on the grass; the sun had to stand in for the missing soap powder, and to gain maximum exposure to it the pieces had to lie flat. I remember an orchard in bloom. I see my mother in the kitchen. Is she washing dishes? Is she peeling potatoes? My one-year-old brother is trying to stand up, holding on to her. The struggle to get milk for Seppi was one of the reasons we had come to the country, guided by my mother's notion that in the country milk would be plentiful. It was not. She, too, needed milk to drink, or at least something more nourishing to eat than leather dumplings. Paying the farmers in cash or goods became problematic. Soon the black market was upon us; the farmers were ever more demanding and the cost of staying ever more expensive. There was, of course, no school. Somehow, my mother acquired a pair of Dutch clogs for me, so that my "good" shoes would not be ruined while I was working in the stables. I was proud of these exotic-looking shoes, but they were made of wood, gave me blisters, and hurt terribly. So I went barefoot and wore the clogs only in the house, or whenever my mother was around.

When we heard that Passau had been "taken," my mother started to make arrangements for us to get back. We were lucky that the Americans had reached us before the Russians; we now lived in the American Occupation Zone. Everywhere there were *die Amis*. (An American student of mine once mentioned that, living in Germany at the time, she had thought that *Ami* was the French word for "friend" and felt good about the Germans calling her that. I, on the other hand, can still hear the angry and dismissive tone when Germans pronounced the word.) There was little food, and there was my mother's constant concern about my father. Where was he? When would he get back? Even: was he still alive? He would be looking for us not in this out-of-the-way village but in Passau; we had to go back. I don't know how we managed to do it. I do remember that when we got back home our apartment—and, worse, our cellar, where my mother had hidden nonperishable food—had been plundered. What had she expected? That refugees in need would honor our right to our property and, as they moved on, leave everything intact?

Waiting for my father became the sole focus of her days. She no longer worked once we came back from Reding, just occupied herself with Seppi and me and waited, waited. We lived on the ration cards, and I stood in line for food. I still spent time in the streets, now always with my brother in his carriage, and our group of children watched *die Amis* do whatever they did. They drove around in jeeps and threw chewing gum to us kids. We heard that their eggs came in powdered form, and their milk, too. They poured vats of leftover soup into the street gutters, and we wondered what that soup tasted like. I saw the first bananas and oranges in my life, but did not know how one would eat them. They were not for me to eat anyway.

Since the Americans had liberated Mauthausen and occupied Passau, they must also have liberated the *Aussenlager* near Passau. I wonder what they found there, what happened to the people there. I never heard one word about it. What we kids did find out, that summer of 1945, was that the Americans had taken over our public swimming pool and we had no place to go—except, of course, to the gravel island in the Inn River. But there was no bridge left to jump from; it had been blown up. The Americans had constructed a pontoon bridge strictly for their own use. That summer we did not swim a lot. I was not too happy to be tied down with the baby carriage, particularly when my friends climbed fences and walls and disappeared into forbidden gardens, but at least I was no longer working on the farm.

Then, one day in late July, there was whispering in the hallway— or did my mother receive a note? My father had arrived. He had escaped from a British internment camp in North Germany and, disguised as a farmer, with pipe and rake and on a bicycle, had somehow managed to cross all of Germany, not quite a thousand miles. (We would hear the stories of his adventures for years to come, until, gradually, he lost his audience.) He needed luck, and he had it. Apparently, a network of returning soldiers, who tried to avoid the unavoidable POW camps until they had seen their families, had sprung up spontaneously, and they all helped each other. My father was one of those who were helped along the way. It was summer; he slept in haylofts, and farmers gave him food. A priest provided him with civilian clothes. A soldier who had made it back to his own family gave him his bike. He also gave him some lard and offered him schnapps before he sent him on his way— hurriedly, since the Allies checked frequently and strictly and nobody was supposed to help roaming soldiers or refugees. At one point, someone threatened to kill my father if he did not surrender his bicycle, and my father handed it over. He finished the day riding on an oxcart; the next morning a trusting widow loaned him her own bicycle, and he returned it many months later.

But he could not manage the last hurdle: crossing the Inn River from the Altstadt into the Innstadt. Many refugees came through Passau: it must have been assumed that war criminals and all kinds of unsavory characters were trying to escape to the West, and Passau was one of the major points of transit. The pontoon bridge was heavily guarded. I had already learned to be in awe of "MP" written in large white letters on khaki helmets. The soldiers who wore them commanded respect; they also had white shoulder straps and twirled white batons, not unlike (as I later found out) New York City police on street patrols, demonstrating their power and strength. My mother was consumed by one question: how could we get out of the Innstadt to meet my father, who was hiding with friends?

This is what memory does: I was not aware of the difficulty of the situation, of the feat my father had accomplished in getting through to us, of the condition of my mother, at first without news of my father and now perhaps unable to reach him. What I remember is that my mother made me wear my best dress—light-blue wool (in July!), albeit short-sleeved, with big pleats from the yoke down, and a stand-up collar embroidered with shiny white thread. I don't remember what my mother wore or whether my brother was with us. I doubt it, though, since he was barely over a year old and might have made noises that betrayed us. We were to hide in a Red Cross van that would take us across the pontoon bridge. My mother could not hide under the seat, because she was too pregnant; was it only I who hid there? Did whoever drove us tell the MP guarding the bridge that my mother had to go to the hospital? Did she look innocent, credible, worried enough? In any event, the MP let the van pass.

My father had escaped the British POW camp in North Germany, but he knew he would still have to go through an American POW camp, since we lived in the American Occupation Zone, and he knew he should do it as soon as possible, in order to get the correct release papers and be able to move about. (De-Nazification, which all Germans had to go through whether or not they had been Nazis, was different from what happened in the POW camps and followed a different, bureaucratic path; that would come later.) My father wanted to report to the camp near Ingolstadt, since Ingolstadt was his hometown. He felt it would be easier to go through camp there than anywhere else.

But now he was in Passau, in July 1945; he must not be seen, because he would be taken away; my mother was highly pregnant; there were these two children, not enough food, and what was going to happen to all of us? My father was eager to get back to Ingolstadt; to make it back there undiscovered, a trip of about 120 miles, would be a feat in itself. But he also wanted to be with my mother when she gave birth. So he stayed in hiding. My mother understood how precarious his situation was, and she did her utmost to cooperate: she gave birth to my only sister, Monika, three days after my father arrived (on the same day that my husband, Bill, was born two years earlier on the other side of the Atlantic). Then my father left.

My father reported to the POW camp in Ingolstadt in early August of 1945; the rest of the family stayed in Passau. My mother tried to breastfeed Monika, but she was so undernourished that she could not produce any milk. My little sister, herself half starved, bit the nipples to bloody pulps. The nurses in the hospital kept trying to make my mother feed her, because there was not much other food around for a newborn baby, until my mother developed a breast infection. With that, she was sent home. I don't remember what we ate or who cooked for us during those last weeks in Passau. My mother's friends must have felt sorry for her: sick, now with three children, her husband in a POW camp, and an uncertain future. There was no way of knowing how long my father would have to stay in the camp. When this new man in all our lives, with whom my mother had never lived and whom I had known for a total of perhaps two weeks, went back to Ingolstadt, it reinforced my suspicion that whenever a man appeared in one's life there would be pain—physical, emotional, and circumstantial.

My mother's breast infection did not go away. There was no medication to be had, no antibiotics or anesthesia. There were mysterious words floating about, words like "penicillin" and "nylon," but they had no relevance to us. We had heard of *Wunderwaffen*, but *Wundermedikamente* were beyond the boldest imagination.

And so, every day, a doctor came, opened my mother's breast wound, and scraped it out. My mother was brave, but the pain was horrendous, and she started to shake long before the doctor appeared each day. (I was so traumatized by what she went through that I was never able to breastfeed my two daughters, did not even want to try.) At the same time, my mother developed pleurisy, and the pain would barely allow her to breathe. There was no resilience or strength left in her body after going through two pregnancies in a very short period, and after all the stress and worries associated with the whereabouts of my father, the end of the Nazi regime, and the efforts to find enough food for us.

My father spent only a few weeks in the camp. Later, as he told the stories from the safe perspective of one who had made it, he would reminisce with his friends about how he finagled his way into assignments that allowed him to leave the camp every day, work outside, and acquaint himself with postwar conditions and possibilities. (These reminiscences usually occurred over several glasses of wine, which made me leave the room in protest and made my mother complain that she had to sit up into the wee hours of the morning with a group of drinking buddies—since my father always insisted that she be with them, sharing their fun. At that time in my life, in high school, I totally sympathized with my mother and was angry with my father for tormenting her so.)

In camp, my father re-established contact with his old friends. He heard there was a bombed-out apartment he could fix up that would allow him to bring his family from Passau. I don't know how he gained access to cigarettes from the PX, but he did. Cigarettes were the most highly valued currency on the black market, and my father started to barter and to do business right away, while he was still in camp. He had to get the apartment ready.

My mother did not want to move back to Ingolstadt—it had been heavily bombed—but she had no choice. Ingolstadt had been bombed because there was a military airport nearby, in Manching, and it had been constantly targeted. (Today, Manching still has a German military airport.) It seemed to me that there were more ruins in Ingolstadt than houses; I was not used to that in Passau. "Why would we want to live in a city of ruins," my mother kept asking, "when we have everything we want in Passau?" But on a deeper level I think she was reluctant to move back to Ingolstadt because there were too many relatives there, all of whom had opinions about her first marriage.

I don't know who told them that I was my father's child. It must have been "Seppe" himself. (All my father's family called him "Seppe," while on my mother's side everybody called him "Bebs.") One of those scenes indelibly etched into my memory occurred early after our arrival in Ingolstadt. I was making my way among the rubble and ruins and the ditches with dug-up water pipes that you had to cross on wooden boards, when an unknown woman called to me from across one of those ditches, "You must be Misslbeck Wuschi!" When I said yes, she said, "Don't you wonder how I know? We both have the same nose, can't you see? We have Misslbeck noses." She was the oldest of my father's siblings, and this was my introduction to the Misslbeck family. Indeed, they never doubted that I was a "real" Misslbeck. (And again I cry as I think back to this scene. Tante Anny died many years ago, but the memory of that chance encounter is as alive and vital in me as if it had happened yesterday.)

With her pleurisy abating but her breast not healing, my mother developed thrombosis, first in one leg, then in the other. From then on, one of my mother's legs was always slightly swollen and would hurt. I was given to understand that one of the blood clots in her veins might start to wander and get stuck in her heart, and she might die instantly. She maintained that, since in her profession she had to be on her feet all the time, she had developed this problem over the years. Only much later, years after we had settled in Ingolstadt, did she have access to support stockings, which helped a bit. In the meantime, she was told to walk a lot and otherwise keep her legs elevated. For the rest of their lives together, one of my father's battle cries over her health would be "Please, put your legs up!"; and we were forever looking for footstools and benches and chairs on which she could rest her legs. I can still see my father fetch a footstool for her, or make her sit on the sofa with both legs elevated, or slide pillows under her legs when she put them up on a chair (which she rarely did, because it was not "polite"). Our family developed the maxim "Don't stand if you can sit; don't sit if you can lie down or put your legs up."

The summer of 1945 was my last summer in Passau. I took care of Seppi, hung around my mother, and on a few occasions looked at Monika behind the glass walls of the *Säuglingsheim* (lying-in hospital). I can still see the main gate, with its glass windows, and the glass door from the stairwell opening onto the second floor, and I still hear the babies crying. But which one is my sister? To which, in a row of little beds, does the nurse point as she hurries by?

Again, my vocabulary expanded. In addition to the generic term *Amis,* there were the loaded words *Amischlampen* and *Amischicksen. Amischicksen* is a very interesting word that made sense to me only after I came to the States: *Schicksen* is the same as the Yiddish *shikse;* in Yiddish it is a disparaging term for a gentile woman; in Bavaria it is a derogatory term for any woman. These women were surrounded by an aura of wealth, or at least of easy living, for they had plenty of cigarettes. I don't recall any of them; the movies I've seen about that period—for example, Rainer Werner Fassbinder's *The Marriage of Maria Braun*—have intruded on my memories. (Of course, some German women genuinely fell in love with their "young Americans," though they

were often left behind when the soldiers returned to the States.)
And there were other terms surrounded by an aura of mystery,
such as UNO, UNRRA, DPs and DP-*Lager*.

What happened to the prisoners in the Passau *Aussenlager*? To
those surviving Mauthausen, Dachau, the many other camps, and
the death marches? What happened to the Jewish refugees from
Poland, to those who had managed to flee the invasion of the Germans into the interior of the Soviet Union? If they made it to the
West, they were now all displaced persons, waiting in yet another
set of camps until they could go . . . where? Many of the Jewish
refugees waited to go to Palestine, others opted for the United
States; very few went back home, particularly when they came
from East European countries where they felt they were no longer
welcome, or where the reality of living under communism did not
seem very appealing. And there was an ultimate irony: many of the
Volksdeutsche, ethnic Germans who had been eager collaborators
with the German troops as they advanced east in the early years of
the war, thought it now advisable to go west, so that frequently the
hunted and the hunters found themselves in the same camps. How
did they manage to get along? Bavaria, in the American Occupation Zone, had a large number of DP camps, but the Western Allies
established such camps throughout Allied-occupied Germany, as
well as in Austria and Italy. It took years for these camps to empty.
In the United States, I met people who had gone from concentration camps to DP camps and elsewhere before they were able to
come to the States. Some of those who tried to enter Palestine ille-
gally were deported to yet another set of camps, the British deten-
tion camps, until Israel was established in 1948.

In September 1945, my father came back to Passau. The apartment in Ingolstadt was fixed up sufficiently for us to move in.
How did he manage to make ruins with no roof over them livable

in such a short period of time? The contacts from the POW camp began to bear fruit, and in addition, there was his father's shop. His father, the artisan and lathe-turner, had died in 1935, five years after my father had left the shop for the Landespolizei in Munich. Now my father remembered the trade he had learned; the shop was still intact—old and rusty, but intact—and, most important, there were great amounts of special wood in storage, which allowed him to make wooden plates, chairs, even small doll carriages—things of special value in a town that had been considerably damaged. His goods were coveted articles on the black market. Soon he discovered yet another new market: he made souvenirs for GIs to take home, wooden plates of various sizes, which the husband of one of my mother's sisters decorated with Alpine flowers, mountain landscapes, log cabins, and an occasional animal you had to guess was a cow. These were big hits, and purchased with the best currency there was, cigarettes. With that currency my father even managed to get an extra washbasin for the apartment, so that we had two of them—one in the bathroom and one in my parents' bedroom. We were affluent by anybody's standards at that time!

The apartment was ready, but my mother was not. She could not get up from the sofa in the living room in Passau, where she had settled down for the doctor's daily visits—the bedroom and the other rooms had long been taken over by refugees; the kitchen was shared, with people even sleeping on the floor there. My brother and I had a small room for ourselves. And there was my father. Not so long ago, he had been a good-looking and spoiled bachelor; now he had a sick wife and three children. But he was on home territory. He was lucky. In contrast to him, there were German soldiers, dressed in parts of uniforms mixed with bits of civilian clothing, always hungry, wandering through town on the way west, trying to be invisible. Meanwhile, women made dresses and skirts out of the old Nazi flags.

When we moved to Ingolstadt, Monika was temporarily left in Passau, since my mother was in no condition to take care of her. In these times of continuous streams of refugees passing through on the way to elsewhere, of roaming soldiers pretending to be somebody else, of displaced persons with no place to go, of liberated prisoners trying to find their families, of group after group of uprooted people waiting to be accepted anywhere, all of them afraid of being put into the newly organized camps and therefore always moving, even someone like my father could not find a caretaker for Monika. She had to stay in the lying-in hospital in Passau for five months, hungry, alone, with no family visiting. Did the nurses ever pick her up when she cried? How often did they change her diapers? Did they even have diapers? What kind of food did she get? My mother cried a lot about that skinny newborn left all by herself in an impersonal place with overworked, indifferent nurses and little food. Finally, by Christmas, one of my father's five sisters, and a Ukrainian refugee who with her whole family had been assigned one room in my aunt's apartment, went to Passau to get Monika. They had a laundry basket, a package of dry baby food (the coveted Hipps-Baby-Nahrung), and no train schedules. There were no train schedules. It took them several days to get to Passau in ice-cold, overcrowded trains, and several days to come back. Monika was the greatest Christmas gift my mother could have wished for—terribly skinny, nervous, easily upset, but finally at home.

For the move that fall, my father had found a truck powered by wood chips, called a *Holzgaser*. (The German word *Holzgaser* may sound innocent enough, but for me it conjures up the trucks in which people were killed with the "gas" of the exhaust fumes.) Our *Holzgaser* had an open truckbed. We—surely my father must have had help—loaded our belongings on this open truck, with boards on both sides of the truckbed sticking up high to hold all our furniture. We left my mother on the sofa in an empty living room, packed the furniture from the other rooms right out from under the refugees, and left Seppi with a girlfriend of my mother's until, two weeks later, my father could bribe her husband with canisters of gasoline. This husband then found a passenger car to transport my mother and my brother to Ingolstadt. How did my father manage to get gasoline, infinitely harder to come by than cigarettes? I don't know. I just know he said he could not function until we were all assembled under one roof.

I did not say goodbye to Tante Betty when we left Passau; she had not yet come back from the country where she and Uncle Avril had gone before the Americans arrived. After I left Passau that fall, I never saw her again, though over the years we would occasionally write to each other. Years later, on one of my visits to Ingolstadt, I was told that she had died. My mother could not even remember how long ago, or how she had heard about it. Her jealousy clearly survived Tante Betty's death.

My two closest girlfriends thought the move was exciting and envied me for it. They promised to visit Monika from time to time in the lying-in hospital, as did my mother's friends. I never said goodbye to Baumeister Max, either. Did he even see me, after my mother had pressed for a divorce? I don't know, but I do know what my mother said when I asked her—"*Du bist ja gut!*," which can mean anything from "What nerve you have!" to "Why in the world would you ask such a thing?" Was I sad when I left? Did I cry? Even today, I don't feel anything when I think back to that epic journey.

So there I was, with my father, on that truck. It was loaded so high that in one of the small towns we could not get through the medieval town gate, and the road around was still in disrepair.

Did we have to unload? I don't remember. Did I try to act brave so my father would not feel bad for taking us to Ingolstadt when he knew my mother did not want to live there? I don't remember. I do remember that on this trip in the overloaded truck my father reached out to me. I now realize he wanted the trip to be a bonding experience; perhaps he was also curious about who this daughter of his was. This trip was the only time, for years to come, when he and I were alone together for any period of time. Since I had not been in school for over six months, he could not even engage in the standard topic that adults address children with. He reached out to me by trying to make me his "buddy," by asking my opinions about the trip and the work ahead. I would be in charge of getting the furniture placed, since I knew Mutti's taste!

I did not dislike my new father, but watched him with the curious attention one pays to an interesting stranger. I did not know him. I cannot even remember when I started calling him Vati instead of Onkel Bebs. I observed his energy, his undaunted positive thinking, his enormous goodwill. On this trip he gave me a new name, and once my mother heard it, she adopted it, too. I became *die Grosse* ("the big girl"). And from then on, *die Grosse* was in charge. *Die Grosse* would manage, *die Grosse* would be there, *die Grosse* could do it, she was so good, so hardworking, so reliable, so efficient. There was not even a question of whether or not I was old enough to be trusted with all the chores. I was trusted because there was no alternative.

When we arrived in Ingolstadt, late at night, one of my father's sisters was there to welcome us and to invite me to spend the night at her house, instead of on the floor of the unfurnished apartment. Curious to meet some of my new cousins, I accepted. I have felt bad ever since that, for that first, important night in the new place, I left my father alone.

From the next day on, the urgencies of daily life—getting the place ready for my mother and brother, getting food and heating material and starting a business—consumed my father entirely. An older woman came and did some cooking and washing for us. The apartment was ready when, two weeks later, my mother arrived. In a sad enactment of the marriage ritual, my father carried his sick wife from the car, over the threshold of the apartment, to a sofa we had prepared in the kitchen, so that she would be part of the daily activities without being sequestered in a bedroom. In those days (perhaps even today?) there were live-in kitchens; they were convenient. Live-in kitchens also saved the expense of heating another room.

From the time I was four years old, I had never had a father around; I was not used to men; I was not used to having a constantly sick mother lying on the sofa; I was not used to having a little brother to take care of all the time; I was not used to being chained all day to unending household chores; I was not used to being *die Grosse,* no matter how much my parents meant it as praise; I was not used to losing the freedom I had enjoyed in Passau; I was not used to not having my friends around; I was not used to being a Misslbeck. Was I jealous of the man who took all of my mother's love and attention and who had—intentionally or not—shaped her life and mine? I did not know then, but know now, that I was traumatized, that I curled up within myself, and that a sediment of anger began to accrue. I worked, took care of my siblings, the house, the food shopping, and my mother as much as possible, and my parents never stinted on their praise for my help. I functioned, and occasionally I even smiled. But I no longer talked much.

Instead, I dreamed—and still dream—of Passau. By now, "my" Passau is probably very different from the actual Passau. Maybe I was never quite that free, even as a young child; maybe I fantasized that freedom later on, as a counterweight to the harnessed existence in Ingolstadt. In my dreams, Passau remains a town of narrow streets and steep stairs, of acute corners and high walls, of tunnels and rivers and rumored underground passages; sometimes it protects you, sometimes it keeps you out, and sometimes it is a labyrinth through which I race in slow motion.

These were the years when the Nazi regime—not an abstract entity but consisting of innumerable enthusiastic supporters, eager executioners, fellow travelers, bystanders, passive resisters—destroyed millions of lives, and inflicted unaccountable pain and immeasurable suffering. During that same time, lulled by the whistling noises of the trains passing through Passau, in daily contact with people of many shades of Nazi allegiance, there grew within me a foundation of strength and self-confidence, of joy, and a sassiness that has by now considerably mellowed. Ineradicably, I carry within me the knowledge that this time of utter catastrophe for so many was also the time of my childhood paradise, and though it was lost, as every paradise eventually is, its memory has shaped me and supports me to this day. I look at my grandchildren and hope that they are in the process of building their own paradises, inaccessible to their parents, to help them navigate the rapids of their lives.

INGOLSTADT

Sometime after my husband, Bill, dropped out of the presidential primary on March 9, 2000, he was invited to give a talk in Germany and I went with him. We both wanted to go to Passau to check my records there. The only day we were free to go was a Thursday in June, on the day of Fronleichnam ("Corpus Christi Day"). In Catholic Bavaria this is a holiday, and all offices are closed. There are impressive processions through specially designated streets with beautifully decorated outdoor altars, and so Bill and I decided to drive to the Bavarian Alps to see some of the last remnants of indigenous culture. In village after village, priests walked ceremoniously under baldachins, holding up monstrances displaying the host, and surrounded by altar boys swinging censors that emitted copious effusions of incense. Farmers and their wives in the processions wore elaborate *Trachten* ("ethnic costumes"), and associations of young men brandished their hunting rifles—all accompanied by the rhythmic murmur of prayers and the singing of hymns. Bystanders crossed themselves and knelt as the processions passed, and the host gleamed in its gold-embossed vessel. I was happy that I could take Bill to see something not many tourists would ever witness, and said to myself, "This is better than digging in the Passau archives."

This part of Bavaria, the Alpenvorland, is picture-perfect charming as it spreads toward the high mountains that close off

The whole family at the log cabin in Schambach, 1949. I'm in the back, between Monika and Seppi.

the horizon to the south. Ingolstadt is situated to the north, in the Donautal. Its beauty is unassuming, yet it touches me deeply. After it became necessary for my mother to move to a nursing home about fifteen miles from Ingolstadt, I would take the bus through the Donautal, a wide floodplain that still bears the traces of early Roman settlements. Once, when Stephanie and the children visited Ingolstadt, we drove to a thermal spa that had been in operation in Roman times and is still in use today. About twenty miles downstream from Ingolstadt, near Pförring, and still a few miles farther, near Eining, are recently excavated remnants of old *Römerkastelle* (Roman fortifications). Just as the Chinese built the Great Wall of China, so the Romans constructed, on a more modest scale, the *Limes,* a fortified and heavily armored wall that closed the gap between the natural boundaries of two rivers, the Rhine flowing north and the Danube flowing east. It extended from the upper part of the Rhine, near today's Andernach, several hundred miles southeast to the upper part of the Danube, and for a few centuries kept the Roman Empire reasonably safe from the invasion of the Germanic tribes. The *Limes* abuts the Danube near Eining, and the *Limesstrasse* to this day attracts those who want to walk in the steps of a distant past.

As I sat on the bus and gazed out the window, I could not help wondering how such a gentle countryside proved, in our time, hospitable to so much political horror. (Not that the Donautal was worse than any other part of Germany.) The bus drove through villages, and the neat houses with flowerboxes in all the windows suggested a fairy-tale existence. I would try to superimpose on what I saw my knowledge of the meanness, the denunciations, the nasty pressures to conform that were rampant during the Nazi regime. Are the pressures to follow the rules that determine at what time you may cut your grass and when power mowers and leaf blowers cannot run, since their noise would disturb the "quiet time" of a neighborhood, or the need to conform to building codes dictating that all roof gables must face in the same direction—are these remnants of a more strident past? Conformity is imposed even in minute details. A former student of mine, coming back from visiting relatives in Germany, told us of an aunt who reprimanded her after she had hung the laundry out to dry (the dryer was for bad weather only). She had not hung all the towels together, and all the sheets, and then the shirts, and after that the undershirts and underpants. Most of my students laughed, incredulous, but some nodded knowingly. They had been to Germany.

I am saddened by Germany's incongruities: its people are kind, and I want to believe that their culture is somehow in harmony with the beauty of their countryside, but I also know that socializing pressures and their transference into politics are stronger than any valley or mountain range, no matter how ennobling or soothing or impressive. Perhaps the determining factor is size rather than topography. For a movement to gain momentum in the expanse of the United States, a tremendous effort and much time need to be invested. Demagogues often fizzle out when they go beyond the boundaries of their home states or regions. Germany and most other European countries are relatively small and densely populated, and movements can catch on and saturate a population much faster. Sitting in the bus, distracted by what I saw, I would find no answers, and so I let the subject drop. I would remind myself that this was just a visit, and that soon I'd go back to the States—not "home," for I found that to be an elusive concept, but back to the place that I had chosen to live in and that had accepted me. America and I mesh—and one reason is that this country draws its lifeblood from the enthusiasm and good will of generation after generation of immigrants.

Not so long ago, I gave a lecture in a small college town. After the lecture, the host and a few of his friends and I sat together and spoke about our roots—not in the sense of who our parents were but what we needed in order to feel rooted in a place, in a time. We came from vastly different parts of the world, some of us from countries that no longer exist, some speaking languages that are disappearing. Did we come from indifferent, accidental places, or had we left a *Heimat?*

Heimat is a German word that has no satisfactory equivalent in other languages. It denotes the region where one has been born and remains rooted even if one spends a lifetime away from it. Perhaps the break in my life when I left Passau at the age of ten also broke any attachment to a *Heimat*. Longing to be in the *Heimat* causes the incurable disease of *Heimweh,* an illness that can be stilled only by being back home. I wonder whether it is not an illness that is beginning to disappear, just as languages and other ethnic differentiations are beginning to disappear. I have friends in New Jersey who change their homes ever so often as the families expand, then contract, or as new jobs require them to relocate. Bill's roots, though deep within Crystal City, Missouri, have spread all over the country; he is truly at home wherever he is. And my two daughters? Do they know their *Heimat* yet? Are my roots still in Passau, a town that I left more than half a century ago and that has changed beyond recognition from what it is in my memory? Where in the United States have I put down my roots? In New Jersey, where I have a deck with a striped awning and lots of sunshine and trees and shrubs all around me? Or is it New York, where I first arrived when I came to America?

In a strange way, I do feel rooted in New York—in noisy, anonymous (not indifferent!), overwhelming New York, where everything is going on at the same time, where even the pavement vibrates with energy, where I am forever amazed at how divergent dynamics can create cohesiveness, where friendliness is a survival technique, and where in times of catastrophe the entire city pulls together and strangers help each other as if this were the most natural thing to do. New York humbles and exhilarates me at the same time. When Bill played basketball for the New York Knicks, we would, after Saturday night games, drive back to New Jersey. Long past midnight, the streets were still full of people buying Sunday editions of the *New York Times* and the Lincoln Tunnel was overflowing with traffic. It was at these moments that I would rhapsodize about "the city that never sleeps."

Why do I love it so much? What experiences shaped me for that? I came from relatively small towns in Germany, so shouldn't I be averse to such a throbbing metropolis? My mother often wondered what she had done wrong in bringing me up—that I did not suffer from *Heimweh* and loved this Moloch. For me, New York is not a Moloch; it is just not an intimate city, and it does not care whether you love it or not. It does not reach out; it simply is. I love the fact that it does not coerce you, has no expectations of you, lets you be, but has more than enough to offer if you want to engage. I live in harmony with the ambivalence of New York: it's a huge metropolis, and people project onto it their fantasies of success and try to look away from the threats of its underside. Perhaps I find the vitality of the city attractive, an energy that scared my mother when she visited here. Perhaps the stones of Manhattan are a larger version of the stones of Passau; perhaps the deep canyons of skyscrapers give me the same sense of adventure and yet of enclosure that Passau's narrow lanes extended to me; perhaps my body remembers the physical mobility and independence I had in Passau when I maneuver my way through Manhattan.

Sometimes I think I might be rooted in my work, or, rather, that my work as a scholar and professor of literature gives me roots. My work is the umbilical cord that connects me to where I came from; it embodies my search for an identity that embraces my German past in all its displacements, and it has structured my new life in my new country. Through Germany's ongoing production of literature, I stay connected to a country that is every year more remote to me. I trust literature rather than the media to tell me in what direction the soul of a country is journeying. Literature shows me the self-perceptions of a nation's citizens, reveals their collective blind spots, traumas, struggles for identity. If not literature, what then? This is an article of faith, and I abide by it religiously.

In 1963, when I became an American citizen, dual citizenship was not an option. It is an option I would not have taken anyway; I exchanged my green card for an American passport as soon as I could. Germany for me, today, is vacation. I love the beer gardens in summer, but I love them as a tourist would—as an attractive exception, not as part of my daily life. Yet I am not quite a tourist, either. I move among the rows of tables and garden chairs and wooden benches on the hard-to-walk gravel with a familiarity and sense of the ordinary that my daughters do not share.

Sometimes I think of myself as a mangrove tree with roots hanging in the air. Is the question of rootedness even relevant in the States? This is a mobile, flexible society. In Germany, people are much more wedded to a specific place, and when a job requires them to relocate, they often prefer unemployment. (Of course, they can afford to prefer unemployment, since the compensation is generous, and with a little "black" labor on the side, they make out fine.) In Washington, D.C., during Bill's years as U.S. senator, we once had a carpenter who was, with his family, on the way from Texas to elsewhere; he followed the jobs wherever they took him. Here, too, history helps shape perceptions and expectations. Are Americans more prone to mobility because most of us came from elsewhere and abandoned, or never had, roots? Or is the hope of economic advancement the driving force that takes us wherever that hope promises to become reality?

I would never want to give up what I have found in the United States, which is not a rootedness but an openness and a constant spiritual and emotional challenge to seek new definitions (including the definition of self) of my aspirations and purposes. It is this openness that makes life in the United States so hard, so competitive, so devastating—and so rewarding.

Am I rooted in the hearts of those I love?

Settling in Ingolstadt was a challenge for all of us. Our apartment was part of the medieval fortifications that surround the city. (They are still standing and inhabited today.) Even though many people had to live under worse conditions than we did, the first few years of the postwar period were not easy. Only with the Marshall Plan in April 1948, and the currency reform a few months later, in June, did the black market collapse and the reconstruction of Germany begin, albeit at a horrendous price—a price that defined U.S.-German relations for nearly half a century. In March 1946, while the Nuremberg War Crimes trials were taking place and the four victorious powers—Great Britain, France, the Soviet Union, and the United States—seemed in agreement about the destiny of Germany, British Prime Minister Winston Churchill gave his famous Iron Curtain speech in Fulton, Missouri. Not too long thereafter, the United States determined that the Soviet Occupation Zone in Germany did not qualify for the Marshall Plan, since the Soviet Union did not accept certain stipulations of transparency inherent in the plan. The currency reform extended therefore only to those parts of Germany that were occupied by the Western allies. A few days after the institution of the reform, on June 20, 1948, the Soviets responded by sealing Berlin off from access by the Western powers. Berlin was situated deep in the Soviet Occupation Zone but administered by the four powers. Denied access, the Western allies organized the Berlin airlift. One year later, the division of Germany became official: in the Western part, the Federal Republic was established; in the Eastern part, the German Democratic Republic. Over the next forty years, the two Germanys would go their separate ways. I registered the events of these four years as a child would, listening to the excited discussions of grown-ups without any real interest or understanding. I saw only what was immediately around me.

Bill once told me that at Oxford he wrote a paper on the terrible conditions in Germany during the winter of 1946, when we settled in Ingolstadt. He wrote about the bombed-out cities, the lack of food and shelter, the shortage of heating material, the lack of building material, the lack of clothes, coats, shoes. What he couldn't write about (because it wasn't, he explained, in the immediate foreign-policy record) was the absence of information about family members, about parents or children lost on the treks from the East, about soldiers missing in action. There were the ration cards and there was the black market; there were the DP camps, fugitives trying to look innocent, and Nazi murderers going underground, leaving the country. What I mostly remember are the frozen ice flowers on the windows of our kitchen and bedrooms, crystallized into beautiful shapes as the steam in the cold rooms congealed.

It was during that winter of 1946 that I saw my father cry. He had bicycled twelve miles over icy roads to get two quarts of milk. When he arrived home, he was so frozen stiff that he fell off the bicycle and spilled the milk. After that, he was able to persuade a *Stadtbauer* on our bombed-out street (a *Stadtbauer* is a farmer whose fields are outside of town, but whose barn and stable are in town—a species that was soon to disappear) to give us, twice a week, a liter of milk. The milk was not pasteurized or homogenized, but then, it was never around long enough to go bad, and nobody thought of asking whether the cows had TB.

When I read the statistics that Bill used in his paper about that winter in Germany, I accept them but I do not feel them as a reality I lived. The reality I lived had to do with such things as the seasonal rhythm of hens laying eggs. To preserve the eggs over an extended period of time, you had to place them in buckets filled with *Wasserglas* ("sodium silicate"). Because the buckets were kept in the basement, groping for eggs in the gelatinous icy substance had to be done quickly, or your hands absorbed the coldness of the *Wasserglas* and sent it through your bones up into your arms. We also had a pile of coal and a pile of potatoes in the cellar, and two large boxes. One of the boxes contained neatly stacked briquettes, the other carrots. Carrots were hard to preserve over the winter. You needed to put down a deep layer of dry sand and stick the carrots into it one by one so they would not touch each other. Then you put another layer of sand over them and proceeded anew. The box was several layers full. The difficulty, toward spring, was groping through the cold sand to reach the carrots near the bottom. Sometimes they were rotten and felt squishy. But going through the potatoes was even worse. By spring they had grown eyes and new sprouts and cockroaches nested among them. You had to clean the potatoes in the cellar before you brought them up into the kitchen.

I remember one of those occasions when my mother asked me to get potatoes. In winter it was always near-dark in the cellar, and the single lightbulb cast more shadows than light. Was I afraid or merely disgusted when I had to fetch yet another bucket of potatoes? Were there mice down there, or, still worse, rats? No, I told myself, never rats, since there wasn't enough food around for them. Did I hear something gnawing, groaning, grunting? Was there some ghost ready to appear from behind some corner? Where did that sighing, creaking noise come from? Was that a baby crying behind the pile of potatoes? Or a dying animal? Was that the shadow of somebody coming after me? And why did the lightbulb flicker? I remember clearly what I did to combat my fear: I tried to walk particularly slowly to that dark corner of our cellar, to prove I could control my panic, and I took twice as long to fill the bucket with potatoes. But I did not go to the corner where I thought the sighing was coming from. When I resurfaced, in the warm, well-lit kitchen, my mother asked what had taken me so long. I don't remember my answer, but surely, for an eleven-year-old kid I had been brave, and I was proud of having conquered my fear.

I just checked in the dictionary the English word for the verb *hamstern*. It says "hoard." But hoarding is not what *hamstern* was; there was no chance to "hoard." In the specific postwar context, *hamstern* meant you biked out into the country, or hitched a ride, or simply walked, from farmhouse to farmhouse, ignoring the disgruntled farmers, ignoring the taunting children who barred your way, ignoring the dogs kept on long chains and barking viciously. You were lucky if you came home at the end of a day or a weekend (having slept in a hayloft or an abandoned barn) with a few eggs, or milk, or potatoes. Most of the time, these few items were bought dearly, with watches and fur coats and Oriental rugs and other valuables that the farmers, on their terms, hoarded. If you had cigarettes to barter with, you did not need to go *hamstern*—the goods came to you. Even farmers, stuffing their houses to the brim with bartered goods, always needed cigarettes. I don't know how many packs of cigarettes a piglet was worth, or the shank of an ox. I do know that butchering on the sly (*schwarz schlachten*, as in *Schwarzmarkt*, the black market) was not allowed.

There is an ultimately funny scene I did not witness but heard described so often and in such vivid detail that I picture it like this: Somehow, a farmer had brought a live piglet to my father's woodworking shop. During the night, the farmer and my father killed it in the shop, with the lights off, so as not to attract the attention of the patrolling MPs. Their only light came from the streetlamps outside. Since a curfew was still in effect, my father and the farmer had to spend the night in the shop. Early in the morning, after the curfew was lifted, they heaved the dead piglet onto a cart and covered it with sackcloth, the farmer set out for his farm, and my father set out for home with the carcass. Perhaps it was the rattling of the cart on the cobblestones, or perhaps the pig had not been bled sufficiently; in any event, a trickle of blood began to flow from the cart. The MPs were still out there. They stopped him. Did they think he had a human corpse under the sackcloth? They asked him to remove it so they could see where the blood was coming from. They knew he was not allowed to have a dead pig on his cart. But then they let him pass. Maybe they were sorry for people who were hungry. My father could have gone to jail. Instead, he rewrapped the pig to avoid further blood trails and arrived home physically drained, emotionally exhausted, and tremendously grateful to those MPs.

I did witness the second part of the piglet story. To slaughter a pig and call it your own was a wonderful thing—but what to do with a slaughtered pig once you had taken possession of it and brought it home? My father had made arrangements with a butcher to come to our house, and he was already there, on the lookout, when my father arrived, and helped unload the pig. This had to be done quickly, smoothly, quietly, so that the neighbors didn't see (and denounce you to the authorities). They pulled the dead pig off the cart (someone must have been there to take the cart away immediately), trundled it through the apartment door and down the hallway into the kitchen.

Big pots of water are already boiling on the stove. The butcher goes about cutting and gutting and whatever a butcher does. I know we are supposed to get not only chunks of meat from that pig, but also sausages and lard. The meat of the sausages has to be cooked for a while before it can be stuffed into guts—yet everything has to be done quickly and there has to be as little smell as possible, so as not to attract the attention of the neighbors. The butcher works, of course, for a share of the meat. And no matter how fast everybody works, it takes hours. Then the doorbell rings. I am told to answer the door and say that nobody is at home.

The electric-meter reader is at the door, and he says it does not matter if nobody is home, he can read the meter anyway. The meter is in the kitchen. I ask him to wait. I run back to the kitchen and tell my father. What can my father tell the meter reader so that he will not come in? I am told to let him come into the kitchen, but slowly. How can I do that? I dawdle. By the time the meter reader and I make it to the kitchen, the big pots and pans have been covered with sheets. But the pots on the stove still bubble, and the smell of sausages fills the kitchen. My father plays the host and shows the meter man the meter, as if the man, who comes once a month, does not know where the meter is. Perhaps my father is trying to distract him from looking around the kitchen. Then they talk a little while. My father wraps something big and chunky in a towel and gives it to him. The meter man walks away with his briefcase full of raw, bleeding meat and calls it a day.

During that first postwar winter, my father would on occasion also bring home loaves of bread. I remember the time he gave me a small loaf of bread, only for me. He took a knife, and with it he made six incisions in the loaf, explaining to me that I now had seven pieces of bread, one for each day, and that I must eat only one piece per day, so that the bread would last me through the week. I did that. Today, I wonder whether that was not asking a lot of a hungry child. Perhaps he was trying to teach me discipline, or to show me that he trusted me to behave as an adult. But what if I had eaten all the bread in two or three days? Looking back, I take my obedience as a sign that I was not really hungry, that we must have had enough food. There were the potatoes and carrots, and also cabbage. Every day, when my father came home from the shop for lunch and my mother was well enough to cook, he would say, "And what magic did you work today to prepare this wonderful meal?" At least there were enough staples to work magic with; others had much less. My father's decision to move us all to Ingolstadt, where he had a network of friends, had proved a sound one.

I did not go to school for a whole year, from the time my mother took us to the country toward the end of the war until spring of the following year. There simply were no schools, at least not in Ingolstadt. I remember when my father took me to register for school, on an indifferent day in the spring of 1946.

He does not enroll me in fourth grade of elementary school to make up for the lost year; instead, he and my mother have decided that I should immediately enter the first year of the advanced track school, which is equivalent to fifth grade. I am apprehensive. I have been in Ingolstadt now for over six months, but I don't know anybody, don't have any girlfriends yet. I would like to ask him to walk down in the street, while I stay up on the sidewalk, since then I would feel a few inches taller, but I don't ask. We walk together on the sidewalk. We pass the Canisius-Konvikt, a Jesuit-run boarding school for boys. We pass the "governor's residence" (an American title for a U.S.-occupied public building, where I applied, years later, to spend my junior year in an American high school—only to find out that I was a year too young). We are almost at our destination. Trees are sprouting tender leaves; some bushes are in bloom; I remember sparse branches in pink and yellow. My first spring in Ingolstadt. My father holds my hand. His hand is warm, dry, fleshy, and holding it gives me comfort. As he holds my hand, he tells me that the adoption proceedings have been started but that it will take a while to finalize my adoption. Since it is only a question of time before I am legally a

Misslbeck, it might be better to start the new life in Ingolstadt right away as a Misslbeck. He will register me in school as Misslbeck, he says. This will simplify everything for all of us— and, after all, I *am* a Misslbeck.

What should I have said? I was ten years old. I felt I had already ruined my mother's life; should I now make life even more difficult for them by insisting that my name was Baumeister when I knew I was a Misslbeck? I think I nodded agreement, but I was numb. My emotional life had closed down. Not at that moment, but in subsequent years, I felt a great sense of loss, a denial of the part of me that had been beautiful and strong and feisty in my previous life. On that walk to school with my father holding my hand, I became a Misslbeck, divorced from my previous life. A few years later (am I dreaming this up? have I been dreaming this up for decades on end?), my mother—or maybe it was my father—told me that the adoption had gone through. It did not occur to me to ask to see the documents.

In the spring and early summer of 1946, soon after school started again, our classes were called out to help farmers combat a threat to their next crop: potato bugs. As in the class excursions in elementary school in Passau when we were sent to pick chamomile blossoms to make tea, we now had to pick potato bugs for the common good, since there were no sprays available. The potato bugs were golden yellow with black stripes and looked a little like scarabs; the thick, fat larvae were salmon red with black dots. They were not half so disgusting as the cockroaches that infested the potatoes in the cellar. The teachers gave us large glass jars filled with a "deadly" liquid, probably gasoline. With some skill, one could roll the insects from the potato leaves right into the glass jars without having to touch them, and they would die. When the jars were completely filled, we screwed the lids tight, handed the jar to the teacher, and had a good time running around the fields before we had to walk the several miles back to town.

Potato bugs were one plague; lice were another. There was no way to avoid bringing lice home from school, even though lice powder was distributed liberally. There were also special louse combs, but they had little effect on the braids of us girls—or on the louse eggs, which would evade even the narrowest teeth of the comb. My mother did not want me to infect the entire family with lice, but she could not simply shave my hair off; that was only for boys. She had heard how one could get rid of lice even if the victim had long braids. You soaked the hair in gasoline; then you put a rubber bathing cap over the victim's head to prevent the fumes from escaping; then you wrapped a towel around the head and waited till morning. I cried all night because my scalp was burning as if on fire, but my mother was adamant: no lice in our family! In later life I wondered why I didn't simply take the noxious cap off without asking her—she was asleep anyway. When the time came in the morning for her to remove the headgear, she also removed part of my scalp, leaving open sores. For quite a while, I had to go to a medical office (to the Ambulante Schwestern) every morning before school to get fresh bandages, and my white turban terribly embarrassed me in class. It happened to be the time of carnival, just before the Lenten season, and my mother suggested I should explain I was in a carnival costume, trying to look like a sheikh.

My mother still had to lie down a lot, with her legs up, to avoid a recurrence of the thrombosis. In that position she could sew and knit. She loved to knit. Of course, in 1946 and 1947 there was hardly any wool to be had for knitting. My mother would unravel those of her sweaters that could be unraveled and knit outfits for my brother and sister. Later, when it was no longer necessary to knit clothes for us, she started embroidering. She embroidered the most beautiful tablecloths and gave me some of them when I started my own household in this country, but the sizes never fit, and the care they required was beyond my patience. I still have them. My daughters cherished the ones with Easter and Christmas motifs when I brought them out, once a year—and now my grandchildren love them, particularly the little figures and animals she embroidered on them.

During those early postwar years, silk stockings were a rarity, and little shops opened up whose owners, frequently widows, knew how to catch runs with special hooks, retrace the fallen stitches, and return the stockings to wearability. The repaired runs showed, but at least they were repaired. Since silk stockings, repaired or unrepaired, were out of the question for a young girl, my mother found another way to keep my legs warm in wintertime. She had a white sweater that was much too large for either my brother or my sister, and I did not need it, since I already had one. So my mother carefully cut the sleeves out of the sweater for use as leggings. Then she knitted feet on those sleeves and— voilà—I had a pair of stockings. To disguise the seam on the inside of the sweater arm, she made it the back of the stocking, and to disguise the origins of the "stockings" even more, she embroidered a long branch on top of the seam with little red berries sticking out. The leggings were white, the branch was green, the berries were red, and the feet she knitted were gray wool, since this was the only color she had. I would have preferred to go without stockings all winter long. It was humiliating to run around with those little branches and berries sticking up the back of my legs. Besides, the wool itched terribly.

These were the externals of my life—but then there were the family dynamics, and they had their own story. Except for a few hurried dates and brief vacations, my father and mother had never lived together. They had never had any time to get used to each other, even to find out whether they were "meant" for each other. Now my father had a sick wife and three children, and we all lived among ruins. Both of my parents came with their own difficult characteristics: my father with his temper tantrums, my mother with her need to "fit in" and her desire to be the queen of her little court. Often these traits meshed, but sometimes there were outbursts.

My mother was a charming and entertaining person. Although I was not receptive to her charms, many people were. My father loved her strength and her presumed naïveté, which allowed him to be the person in charge. I think she often faked it (a very common marital pattern). She had strong opinions, and there were many topics she and I would argue over, vehemently, once we got into them. She could not understand how anyone might not agree with her, when she meant so well and knew "instinctively" that she was right. Sometimes I fantasize about what it would have been like to have a mother with whom one was in agreement—for example, in relation to men, or neighbors, or fashion, or music, or art, topics of concern for a teenager—and who took a genuine interest in one's opinions. I have no idea; it is like trying to imagine a country that does not exist. My mother cared about all her children deeply, but her concerns were conventional. Even in the year before she died, though bedridden in her nursing home, she was preoccupied with our well-being: that when we came for a visit there was enough food in her now empty house, that it be warm, clean, comfortable, that someone should pick us up at the airport, that we should have a good journey. She was never interested in what we had actually done with our lives, because, in a deeper sense, she rejected our independent selves. Monika is a painter; why did she not do something more conventional? (My father loved and took delight in Monika's career as an artist.) Monika's husband is a filmmaker, also a not very stable profession—"stable" in the sense of bourgeois stability, with a steady monthly income and a pension calculated years in advance. My husband, Bill, was a politician, something she came to dislike in my father because it kept him away from her for so many hours a week. Although she asked Bill questions about what he "did," she did so out of politeness and not true interest, either in Bill or in what he did in the Senate or in how the American political system works. In her eyes, I was perhaps more conventional, because I was a college professor, but, then, I held opinions she did not approve of, and she certainly did not read what I wrote, although she kept the books on display on her coffee table.

She adored my brother, Seppi (as we all do). He took over my father's woodworking business, which had grown into a tool-and-dye company in Ingolstadt, and made a tremendous success of it. Yet she could not understand what it took to convert a business that came basically out of the old guild system, with my father's efforts at modernization, into a technologized and competitive company that is now a supplier for the automobile industry worldwide. Before her stroke, she was concerned with my brother's plans for expanding the business and afraid of the rapid growth of the company rather than enthusiastic about it. Her need in life was security and stability; anything that went beyond the horizon of what she considered safe was a threat.

My father found my mother's bourgeois aspirations adorable, as you adore a child's efforts to appear grown up, but he rebelled with the vehemence of a four-year-old when she tried to confine him. Though my father loved my mother as dearly as she loved him, he made fun of her desire to be "respectable," to wear the right clothes, to "air" her jewelry at the right social events. He joked that if she wanted to look like a walking Christmas tree, sparkling all over, that was fine with him. When she became hysterical because she had once again misplaced a ring, he would laugh and find her cute and her anxieties most charming, and he would crawl around on all fours to dig the ring up under a carpet or the leg of a chair; he would go through the pockets of her aprons, stuffed with Kleenex; sometimes he would find the missing bauble in a soap dish or an ashtray. My father, volatile, generous, full of energy and good spirits, was the heart and soul of what we called the family circus. He was the ringmaster, yelling and screaming (sometimes in earnest, sometimes in fun), letting his good spirits or his temper fly. My mother was his sidekick, forever ready to engage, to challenge, or to enhance his performance. My brother and sister were seconding, refereeing, applauding, trying out their own little parts, and there was *die Grosse*, standing apart, observing—sometimes smiling, sometimes turning away in disgust.

When I had dinner with Monika recently, she described for me a scene that had occurred after I left home. It was my father's birthday, and my mother had invited all the Misslbecks to attend. She had prepared a luscious late breakfast. There were soft-boiled eggs, my father's favorite cold cuts and cheeses, marinated fish, and the traditional *Stamperl* for toasting my father's health. (A *Stamperl* is a shot glass full of schnapps, to be downed with the toast.) The only person not present for the celebration was my father, who had left for the company very early in the morning, promising to be back in time. My mother became upset that even on his birthday, with everybody waiting for him, he would not be punctual. Finally, my father arrived. My mother reproached him. He became defensive, and my mother kept pushing, perhaps because she wanted his relatives to see how unreliable he was. And so my father exploded. He grabbed a soft-boiled egg, threw it against the wall, and screamed, "I don't give a shit about this birthday!" (*"Auf den Geburtstag, da scheiss' ich drauf!"*) My mother did not take this in silence. My grandmother at this point discreetly reached for her *Stamperl* and emptied it in one gulp. Eventually my parents together cleaned the egg off the wall, and by the time they were finished they were laughing, kissing, and admiring each other's tempers. My sister and I screamed with laughter as she told me the story.

Yet my father also cherished the decorum my mother insisted on. On weekends, for example, we would traditionally be in Schambach. (Schambach is the name of a small village in the Jura mountains north of Ingolstadt, but also of our little house there.) My father had bought the cabin soon after the currency reform so that my mother and brother could recover and heal—my brother from the asthma he had first contracted as a baby in the dank air-raid cellar; my mother by being able to breathe good fresh air, rest, and take long walks; and Monika was to be "fattened up" on rich cow's milk, still warm from the cow's udders. On Mother's Day, my father would get up before anybody else and go out to pick a bouquet of wildflowers. He would arrange them as a wreath around her breakfast plate and wake her up by singing opera arias on his knees at her bedside. I pooh-poohed such florid scenes as theatrics and pretended they turned me off. But they did not really. I felt at home with them; it was just that I was an adolescent by then and never wanted to be drawn in.

For many years after we moved to Ingolstadt in 1945, I was angry. I could not be openly angry at my mother, who had sacrificed her life and her happiness for me. Instead, I nursed a suppressed kind of anger—at her sickness, at her need to have me in the house, at her lack of nurturing, at having to take care of my siblings, at being deprived of the unencumbered adolescence others had. She was oriented toward men, not toward children, and men were drawn to her. I still see her spreading her ten fingers wide and saying, sometimes in triumph, sometimes almost matter-of-factly, but always as a challenge, "I could have had at least one man for each of these fingers, but I only loved my Bebs, your Vati." These passionate confessions did not create a nurturing atmosphere for her children. (As I became a wife and a mother, I had great difficulty in differentiating between a warm, nurturing, but in my eyes all-too-calm love, and the expectations of an intense and consuming if volatile passion, which for me was normal.) My father called her *Mutter Erde* ("Mother Earth"), and Italian friends called her *Zia Terremoto* ("Aunt Earthquake"), and both nicknames she relished. She was generous when she could rule, but she needed to be acknowledged and deferred to as the center of our world.

And I was angry at my father for having intruded and destroyed the wonderful life I had had as a Baumeister, before he arrived, before my mother had all these pregnancies and got sicker after each one, while he had no time to cultivate a relationship with me. Ambivalence galore: I was angry with my father for making my mother sick, yet I also wanted him to turn around and look at me. I was jealous because he lavished so much attention on my mother; I felt I deserved it more than she did! I was doing all the work! I practically stood in for his wife! Would I have been less critical or dismissive of my father if he had spent more time with me, shown more interest? But how could he? He had a large family to feed and provide with decent shelter. In the first few months this was problematic, for whenever it rained the apartment above us, which had only a makeshift roof, leaked its water puddles down to us. (I think he finally helped the people above us to put on a more substantial roof.)

Of course, I wasn't angry all the time—not overtly. In my conscious mind, my mother was a saint who could do no wrong. My father's flamboyant moods captivated me as well as turned me off. How can one resist high spirits, good will, and exuberant behavior? And there were kind and tender moments with him. Perhaps they are memorable because they were rare. One such time was our ride to Ingolstadt in the overloaded wood-burning truck, when he tried to enlist me as his little helpmate, when *die Grosse* was born. And one summer day, we were swimming in the tame little Altmühl River, near Schambach, where we had the wood cabin, and he told me to hold on to his shoulders so the current (slight, compared with the Inn!) would not carry me away. I held on, tried to kick my legs in tandem with his, and saw the freckles on his shoulders.

I was more openly angry with my brother and sister during those years in Ingolstadt. They were always, so it seemed, in my way. When I was fifteen and sixteen, I had a young "admirer." (The German *Verehrer* indicates a more distanced relationship than "boyfriend." In fact, I hardly ever had a boyfriend, I had no time for them!) This *Verehrer* would play tennis with me at six o'clock in the morning, before I had to get my brother and sister ready for the day and take them to their school on my own way to school. I wanted just one hour in the early morning to play tennis and warm my heart with the thought that there was a young man who would get up that early in the morning for me. The tennis club was close to our apartment. It was not long before Seppi and Monika realized where I was when they woke up, and so they would walk, hand in hand, as they always did, in their pajamas to the club, and to assuage my anger they offered to pick up the balls! I was usually not pleased.

No matter how hard I pushed them, all three of us were nearly always late for school. The nursery school accepted children as soon as they were out of diapers, and Monika started going there when she was barely two. But she simply could not walk fast enough. Seppi dawdled just because he felt like dawdling. In first grade, he was on several occasions severely punished by his teacher—a war veteran from the Russian Front, still half starved, traumatized, and a nervous wreck—for being late. The man had no patience with lively first-graders, and my brother more than once got it with a special cane called a *Spanischer* across his outstretched hands, palms up. (A *Spanischer* is a long, thin, extremely flexible kind of reed that can cut like a knife. The term is an interesting South German/Austrian word dating back to the Habsburg Empire, when Austria and Spain were ruled by the same emperor—interesting because it indicates the impression the Spaniards left on the Austrian mind, just as the South German word *grantig*—"disgruntled"—derives from the Spanish title "grandee.") My brother never said anything at home about it, but one day my mother saw his partly blistered, partly bloody palms. My father went to see the teacher and had one of his famous outbursts, shouting, "I feed my son, I clothe my son, I shelter my son, I take care of my son, and when it comes to punishing him, I don't need anybody else, either."

My behavior never necessitated the use of a *Spanischer*. I don't know whether I was afraid of physical punishment because I had never been beaten, or whether, as a quiet student, I never provoked pedagogical ire. Only once, in a high-school history class, did I drop my reserve and ask questions I should not have asked, since the teacher was not prepared. But she wielded the equivalent of a *Spanischer* when, at the beginning of the next history class, she announced that one of her students had tried to embarrass her and, with a nod in my direction, said, "Know that I am speaking of you." She would not have that, she said. From now on, she would not answer any of my questions. I was a junior at that time, history was my favorite subject, and I would have that teacher for another year. But I never again opened my mouth in her presence. (History, as it was taught in German high schools in the early 1950s: we learned a lot about the Germanic tribes but nothing beyond the end of the nineteenth century and Bismarck. The twentieth century, Germany's recent past, the Holocaust, and World War II did not exist.)

I attended the only girls' high school in town, which was a Roman Catholic school run by nuns. The boys' high schools were public in the American sense of the word, yet admitted no girls. (Segregation by gender in the high schools was then so strict that even the daughter of an inveterate communist had to attend a religious institution; however, all high schools had to follow the same curriculum, imposed by the State Ministry of Culture and

Education.) Upon entering the building, we had to go to the basement and change from street shoes to house slippers, so that the beautiful wooden floors would not be damaged; that took up a few additional minutes, and sometimes, when I was more than a few minutes late, the entrance to the building was already locked and I had to ring and wait and ring again. To this day, I cannot stand having people be late, and I am rarely, if ever, late myself.

My brother remembers another instance of my adolescent anger. He must have been about five or six, and I had asked him to dry the dishes. Outside, his friends were waiting for him, urging him to hurry up since they were going on a trip with one of the parents. He cried and wanted to leave, but I insisted that he do a good job of it, and made him dry some of the plates twice. By the time he finished, his friends had left. I can also remember the last time I mistreated my sister (then I thought I was "disciplining" her to become an orderly adult). She was six years old. I don't remember what she had done, but I was so furious that I pulled her hair. With tears streaming down her face, and barely able to speak because her voice was so choked up, she exclaimed, "You can beat me as much as you want, but I will never obey you." I never again touched her. These scenes, too, have become part of our family's mythology. The three of us often marvel at how close we are to one another as adults, under the circumstances.

My mother never reprimanded me for being the stern, unbending, even mean-spirited taskmaster. Asked why she never interfered when I "educated" my brother and sister, she would say, "Wuschilein is doing all the work, she is bringing them up, so she also has the right to punish them when they deserve it." Now I live in a country, and perhaps at a time, in which disciplining children is not an acceptable idea. Did my brother "deserve" not to go with his friends until the dishes were done? No. Underneath my schoolmasterly exterior I was jealous—jealous and therefore angry. Why should he run off and have a good time when I was stuck with the chores? It did not matter that my brother was just out of infancy and I was already in my teens; my injured self was that of a child, and there was no generosity in me, no perspective: I could not allow him to have fun before he had "earned" it.

For that matter, why was I so obsessed with cleanliness and orderliness, two qualities I later came to identify as characteristically German, and always negatively? (The numbering of the concentration-camp inmates, the counting of their possessions, the keeping of endless lists.) I think orderliness gave me a sense of being in control of my surroundings, and cleanliness gave me a sense of comfort and stability. Truly disturbing to me today is the realization that I had already co-opted the values of the society around me to such a degree that abiding by them made me feel good. Orderliness and cleanliness are also effective tools with which to dominate others. My father, for example, coming out of the military, taught me how to clean shoes. Every evening, six pairs at least were lined up, and he showed me how to make the leather shine even if there was no shoe polish to be had. (You spit on the leather or breathe on it, and then you rub.) There was to be no dirt left on the sole. My father showed me kindly, once, and I followed his orders until I left home. As a result, to this day I do not polish any shoes. Nevertheless, what I was subjected to, I then passed on: When Monika and Seppi played outside in the mud, I made them wipe the mud off, and there was trouble if they did not do it right! They were to see that their clothes remained rather clean all day! (What a harness on a child's spontaneous playfulness!) I justified this edict by the fact that at the end of the day you could not simply throw your clothes onto the dirty laundry pile: there *was* no dirty laundry pile. There was not much soap, no washing machine, and only once a week a washerwoman would do the entire family's laundry, including sheets and linens. All clothes were worn several times before being washed, though in between wearings they were "aired out" for a day or so. Once, when the wash was hanging in the backyard to dry, it started to rain and I forgot to bring it in. The sheets hung almost to the ground, and the impact of the raindrops spluttered wet soil onto them. They had to be washed again, a calamity I have not forgotten to this day.

In another instance of this domineering orderliness, I had a run-in with my mother. Our kitchen had a wood-burning stove; the top was for cooking, and there was an oven for baking; on the side was a built-in deep oblong container for water, which we kept filled, and which was hot as long as the stove burned. This *Wasserschifferl* was a perfect humidifier when the stove was lit. I had to clean the top of the stove, but there were no cleansers to be had. Somebody had told me to use a cork and vinegar, and I scrubbed until at least the iron rim of the stovetop was sparkling. My mother one day took water out of the *Wasserschifferl* and spilled a few drops on the freshly cleaned stovetop. Water on an iron surface cleaned with vinegar immediately created rust spots. I was beside myself. I screamed at her, at how sloppy and careless she was. She was not appalled by my outburst; in fact, she apologized for making these stains. I had appropriated cleanliness as a tyranny, and I had learned to use the weapon pretty well—but this tyranny is possible only in a culture that has accepted cleanliness as a supreme value.

I look at kids today and they seem to yell at their parents all the time, even hit them. Is the underlying frustration the same? I don't think so. Stephanie told me that recently she saw a child who hit his mother at the schoolbus stop because she made him wear a jacket; Stephanie explained to me that the child was trying to "separate" from his mother, establish his own identity. The mother apparently understood and was not distressed by his behavior. When I yelled at my mother, this did not mean I wanted to separate; on the contrary, I wanted her to conform to my expectations. In later years, I would not allow my daughters to yell at me. Did I thwart the process of their "separation"?

As I think back to my time in Ingolstadt, I know that all my little complaints were made in the context of relative abundance. I remember feeling miffed, or humiliated, but not because I suffered. My parents had suffered, and my father worked day and night to provide us with essentials, but what we went through was, for me, an ordinary, everyday life. In America you see the contrast between rich and poor daily. Poverty discriminates; it makes you angry or envious and violates your sense of justice, or it serves as a stimulus to create a better life for yourself. In Germany at that time, nobody was better off, or seemed better off, than we were, and a lot of people were worse off. Once school started again, there were a lot of refugees in our classes, and for some the Quaker school-lunches (*Quaker-Speisung*), provided by the American Society of Friends, were the only real meal of the day. Sometimes there was soup or stew, sometimes pudding or eggs, and always milk. I was so little starved that I could afford to be picky; when I did not like my soup, I would give it away.

Over the years, we rearranged the rooms in our apartment many times, but no rearrangement created more space. For a while, a section from the kitchen was cut off by drywall to create my brother's *Kammerl* (his little "chamber"). For a while, the bedroom I shared with my sister was in the tower of the old fortifications: one side of the room was a semicirccle, and cut into the thick wall of the semicircle were small windows, which became my closets. In one of those spaces I kept my schoolbooks and Tante Betty's letters; the other window space eventually held a record player and some records. Here I heard for the first time Rosemary Clooney sing "You Belong to Me" ("Fly the ocean in a silver plane . . .") and kept a copy of Thomas Wolfe's collection of stories, *From Death to Morning*, borrowed over and over from the Amerika Haus.

The tower room on the third floor was my Grandfather Keller's—he was my mother's father, and when we arrived in Ingolstadt, he had been widowed for about a year and had been living by himself. He was seventy-six years old, and I adored him. He was tall, bony, with sharp features, brown eyes, and salt-and-pepper hair. (Perhaps my preference for tall, dark-haired men originated not with Baumeister Max but with Keller Opa.) There was only this one room on the third floor, cut into space taken from the attic. Also in the attic, freezing cold in winter and burning hot in summer, under a slanting roof, my father managed to have a toilet and a washbasin installed for him. When he wanted to take a full bath, he had to come down to our apartment on the first floor. Keller Opa moved into the third-story tower room once it was completed and lived there until he could no longer climb the stairs and had to go to a nursing home.

He was born in Pomerania—then Prussia, now Poland—the younger son of a *Gutsverwalter*, an estate manager who probably administered the estate of a *Junker*, a member of the Prussian landed nobility. His mother was a Pauline Raschke. When my Uncle Fritz, his son and my mother's brother, wanted to marry in 1939, he had to produce an Aryan certificate. There was some anxiety about whether his Grandmother Pauline qualified as an "Aryan." She must have, because Fritz was allowed to marry. My mother would mutter under her breath that Pauline was Polish and that our family had inherited our high cheekbones from her. I was so annoyed with my mother's secret-mongering (an understandable response to the Aryan-purity drive of the Nazis) that I smartly replied that if a Prussian man had married a Polish woman she must have been very rich. My mother, not seeing the affront, agreed that, yes, Pauline had brought three mills to the marriage. My grandfather grew up on that *Junker* estate; he became a miller and was also trained as a sheep breeder. When my mother and her sisters talked about "Papa" (as they called their father, always pronouncing the word in a heavy French accent), somebody would inevitably mention that until he was twelve he had continued to nurse with some of the Slavic women working on the estate who happened to be nursing their own babies. My grandfather would laugh, to my mother's great outrage, when he recalled (or did he just invent?) how he would drop the heavy sacks of flour and run after one of these young women, fondle her breasts, and drink her milk. My mother would be beside herself, and I would watch the interaction, delighted.

There is a saying in German that even the devil cannot ride "wild" people (*den kann der Teufel nicht reiten*), and this is how, as a child and young adult, I pictured my grandfather. In my mind's eye, he would ride wild horses in an unimaginably vast Pomerania, jump off them while they were galloping at full speed, run toward the maids, suckle milk from their breasts, then jump back on his horse and disappear over the horizon. As the younger of two sons, there was no chance that he would inherit anything, and he left home as a sheep-breeder journeyman. When my cousin Inge and I tried to piece together his journeys, to figure out how he arrived in Lorraine to marry our grandmother—Emma Müller, one of three daughters of a former shepherd and sheep breeder—I would always say, "Follow the sheep"; and the sheep trail guided us.

My grandfather was no longer a young man when he married into the sheep farm in Lorraine. Perhaps he saw in Emma a respectable high-Victorian lady, gentle and sweet, but with enough sparkle to attract him. They were married in 1909; my grandfather was forty, my grandmother twenty-nine. I don't know whether their personalities meshed. I know little of their lives together except what my mother told me. And my mother remembered mostly the occasions when her mother would say, in Ingolstadt, "Come, children, sit with me—I will tell you about back home," and they would hear what they thought were versions of fairy tales. In these tales, "Monsieur Keller" was mocked by the three sisters, and though he was wild on a horse, they, too, knew how to ride, and raced him, and laughed at him. Just as my mother had four years between my birth and the outbreak of World War II in which to live her life as fully as she knew how, my Keller grandparents had five years between their marriage in 1909 and the outbreak of World War I in 1914; and just as my mother's life had changed dramatically by the end of World War II, so my grandparents' lives were thrown into a radically new phase with their forced departure from Lorraine at the end of World War I. When I think about my grandmother now, I find her life a striking example of how war and politics can derail an existence that once was carefree and prosperous. I picture my grandmother, in her youth in Lorraine, as lively, and my grandfather as "alive." When you are lively, you can also become sad; life can teach you lessons, whereas being alive is a quality independent of circumstances. My grandfather was like a cat, always landing on his feet. He was not rooted, as my grandmother was. He was, in my mother's words, an "adventurer."

He did not consider himself a refugee, as my grandmother did after 1919, but he had no roots. Maybe I learned from him that displacement was a natural condition, that life dishes out events for which you are not prepared, and that your identity arises from your way of coping. Displacement broke my grandmother, and it was a challenge for my mother, which she never quite overcame. For my grandfather, it was a state of being. He showed me that living without roots can give you a sense of freedom. He never evinced any of the disorientation and pain that may come when you are no longer "home," no longer in a place you can unthinkingly, instinctively take for granted. He never entered that territory where you see two or more sides to every circumstance, where you constantly compare and evaluate rather than just "be." There was no ambivalence in my grandfather, as there is in me.

The deep emotional attachment I had felt for Tante Betty was now tranferred to him. He could do no wrong. He was extremely charming and, to my mother's great distress, an outspoken ladies' man. But he was not condescending to women or puffed up with his own virility—he simply liked women, liked their company, liked entertaining them. My mother would be furious when a woman spent the night on the third floor and was heard coming down the stairs and leaving the house in the early morning. My father laughed and shook his head and complimented my grandfather, and I was happy that my grandfather stood his ground and refused to be intimidated by my mother. He would goad her, telling her that he was having fun, that she could disapprove as long as she wanted to, that he had no intention of giving it up. But it was after one of those nights when I went to my grandfather's room to clean up, that I found him on the floor, in the corner between the sofa and his desk, slouched over, his dentures all askew, half out of his mouth, unable to speak. He had had a stroke and could not move, although he recovered within a few weeks. After that, the overnight visits from his girlfriends stopped; he did still take them out to restaurants where in those postwar years not much more than beer was served.

Why did I so adore him? Because he showed me a kind of freedom I did not realize existed; because he stood up to my mother and she had no hold over him; because he treated me like a young woman. Who else was enchanted with me? Who else would sit with me and tell me adventure stories? In those early postwar years, he grew his own tobacco and hung it outside the central tower window on several rows of string to dry. (To this day, smelling tobacco gives me a sense of comfort, though I don't smoke.) He fermented his own wine; the apparatus was hidden in the curved space between the tower and the back of his desk, and

I had to be careful, when I cleaned, that I did not disturb the arrangement of bulbous and bubbling glass containers. In winter, when I was done with the cleaning, my grandfather and I would sit under the lamp at his table, and he would offer me a glass of wine and tell me stories. I will always hear his "*Wuschelche, komm setz dich, trink ein Gläschen Malaga,*" and I felt grown up and appreciated. He treated me with the same courtesy and interest that he accorded his lady friends.

When I was growing up in Germany (I cannot speak for the rest of Europe or for Germany today), children were used to having alcohol around them; perhaps that made them less curious about drinking than American teenagers are said to be. When my brother was five years old, my father routinely sent him to a nearby inn to get a stein of beer. There was no question that the innkeeper would fill the stein for this youngster. Once, my brother was accompanied by a group of his friends; he let them all take a deep draft, and by the time he got home the stein was almost empty. My father found that wonderful and sent him back to get more. Before the invention of plastic pacifiers, the usual pacifier for babies was a rag that was tied into a lump and dunked into beer, so the baby could suck on it and fall asleep immediately.

By the time I was sixteen, my father had acquired our first car. He wanted to celebrate the occasion with a trip, and we drove to the Auracher Löchl in Kufstein, a famous wine restaurant in Austria, just over the border. It was treacherous wine, and both my father and I got so drunk that he could no longer drive and my mother had to chauffeur us back to the hotel. En route, I had to throw up! My mother had to pull the car over, and my father stumbled out so I could emerge from the back seat. As he held the door open for me, swerving and holding on to it, it slid from his grasp. He grabbed at me, and together we fell down the embankment into a ditch. I am almost as disgusted with us now as my mother was then. At the time, I was too dizzy and sick to have an

opinion about anything at all, but to this day I have never wanted
to feel that bad again.

When I think back to the stories my grandfather told me, I see
how clearly he was a person of his times. He was born in 1869,
shortly before the Franco-Prussian War and Germany's unifica-
tion under Prussian leadership in 1871. He grew into adulthood
during Germany's ill-fated bid to become a European power, a
Grossmacht, which ended with its demise in 1918, at the end of
World War I. For nearly fifty years, he participated in Germany's
rise, and when he had almost reached retirement age, he had to
cope with its fall and the aftermath. Though he was a Prussian
imperialist, he saw his times not from a political angle but as a
Lebemensch, a person who enjoyed life. According to his stories,
he had been to Africa, to Turkey, to the Near East, to Egypt. He
spoke about the Boer War, at the turn of the century in South
Africa, as if he had been there, and he may well have been. I picture him there. German Southwest Africa was acquired in 1884 in
imperial Germany's late bid to become a colonial power, and it
was only a few hundred miles from the Transvaal and the Orange
Free State, where the war was fought. Sheep were an important
element of the economy of German Southwest Africa. As a sheep
breeder he could easily have found himself in this newly acquired
territory, but he must not have been very successful, since he did
not stay. Might he have been there in 1904, when the Germans
decimated the Hereros? Imperial Germany had also established
ties with the Ottoman Empire through the projected building of a
railroad from Berlin to Baghdad; and, again, this occurred at a
time when he could have been there. Only later did I realize that
all the places he claimed to have been around the turn of the century were extensions of Germany's colonialist and imperialist
aspirations. He may have been "on the road," but it was always a
well-traveled highway.

He introduced me to his sixty-five volumes of Karl May, the

nineteenth-century German writer who sat in his prison cell, having been convicted of financial irregularities; he invented a life full of adventures and made generations of Germans, including Adolf Hitler, fervent fans of his novels about the American West and the Middle East. It was also my Opa who got me hooked on James Fenimore Cooper's *Leatherstocking Tales* in German translation and on Cooper's *The Red Rover,* which he gave me to read in a well-worn edition. I saw myself, one day, participating in all the dangers these heroes encountered, unafraid of the big oceans, ultimately settled, finding a happy ending. My grandfather painted before my mind's eye big ships on big oceans with big storms. And he told me about this funny, crippled man he had met at the Moulin Rouge when he and his future father-in-law spent time in Paris, after the shepherds had walked the sheep to Paris and they had been sold. (How much money did the two men spend on these trips?) When did my grandfather come back from South Africa, if he ever went at all? I tried to check the dates. The Boer War ended officially in February 1900 and Toulouse-Lautrec died in 1901. Could he truly have been in both places at the correct times? (If indeed he met—or even saw—Toulouse-Lautrec, he would no longer have been in South Africa when the Hereros were destroyed.) And then I stopped wondering. I felt petty. Why would I destroy the glory of his stories by holding them up against a checklist? I don't know how many of these stories were based on facts, how many he invented, how many came from books he read. But did it matter? I was enchanted. He opened my imagination to dreams and possibilities. He told me ghost stories in *Plattdeutsch,* and they always ended in laughter. He had an old-fashioned *Bücherschrank* (a large library cabinet of dark wood, with glass doors). It was full of leather-bound issues of the popular magazine *Gartenlaube,* dating back to the beginning of the twentieth century. Curious to read these issues, I learned the Gothic alphabet. I remember the atmosphere of his room, the tobacco smell, the pipe of his cast-iron stove glowing red-hot, the wine bubbling away behind his desk, the parrot printed in lively colors on the velvet blanket covering the back of his sofa, the excitement and curiosity that came with the stories. I do not remember much of the stories themselves.

Here is a scene that carries echoes of my early life with Tante Betty but that would not exist without my grandfather. I see it in my memory in shades of brown, red, gold. Our kitchen at night, dark in the corners (this must have been in the early postwar period, since there's no electric light), two large candles on the table; the stovepipe glowing, the room silent. My father is bent over his notes, calculating; my mother is darning or knitting; my grandfather is reading; I am bent over an atlas trying to figure out how to get to America without having to cross the Atlantic, since I am afraid of it (though I have never yet seen it). Can two candles serve so many people? Four faces bent close together, their prominent features catching the golden light, the rest of their faces in shadow. What did I know about America then, except what I learned from the *Leatherstocking Tales* and when I observed the occasional GI or MP in a jeep on the streets? Why, even then, did I want to go there? I felt that night that I was trying to solve a practical problem, not address a dream: how could I not cross the Atlantic and still get to America? The answer I found was to cross Siberia all the way to the Bering Strait, wait there till the passage was frozen over, and then walk to Alaska. I was profoundly satisfied with that prospect.

For years, my grandfather leased a small garden plot—a *Schrebergarten*, named after Daniel Schreber, a doctor who was part of the health-and-fresh-air movement of the mid-nineteenth century in Germany. There, he bred rabbits, planted vegetables, kept a few berry bushes and (of greatest interest to me) an apple tree. In my early teens I would climb up into its branches and read. It was the only place where I could read without being disturbed. For a while, Johanna Spyri's *Heidi* books were my favorite, since Heidi was a little Cinderella, attached to her grandfather. Later, I switched to picturesque pirates and exotic, brave Indians. What a poverty of resources for a curious child!

Schrebergarten are still popular in Germany, particularly for people who live in apartments and have no immediate access to land. They are small plots arranged in groups, sometimes more than a hundred of them together, leased from the municipality that owns the land. The leaseholders usually build little huts on them (some nowadays are as elaborate as weekend houses), large enough to brew coffee in, or to keep a few bottles of beer and some tools. On special occasions, the woman in the garden next to my grandfather's would have enough coffee to brew two or three cups, and she would invite us to share it with her. She, too, liked my grandfather, and accepted me as if I were an adult. A sip of coffee was a very special treat then, and as currency it was worth almost as much as cigarettes.

My grandfather had a sofa in his hut, a small gas burner, and there was an adjacent outhouse, where he also kept tools and raised his rabbits. A big old bathtub collected rainwater to splash in, and for the daily watering of the plants there was a water pump. For me, it was heaven. I never developed a relationship with any of the rabbits. They were food, and were regularly slaughtered. Eventually there were enough skins for a winter coat for Monika. I still see my mother in a rabbit-fur winter scarf and myself in a rabbit-fur vest.

Rabbits were not all that my grandfather kept. Before the currency reform he also kept chickens, and we anxiously waited every day for their eggs. The chicken coop was not in the *Schrebergarten* but in back of our apartment, inside the old fortification. The coop had a high, loose wire fence around it and opened into our woodshed, where my father had a pole installed on which the chickens could sit and spend their nights. The son of one of my father's workers constructed the fence, installed the pole, and on occasion came around to bring wood to fire our kitchen stove. He was an apprentice in my father's company, perhaps sixteen years old, with black hair and black eyes, and I had a crush on him. He never noticed. Once a week I had to clean that perch and the area beneath it, and it always seemed an indignity to me. My grandfather fed the chickens and took the pile of chickenshit to his garden for manure. Today, I cannot understand how we (or any other families) were allowed to keep chickens in the middle of town. After the currency reform of June 1948, the black markets collapsed, *hamstern* was no longer necessary, and we could do away with our chickens and rabbits. My grandfather had contributed his share to feeding our family and could now slaughter the animals one by one. To this day, I cannot fathom how difficult it was to gather enough food during those years.

During the summer months, when I was not at school, I would bicycle with my grandfather almost every day to the *Schrebergarten*. Most of the time my brother and my sister had to come along. My grandfather and I would divide them up among us, but if he had to go earlier, or stay later, I had to balance both of them, Monika in a basket wrapped around the handlebars, Seppi on the luggage rack on the back, where he had to hold on to me in order not to fall off. If I saw a kid today trying that balancing act with two small children, I would shake my head and wonder what the parents were thinking of to allow it. What did my mother think? She would praise me for being so responsible and reliable; I think she never saw that this was a dangerous situation, and since she did not worry, neither did I.

My grandfather also grew flowers in the *Schrebergarten*, and from early spring through fall we had vases full of them in our apartment. The only flowers I can, even today, name are those that he grew: roses and gladiolas, zinnias and columbine and larkspur, sweet peas and peonies, snapdragons and dahlias and phlox, freesias and lavender and any number of herbs. I can still smell—and taste—the fresh, tender lettuce my grandfather grew, and savor his tomatoes, the likes of which I have found nowhere else in the world. Together with a boiled potato and curdled milk, they made a good summer dinner.

My grandfather gave up his garden after he twice fell off the bicycle. This must have been around the time when he moved into a nursing home in Ingolstadt. There, true to his nature, he proceeded to pinch the fannies of the nuns who ran the home; they seemed not to mind, actually interpreted this as a sign of renewed vigor, but my mother was, as usual, embarrassed. However, not embarrassed enough: it was she who told me, half smiling, about Opa's latest exploits. By that time I had graduated from high school and left Ingolstadt, and I saw my grandfather only occasionally, when I came home to visit. But he did not vanish from my life, as Tante Betty had. Though I was not there when he died in 1956, I came to the funeral. Every time I am in Ingolstadt, my first outing is a walk to the cemetery to visit the graves of the Misslbeck and Keller families. (It is a tradition that Bill and my daughters have also accepted and that we keep in this country, too, when we are in the towns where our dead are buried.) I walk along the path with *Schrebergarten* on one side and a little brook on the other, walk by the little zoo, the Wasserstern, that my father's father had helped found almost a century ago, and walk into the cemetery; it looks more like a park than a cemetery, the graves competing in their display of flowers and ornaments. (Bill was there with me for my father's funeral in December 1974, while he was playing basketball, and he had to miss a game; he was also there for my mother's funeral, in the bitter month of February 2001.) My grandfather is buried next to his wife in the Keller grave, just as my parents are buried together in the large Misslbeck family plot with my father's parents, his stepmother, and one of his sisters.

When the time came for me to decide which advanced high-school track to pursue, it was my mother who stood by my wish to take the one leading to university admission, while my father wanted me to end up working as a secretary in his company, which had begun to take off. We had vehement discussions, my father insisting that he had no use for "eggheads," whereas I saw university studies as a chance to leave home. I know my father felt rejected, but my mother supported me. The German school system was then (and still is) a frozen structure: at age ten, you must decide whether you will eventually go on to trade school, which is what both my mother and my father did; whether you will switch to a *Realschule*, which leads to a career in middle-level management; or whether you go to a *Gymnasium* or its equivalent and thus qualify for admission to the university. I ended by going to an *Oberrealschule mit gymnasialem Zweig*, which means I had chemistry and physics and studied Latin (but not Greek, and would thus never be able to study medicine at the university), as well as English and French. With good enough grades, I could then qualify for admission to a university.

Even though my father was opposed to my taking the advanced high-school track, he understood my need to get away from home; perhaps he was thinking of himself at my age. In my junior year in high school, he made it possible for me to go to France for almost two months. This was at a time, 1951–52, when West Germany was still sealed off from the rest of Europe and it was very hard to travel. Nevertheless, he wanted to show my mother his French friends and where in France he had been stationed during the war. Today, this naïveté takes my breath away. Didn't he know he might embarrass his French friends? Didn't he understand that Germans and anything to do with Germans were not welcome in France? Didn't he know what had happened to French collaborators and Frenchwomen who had fallen in love with German soldiers? Of course he knew, for one of his postwar friends had fathered a child in France during the German occupation and after the war could not find any trace of mother or child; he told my father he was afraid to think what might have happened to them, and that he had heard of women who had their hair shaved off and were driven through the streets for bystanders to vilify.

But my father felt that he had been friends with the French people and had nothing to hide. So my parents went to France. From what they told us when they came back, people there remembered my father and were friendly. My mother, for her part, was delighted to meet the people my father had known during the war. Of greater importance to me was that they went one evening to the Paris Opéra. During intermission, they overheard a couple speaking German to each other. For my father that meant he would go over, introduce himself, and strike up, not only a conversation, but a friendship. The couple lived in Fontainebleau, where the man designed airplanes for a French company, as he had during the war for a German company. My father arranged for me to visit them for six weeks. The impossible happened: in the middle of the school year, I was allowed to go to France and live with that family in Fontainebleau. I had never seen baguettes, tasted mayonnaise, or drunk café au lait out of cups as large as bowls. I did not realize that you use mayonnaise instead of butter, and I loaded my baguette with butter and spread mayonnaise on top of it as if it were jelly. We hardly ever spoke German to one another, and they introduced me to their friends, all of whom were French-speaking. When I came back to Ingolstadt, my French was pretty good, and for years it was better than my English. Since then, I have been very attached to France and things French. I love it when the French are grumpy—I find it amusing—and the petty, bureaucratic spirit that so appalls me in Germans does not bother me in the French.

Family myth had it that my mother's mother, Emma Müller, was French, and that Lorraine was her birthplace. On this first trip to France I felt I was coming home. When my cousin Inge and I went to Metz in the late fall of 2001 and checked the records, we discovered that this was not so. Both of my grandmother's parents were from Hessia, about seventy miles northeast of Frankfurt, in the Vogelsberg region. After the Franco-Prussian War of 1870–71, Alsace-Lorraine became German, and the Müller family crossed the border from Hessia to Lorraine and settled at Cheval Rouge ("Red Horse"), a farm perhaps 150 miles from where they came from, and not far from Metz. My grandmother was born in Hessia in 1880, but, judging from her attachment to Cheval Rouge and the French language, she must have been quite young when they arrived there. There were the three sisters, whom my father remembered as lively, even frivolous, laughing when they were together, reminiscing about life on Cheval Rouge, speaking a language that was neither German nor French and comprehensible only to those who came from the region.

The farm was not really a sheep farm, although sheep were raised; it was more a farm for milk cows that provided Metz with milk. Looking at the photographs and the items the family salvaged when they had to leave France in 1919, they must have been well off. I wanted to know how they managed that. The money must have come from a combination of sources: perhaps to some extent from the sheep, which were raised not for their wool but for their meat; from the milk; and from the fact that Cheval Rouge— true to its name—was a *relais* station to change horses at a time when cars were not yet the common mode of transportation. When Inge and I went to Cheval Rouge, the house still stood and the current owner gave us a tour of the premises. She told us that the road would soon be replaced by a superhighway and Cheval Rouge would be torn down. We came in the nick of time!

Inge and I also visited the village in Hessia where our great-grandparents had come from. There, a local historian read us the annals her grandfather had kept, in which he noted that the shepherd Ludwig Müller had loaded all his sheep on a train in the direction of Frankfurt; from there, Inge and I assume, he continued onward to Lorraine. I have no doubt that these were the sheep with which our great-grandfather hoped to build his fortune.

Leaving one's country for economic reasons, as the Müllers did, holds a promise that perhaps helps overcome *Heimweh*. As I traveled through the United States during Bill's bid for the Democratic presidential nomination, I was impressed with the usefulness of ethnic neighborhoods, with the stabilizing force these enclaves are for new arrivals, with the guidance they provide and the shelter they afford against too violent an onslaught from a foreign civilization. Having to leave one's country for political reasons, as my Keller grandparents did, must be much more painful; these refugees are not driven by the hope of economic success but feel rejected, expelled, outlawed. I often meet the offspring of such refugees, and we talk about the toll it takes on the next generation, the one brought up by refugee parents. My grandmother did not fear for her life; she and her family simply had to pack up and be gone. She was not thrown into a culture alien to her and did not have to cope with a totally new language. Yet she saw herself as a refugee, and she impressed this sense of loss on her children. She ended up in Ingolstadt. It broke her heart, slowly but inexorably, and when her only son was killed in World War II, she gave up any desire to stay alive.

My mother has left me with one memory of her mother which was as indelibly imprinted on her mind as it is now on mine: an image of absence. My mother, then still living in Passau, had been notified that her mother was dying. When she arrived in Ingolstadt, my grandmother had already died, and her body had been taken away to the funeral hall, adjacent to the cemetery's chapel. My mother entered the apartment and found it deserted. In the bedroom, the bed was unmade and still imprinted with the outlines of my grandmother's body. On the night table lay half a praline with the marks of my grandmother's teeth in it. These were the traces of a farewell my mother would need to talk about over and over.

There is an expression in German for when you want to say you are living extremely well and are enjoying life to the fullest. You live *wie Gott in Frankreich* ("like God in France"). My grandfather and everybody at Cheval Rouge lived like that. Then, in 1914, the Great War started. Lorraine and the Argonne region became battlegrounds for bitter and disastrous fights. Sedan and Verdun, not far from Metz, are still names fraught with an air of doom. The Siegfried Line must have run close by Cheval Rouge. It was here that my grandfather met Fritz Todt.

Todt, an engineer by training, was a young officer stationed on the Western Front to observe the first attempts at air war. Later, during the Weimar Republic, he worked as a civil engineer, building hydroelectric plants and roads. He was one of the very early members of the National Socialist German Workers' Party (NSDAP), Hitler's party, joining in 1922, and from 1931 on he was an active member of the SA. After Hitler was appointed chancellor in 1933, Todt became inspector general, first for the construction of the German road system (the *Autobahnen*) and later for all military construction projects in the Third Reich. The "Organisation Todt" built the fortifications along the Western frontiers of Germany. Todt was killed in a plane crash in early 1942. Its cause was suspicious; Todt had started to criticize Hitler—not for his racial policies but for his mismanagement of the army—and Hitler allegedly wanted him out of the way. Once Todt *was* out of the way, Hitler staged an enormous funeral for him.

During the second half of the Great War, Todt was stationed

at various places on the Western Front, but always in the vicinity
of Cheval Rouge. He must have visited the farm frequently, perhaps with some of the other officers. They undoubtedly enjoyed
hunting with my grandfather, and on hunt mornings they would
be fortified before they set off with hot red wine mixed with egg
yolk. They shot pigeons and had them for dinner, well seasoned,
roasted. They "lived like God in France" even in the middle of
the war. (At the time, my grandfather was in his late forties. His
only son, my Uncle Fritz, was a small child. They did not have to
fear the draft. But a story that my mother used to tell always made
me shiver. There was a mother in the neighborhood, and she was
so afraid her son would be drafted that she locked him up in a
chicken coop. They found him, of course, but by that time he was
no longer "right in the head." The image of a young man locked
up with the chickens left a deep impression on me.)

When the war was over, Alsace-Lorraine was returned to
France. According to my mother, the Germans in the area were
given a choice: to become French and continue to lead their lives
in the customary way, or to remain German and leave. My grandmother would have opted to stay, but for my Prussian grandfather it went without saying that he and his family would return
to Germany. My mother was wrong: the political arrangements
of the Versailles Peace Treaty stipulated that native-born German couples had to return to Germany. My grandparents had no
choice. They became refugees. They were allowed to take twenty
kilos of luggage per person. But how did the very special set of
china that Monika now has, and the beautiful Baroque prints that
I have, end up in Germany, together with all the leather-bound
volumes of *Gartenlaube*? Certainly they could not have been
Handgepäck ("hand luggage"). On the journey, my grandmother
held my mother, a three-year-old, in her arms for three days and
nights; when they arrived at their arbitrary destination, Ingolstadt, her arms were completely immobilized.

Ingolstadt had been a garrison town, which meant there were now lots of empty barracks, and since the refugees had to be sent somewhere and given provisional shelter, this is where they were sent. Ingolstadt developed a small colony of these "Wackers," as they were called. I do not know where the term comes from—it is of course derogatory. Occasionally, when I accompanied my mother into town, she would meet some friends from that long-ago transport. They would laugh together and reminisce and pronounce words in the strange way their families spoke at home. These refugees were a prelude to the massive dislocations of millions of people after World War II, and to the millions of refugees in the six decades since then, from all over the world. I meet them in this country. They all seem so courageous and determined to create a good and productive life. But then I remember my grandmother's melancholy and think of my mother, who never could shake the feeling that she had come from the "barracks." Sometimes, when she and I took walks around Ingolstadt, she would point out a nice house and say, "Papa wanted to buy this house when we came from France, but Mama did not want it. She did not want to have anything to do with the Bavarians." I have often wondered whether my mother would have felt differently about herself if she had grown up in a house her parents owned. I was never a refugee, but I have some experience of cultural dislocation and the pain that comes with the frequent awareness that you are not "from here," where things are done differently.

My grandfather had to confront a harsh reality in 1919. He was now fifty years of age, had a dejected wife, five children, no job prospects, and was without the hometown rootedness that carried my father and our family through the rough times at the end of World War II. Germany did not need sheep breeders at that moment in its history. In 1945, the Allies would remember the mistakes they had made in 1919. The Versailles Peace Treaty of 1919 was a disaster for Germany, which was made to bear all payments for war damages done to other nations and to themselves. The Russian Revolution of 1917 exerted a powerful influence on Germany and set an example for a possible future—exhilarating or frightening, depending on one's political convictions. World War I ended with a revolution in Germany and a subsequent series of mini-revolutions in the various states, uncoordinated and doomed to failure from the start. (I get a whiff of the magnitude of the turmoil of these times when I consider that conservative, Catholic Bavaria was, for a few precarious weeks in 1919, a Soviet republic!) These were the conditions that gave rise to Hitler's vociferous and hysterical tirades and to the "stab-in-the-back" legend, when the socialists allegedly stabbed the soldiers who were bravely fighting on the front lines in the back, at home, by staging a revolution. Hitler's party slowly grew in strength by fighting the communists, and it was supported by the (unconstitutional) *Freikorps,* right-wing paramilitary organizations recruited from returning and unemployed war veterans.

The years after World War I, until 1924 and the Dawes Plan, saw a hyperinflation of unimaginable dimensions. (In its latest phase, the dollar's exchange rate had risen to one trillion marks per dollar.) My father, who was then in his early teens, spoke of taking armfuls of paper money just off the press to buy one loaf of bread. My grandfather, forever doing things in grand style, would light his cigars with the money.

Under these circumstances, what was my grandfather to do? He and his family, like so many others, were caught in the crucible of historic forces and personal destiny and had to find a new life for themselves. Perhaps only in insular America can the notion persist that wars are "out there": they will be won or lost, but life at home can go on without major upheaval. Society as a whole does not disintegrate. Refugees come to this country, but this country on its own soil has created no refugees since the Civil War.

My grandfather must have left Cheval Rouge ahead of his family to go job-prospecting, since my mother never mentioned his presence on the family's epic train journey to the barracks. He went to see his friend Todt, and Todt found him a respectable job with Sager & Woerner, a construction firm in Munich. I still do not know what his title, *Schachtmeister*, meant, but after the Ingolstadt barracks, in the precarious early 1920s, it came with a house in Eitting, where my grandfather worked on draining the Erdinger Moos, the moors around Erding, the site of today's Munich airport. Nearby, Todt was supervising work on the *Isarkraftwerke* (hydroelectric plants on the Isar River). My grandfather was up and at work at 5:00 a.m., and before he left for work he still drank red wine with an egg in it, as he had done in France. Today, one would probably say that he worked endless hours of overtime, but then there was no overtime; people were happy if they had a job at all.

There are photographs of my mother and her older sister Dora sitting on a sled pulled by two huge dogs. Apparently the dogs accompanied the girls to school every day and were there to pick them up. The girls had a long way to walk on deserted country roads, the political situation was unstable, and my grandmother was worried. My mother still remembers the playhouse the workers built for the girls, and the brook behind the house in which she almost drowned. In the 1960s, she wanted to see whether the house they then lived in still existed, and she and my father drove there (Eitting is only about fifty miles from Ingolstadt). Forty years after my mother lived there, some people remembered the Keller family and recognized her by her gorgeous thick chestnut-colored curls. Even before she died, when her hair was all white, it was still thick and curly.

In the 1930s, my grandfather tranferred to construction sites of the new *Autobahn* to be built south of Munich, in the direction of

Garmisch-Partenkirchen. When I was four and five years old, the words "Irschenberg" and "Mangfallbrücke" had an almost magical quality, and when, in the summer of 2000, Bill and I drove that part of the *Autobahn*, I started to cry, remembering the magic of the words. Today, as I was writing this, a book about Todt that I had ordered arrived. When I read about this particular stretch of the *Autobahn* and saw the letterhead of Sager & Woerner, I cried again. I don't know whether I was crying over the loss of my grandfather, who re-emerged as a living presence as I looked through the book, or because I felt that the present can never recapture the past, or because that time and those projects are so indelibly tarnished.

Dachau is very close to Munich, and I recently began to wonder whether slave labor was used on my grandfather's construction sites. As I found out, before the war slave labor was not used in broad daylight in the midst of Germany. (It was, however, used inside factories and plants, out of the public eye. And when the bombardments started, slave workers had to clear the rubble in full public view.) What did my grandfather know about slave labor? How long did he work for Sager & Woerner? In 1933, when Hitler came to power, Opa was sixty-four years old. He could have worked on construction sites until he was seventy or seventy-two. I do not know. All I know is that the working conditions on these sites, even for nonslave labor, were horrible. There was great time pressure for the completion of the *Autobahnen*, the workers were treated roughly, and he must have been aware of that.

Soon after the calamitous Versailles Peace Treaty, the party program for the NSDAP was formulated, with the Austrian Adolf Hitler as its head. In November 1923, Hitler tried to overthrow the Weimar government but failed. In a political atmosphere where fear of the communists far outweighed any fear of right-wing radicals, he was given a five-year jail sentence, to be served at the fortress of Landsberg in Bavaria. That is where, during 1924, he received his friends and supporters, continued with his plans, and wrote, under rather pleasant circumstances, his battle cry, *Mein Kampf*. He was set free after a year. When I am in one of my counterfactual moods, I present this scenario to my students: Imagine a Canadian national coming to the United States, founding a party here with the express and loudly stated purpose of overthrowing the U.S. government, and then trying to do just that! He does not succeed and is given a jail sentence of five years, four of which he does not have to serve! After his release he is allowed to continue to live and work and instigate and organize anew—in the United States. And all this while continuing to be a Canadian national! If only Adolf Hitler had been given a more appropriate sentence! If only he had had to serve his full term! If only he had been sent back to his country! If only he had remained blind when he was wounded toward the end of World War I! If only he had been accepted as a young man into the art academy to which he had applied! If only the most able politician of the Weimar Republic, German Chancellor and Foreign Secretary Gustav Stresemann, had not died at the most critical moment of Weimar history, in 1929, twenty-six days before the stock market crashed! If only the stock market had not crashed and stability had been maintained. If only, if only . . .

In February 1925, a few weeks after his release from jail, Hitler established a new NSDAP. I needed to know about my grandfather and his relation to Todt. Did they stay in contact once Todt had found him the position? Todt proselytized vigorously. He must not have lost much time in impressing on my grandfather that he should join the Nazi Party, which my grandfather did in April 1925, two months after it was reconstituted. According to the information I solicited and received from the Bundesarchiv—the former Berlin Document Center, which houses the records of the members of the Nazi Party—my grandfather had a very low party number, meaning that he was one of the first to join. But also listed on the copy the Bundesarchiv sent me was another date—the date when my grandfather left the party. He was a member for seven months, from April to November 1925. I was relieved, and also a little proud of him. I have never been able to see my Grandfather Keller as a member of the Nazi Party, or, for that matter, as a member of anything. He was not a belligerent individualist, he just did his own thing. He could have remained a silent, inactive party member, but he took the trouble to deliberately resign. I assume he joined in order to please Todt, and I doubt that Todt ever found out how quickly he left the party again.

The story of my grandmother's father, Ludwig Müller, is a different matter. When the family had to leave France in 1919, he was a seventy-one-year-old widower. He went back to Hessia, to his native village, where he died in 1937 at the age of eighty-nine. My cousin Inge found a newspaper containing a long obituary and a photograph that shows him with a long beard, in a military cap and a uniform with lots of medals on the left breast. The obituary noted that he joined the SA when he was already over eighty years old (so it must have been around 1928), praised him for being an "enthusiastic admirer of the Führer," and mentioned that the Führer even sent him congratulations on his eighty-fifth birthday. I cannot help wondering where he would have gone with this fervent admiration of Hitler if he had been a generation younger. Would he have been one of those brownshirts that smashed the windows of Jewish stores? What drove him into Hitler's arms? The defeat of 1918? The expulsion from Lorraine? Perhaps he felt suddenly empty-handed, at the end of his life, having passed his adulthood in the intoxicating aura of German imperialism. I see him as one of the innumerable Germans seduced by the promise of Hitler's rhetoric.

The last few years in high school were a quiet time for me. Perhaps I had outgrown the "hormone hell" of my early teens. Until fairly recently, I maintained that I had never suffered from "hormone hell," since that was a luxury not open to all young women. I thought of the many refugees struggling for survival and could not conceive of their indulging themselves in moods when their lives were at stake. If you had to steal potatoes or search for a lost parent or live in fear of being raped, you didn't have time for hormone hell. But I know that the anger of my early teenage years, although it appeared justified, was excessive. I do not know whether it was excessive because of the rumblings of that suppressed teenage chemistry or because of a deep-seated sense that my world had gone awry at a time so long ago that it had sunk into the unforgettable forgotten.

In those last few years in Ingolstadt, my mother and I took many walks. She still had to walk when she did not have her legs up on the sofa, and I was a natural companion. In the early 1950s, a building mania, forerunner of the economic miracle, seized Germany, and began to bulldoze the ruins and the past that they evoked into the ground. My father was one of those seized. He acquired a large plot of land on the periphery of Ingolstadt. An architect was consulted, plans were drawn up for a house and, adjacent to it (still the thinking of the old guild system), a small factory, for about eighty workers. On our walks, my mother and I discussed these plans, and in the summer of 1953, after I graduated from high school but before I left home, I helped my mother, in a grandiose gesture of farewell, move into the new house. In this house, I finally had a room for myself, but I occupied it only occasionally, as a visitor. My mother, however, often reminded me that my room was waiting for me and that I should come back to it. My parents would live in this house until 1974, when they left it to Seppi and his burgeoning family and moved to a smaller place, also on the periphery of town, about three miles from the old house. My father died the same year he and my mother moved into this last house, and my mother lived there until she needed to go to a nursing home; however, she kept the house open for us until her death in 2001.

But mostly my mother spoke on these walks about her marriage. She told me that she suffered because the business was taking off and she and my father had to entertain a lot at home, with dinners having to be cooked. By now my father was well into town politics, and this distressed her even more. In the immediate postwar years, while the Allied forces occupied Germany, they were eager to have Germans establish a working democracy. The Social Democrats and the Christian Democrats evolved as the two major parties. Since neither of them held an absolute majority, they needed the votes of the Free Democrats to pass their legislation. My father did not like the Social Democrats. For him they were too "red." And he did not like the Christian Democrats, who for him were too "black"—i.e., too conservative—and, particularly in Bavaria, dominated by Catholic politicians. He had therefore decided in 1949 to found his own party, the Independent Voters (Unabhängige Wählerschaft). He was able to line up a respectable party list, and when he ran for city council he won. Like the role of the Free Democrats on the national scene, the part played by the UW was important in city politics and, way beyond the significance of their numbers, his group could frequently determine the outcome of an issue.

On Sunday afternoons in Ingolstadt, half the town would take their Sunday constitutionals. We would walk in formation, a procession that was constantly interrupted as my father stopped to greet people, discuss the latest votes, present the most recent problems, explain the backgrounds and undercurrents of issues, gesticulate as he broadcast his opinions. Our family parade had an order: in front came our dachshund Morle, a nickname for *Amor,* given to him by my mother. He knew the way and knew when to stop; behind him the three children, I in the middle, holding my brother and sister each by the hand; behind us our parents, my mother with her arm hooked through my father's. When we stopped, my mother unhooked her arm, my father lifted his hat in salutation, then came the handshake or the slap on the back, depending on how good a friend the other one was. Sometimes there was only the lifting of the hat, a courtesy without cordiality.

For many years, my father served on the Ingolstadt city council, and the last six years of his public life, until 1972, he would be *Bürgermeister,* a deputy mayor. For many years, he was also president of a sports club, the MTV, where many years before he had met my mother. Then there was the Kegelclub, a bowling club frequented by all the town dignitaries, and the Rotary Club, and all the many other social and business obligations, especially evenings at the opera. But above all, he had to chaperone a fast-growing company into the postwar economic miracle and sustain its rapid expansion. For my mother, the political aspects of my father's life seemed the most easily dispensable, and therefore she complained most about them.

I remember in particular the weekend spectacles around the telephone, which traumatized me so much that to this day I prefer to have others answer the phone. On a Sunday morning, the phone would ring. As the phone rang, there would be a family consultation as to who the caller might be and who in the family would answer the phone. My father would pretend he could not answer, since, if the call was for him, which it usually was, he would be hooked, get involved, stay on the phone forever, ruin the Sunday he had promised my mother. My mother could not answer, either, since she would then have to listen to the entire story and give her opinion, and that would make my father impatient. Until I left home, I was the one who had to pick up the phone after the family consultation established that my father did not expect the call, did not know who the caller might be, and appeared upset at the insensitivity of people who would call on a Sunday morning, when he wanted to be with his wife. I would pick up the phone and say, "Here Misslbeck" and wait for the other person to say his name. Then I would say, "Oh, Mr. So-and-so!" and look at my father, who would either nod his acceptance or shake his head in rejection. If my father shook his head and I told the caller he wasn't home, the caller might ask for my mother. I was then to say, loudly, "Oh, you would like to speak to my mother?" and wait for my father's next signal. Sometimes I misinterpreted his signals and said the wrong thing. If I said he was not home when he wanted to speak with the person, he would rush to the phone, grab it out of my hand, and say something like "Oh, hey, buddy, I just walked in the door and heard Wuschi say you were on the line." The consequences were worse when I said he was home but the caller was someone he did not want to speak to, or at least wanted my mother to think he didn't. Then, if they started to argue, I felt it was my fault. Why did I allow myself to be drawn into this circus? If I left the room when the phone rang, my parents would call me back, and I did not have the courage to stand up to them, since this was a situation in which they clearly needed me.

My father was frequently absent, my mother complained; besides the city council, being president of a sports club, too, took time away from her; he enjoyed being out, having friends in, staying up late, and he always wanted her to be with him. She was not well, she said—she was exhausted, even bored. He was living "too fast."

What should I, a fifteen- and then sixteen-year-old, have said to console her? Only in retrospect did we understand that, indeed, he *had* been living too fast: he died when he was only sixty-two years old. He often said that he would not grow very old, and perhaps felt he had to cram as much living as possible into the time he had.

My teenage years were a time when my mother reveled in our close relationship. Yet this was not the relationship of a mother to a daughter, or even that of two friends of unequal age. It was something more intimate. Was it symbiotic? My mother taught me that when you love somebody there is no boundary between that person and yourself. She took it for granted that I would agree with whatever she said and thought. I was swallowed up in her, and I allowed this to happen. I allowed her to possess me as she pleased—she, in whose life I had played such a singular role. I was not even conscious that I wanted to please her; it was natural for me to do or to feel as she said. I would be angry at my father for insisting that she stay up with him and entertain his buddies (she the prize object, his trophy to be displayed), and then I was angry at my mother when, the next day, she seemed perfectly happy and reconciled to my father's ways and made excuses for him. I despised her for her lack of character; I was angry at him for creating unrest and tension.

Should my mother have told me all the grievances of her life? Probably not. Of course, it was gratifying to see her as a saint, a martyr, and to see my father as the major disturbance in our lives. I would picture her during the war, in Passau, with the belt wrapped around her head to contain her migraines, not knowing where my father was or whether he was still alive. I would see her waiting for his letters, which could never give her the assurance that he was still alive, only that he had been alive when he wrote them. As a teenager, I did not understand that my parents' consuming relationship fed on the tensions between intense love coupled with the desire to possess one another, and the vehement efforts by each of them to break loose from the domination of the other. All three of us children learned from their example that love is utterly consuming, even merciless, and gives no respite. If there was momentary peace, did that mean that you now loved me less? Love was not a haven, a sanctuary, a place to rest and be restored, but a stormy, exciting, and terrifying voyage in which nothing could be taken for granted.

Did I, as a teenager, dream of romantic love? In my early teens I had had a crush on the apprentice who built our chicken coop. Later, I had a crush on Stewart Granger, who played a pirate in a movie entitled in German *Der Herr der sieben Meere* ("Master of the Seven Seas"). But boyfriends I had none. I had "admirers," young men who would try to cross the moat surrounding the fortress of myself, but I was not willing to engage in the turmoil of love. My father would make fun of me when I turned my head away as he teased me about not having any boyfriends, and my mother sometimes suggested, not so jokingly, that I should become a nun. But, then again: Once, when my mother and I were picking up my father from some event in town and stood in the street talking, a young man walked by whom I (finally!) found attractive. More as a joke, I said to my father that there was a man I would not mind meeting. What did my father do? He ran after the fellow, greeted him, said he knew his parents (which was true), asked how they were, and led him back to meet my mother and me, waiting at the street corner. By then, I had already left Ingolstadt for good, and this young man, too, lived elsewhere and was just back for a short visit. We dated for a while, but when I left for the United States, it was over.

Our graduating class consisted of twenty girls. In Germany in 1953, unlike today, it was not common for girls to go on to the university, and we felt we were a special crop. I was, according to my father, an egghead, and therefore good for nothing but to matriculate at the University of Munich. But Munich was too close to Ingolstadt, as far as I was concerned: it was only fifty miles away, and some students who could not afford a room in Munich took the train every day. And what could I do with a *Staatsexamen* except teach, and teach at the very same advanced high-school track from which I had just graduated? I wanted to get away, travel, see the world. My choice was therefore a well-known language school on the other side of the Black Forest, the Sprachenschule Vorbeck in Gengenbach. The school offered diplomas in translating and interpreting in English, French, and Spanish. That sounded perfect to me, and my mother seconded my decision. She still thought knowing a number of different languages might protect a woman from being raped. I thought it would open up the world. And it did.

The school was close to the Rhine River and the French border. One of the students I met there had French connections through her father, and after graduation, he found a job for me in Paris—an extraordinary feat, considering that it was 1955 and I was German. The job was an apprenticeship in a bank and paid nothing. I had no intention of ever making a career in banking, but this job offered me the only opportunity to live in Paris. My father, who loved France and had already sent me to Fontainebleau, did not hesitate for one second to finance my stay, but I had to make my own connections. Through a friend of a friend, I found a room at the Union Chrétienne des Jeunes Filles and met there enough people my own age not to feel alone. I began to understand how people felt when they said they were happy. I began to feel happy. To be in Paris in the mid-1950s—when Juliette Greco was singing in the *caves,* when to know Dixieland jazz and Sidney Bechet was an absolute must, when Sartre was composing his masterworks in the Deux Magots, and Arthur Miller's *Les Sorcières de Salem* (*The Crucible*) was all the rage and

I had to skimp on a few dinners to afford the price of the ticket—
was sheer heaven. And I was in that heaven! Even the métro, a toy
system in comparison with the New York subways, was mesmer-
izing, and I felt like a true Parisian when I no longer needed a map
to find my way underground. How could life ever get any better?
One decade after the end of World War II, in the heart of a former enemy country, I spoke a lot—in French—about my grandmother from Lorraine, to break down any occasional hostility.
The most amazing moment of acceptance occurred when I
was asked from which part of Germany I came and I replied,
"Bavaria." *"Alors, mademoiselle, il faut bien le dire—vous n'êtes
pas allemande, vous êtes bavaroise!"* The deep sense of history cultivated by the French had allowed my questioner to recall that in
the Napoleonic Wars of a century and a half earlier Bavaria had
sided with the French.

Since my father had agreed to pay for a four-month stay, I
knew that paradise would not last, but I also knew that, with luck,
I would be back someday. When I returned to Ingolstadt, my
mother thought the time had come for me to show my father that
I could earn a living with the investment he had made in my education. Yes, of course—I needed only to find a way to combine
my earning capacity with my desire to see the world. After 1948,
Germany had gone through a series of "waves": the *Fresswelle*,
when you could finally eat all you wanted, with the result that
everybody put on weight; the *Wohnwelle*, when everybody wanted
to get out of the make-do ruins and began to invest in a *Bausparer*,
a tax-deductible savings system designed for home constructions,
of which my parents took advantage when they built the house in
1953; and the *Reisewelle*, when Germans again began to travel. At
first, their preferred destination was Italy, a country that had been
Germany's ally a decade earlier. I applied and was accepted as a
travel planner in a newly established travel agency. It was primarily a desk job, but just to hear names like Portofino or Rimini
or Forte dei Marmi made me feel as though I were almost there. I

even had a chance to fly (fly! in 1955!) to the Spanish island of Mallorca and report on my experiences for a travel journal.

Was this to be the egghead's future career? The short trip to Mallorca made me think that journalism was perhaps another way of seeing the world. My restlessness increased. And so I matriculated at the University of Munich in journalism and, of course, Romance languages while I was also working at the travel agency. There are lots of students in this country who hold jobs while they get a university education. This is always difficult for them, since there are papers to be written, exams to be passed, and, in many classes, demerits for absence. The incredible thing, from an American point of view, is that in the German university system nobody really cares whether you attend the lectures or seminars as long as you qualify for the final exams. But I would never reach that point.

After I came back from Paris, and before I found the job at the travel agency, I briefly worked as a translator at a trade fair in Munich, escorting foreign visitors around the fair and explaining to them what they saw. Two young Americans, who must have been GIs on their day off (they did not wear uniforms), took the tour with me, and afterward we celebrated our new friendship at one of Munich's beer gardens. That summer I also worked as a receptionist at a hotel in Switzerland, above the Lake of Lucerne. I acquired a Swiss accent. I would save my days off and go hitchhiking into the Ticino, to Lugano and Locarno, always alone, but delirious with the happiness of being out, seeing the world. I picked up some Italian. My two American friends, who appeared as interested in absorbing the culture of Europe as they may have been in me, visited and stayed a few days at the hotel. I mentioned them to my mother. She suggested, perhaps following her mother's example of "receiving" her daughters' "suitors" over tea and cookies, that I invite them for Christmas. I invited them and they accepted, gladly. Somewhere are still some photos of them stretched out under our Christmas tree.

After I came to the United States, I regretted that I did not have their addresses. I knew that one of them lived in New York City, and it would have been nice to have a contact there. In Germany, he had recommended that I read *The New Yorker* to perfect my English, and I followed his advice. (It took me years and a fairly deep immersion in American culture to understand the cartoons.) My mother told me many years later, when we were reminiscing about my travel-agency days, that "the Americans" had written to me on several occasions.

How often had they written? She was vague about it. Had they both written or only one of them? Which one? The one from New York? She said she could not remember. What had she done with the letters? She had destroyed them. Why had she not forwarded them to me, wherever I was? Because she was afraid that if I ever went to the States (aha! so she thought I would one day go to the States!) and they were my contact persons, I might fall in love with one of them and stay there.

I can still feel the nausea rising from my stomach to my throat as she told me about this act of betrayal. She had no sense that she had betrayed the trust I had unthinkingly invested in her—to her, forwarding mail was a minor matter! She hoped that if I was alone in New York I would return to Germany all the sooner, since my eventual return to Germany was the only frame of reference she had—and my room in the new house was waiting for me. Again I can hear her "*Du bist ja gut*" in defense of her position. In fact, my anger was, to her, a betrayal of her good intentions and her love for me. She, as my mother, knew better than I (her symbiotic mirror reflection) what was best for me. And that was to be back "home," close to her, where I always behaved so well, in ways predictable to her—where I was her Wuschele.

It is in the nature of betrayal that the person betrayed does not know it at the time—when there might be a chance of salvaging the situation. The secrecy, the sly serving of one's own purpose at the expense of the other, constitutes the betrayal. My mother's action was an admission of weakness and a refusal to try to achieve her goals by honest, open means. She must have known that if she was forthright with me she would never persuade me to stay at home. Therefore, betrayal (or, in her mind, a necessary intervention) was justified. Did she, when she told me of the destruction of these letters, sense the deep irony? By then I'd been married for many years, in America, and with American children. She had tried to influence my destiny, but destiny had not bowed to her wishes.

The letters were immaterial to me; what mattered was my mother's interference. And it sickened me, despite the many years that had elapsed. As I grew toward adulthood, I had not made a conscious decision to trust my mother—I had simply trusted her, over a lifetime, again and again. In my scheme of values, betrayal uproots your trust in the betrayer, and if the betrayer is important in your life, the betrayal attains a dimension way beyond what seems warranted. By this time, however, I had learned to extract something positive from defeat. I had accepted the old existentialist position, which for me culminates in Camus's statement "*Il faut imaginer Sisyphe heureux*" ("One must imagine Sisyphus"— forever rolling his rock back up the mountain—"as happy"). To live without trust threatened to diminish my own humanity, to reduce me to a skeptical disbeliever, a disappointment to myself and others. To imagine Sisyphus happy may be a pitiful rationalization, but it is better to be periodically duped and disappointed than to be permanently damaged in one's relations with others, with "the world." This is a philosophical position that takes a tremendous amount of courage and deliberate blindness. And I know that rationalizations are crutches. Do I need crutches? Yes. But I can walk with them!

One day, working in the travel agency in Munich, I began to see prominent advertisements in the newspapers: Pan Am was looking for young women to work as stewardesses. Most important prerequisite: the women had to know several languages. Pan Am was at that time opening routes around the globe and needed appropriately trained flight personnel. How many languages? Three, four, five? Would I qualify? I remember a cold, rainy Sunday in March in Ingolstadt. The entire family, dachshund included, were walking home from a restaurant after the big Sunday lunch. (By 1957, almost ten years after the currency reform, restaurants had started to do business again.) Interrupting our stroll, occupying the entire width of the sidewalk, my mother in the role of referee, my father and I made a bet: would Pan Am take me? He said no; I said yes. He was wrong; I was right.

This was the chance I had been waiting for! I did not even have to cross the Bering Strait to get to America—I would fly! I was determined not to let this opportunity go. In April 1957, at the age of twenty-one, I left for the United States.

AMERICA

When I came to America, I came with the psychological baggage I had accumulated over twenty-one years of life. But along with it I brought skills and values. By the time I came to America, I had started to grow rings around the core of my life. I brought openness, strength, perseverance, and an ingrained sense of justice. I wanted people to be forthright with me, as I was forthright with them.

I had been excited, full of joy and curiosity, when I worked in the Paris bank. But now I was happy beyond anything imaginable. I felt I had fulfilled a dream of long standing, and I had achieved this triumph all on my own! I was being paid to indulge in the most glamorous hobby I could think of. I roomed with three other young women; we lived in Queens in a one-bedroom apartment to save on the rent, since a couple of us would always be on a flight. I was assigned to fly from New York as far as Bangkok and Johannesburg, and I had layover time (oh, the glory of layover time!) in all the major cities in Europe. I met the people, spoke with them in the languages I had learned: English, French, Spanish, a little Italian, and of course German. (Italian I spoke mostly with my hands, but everybody knew what I was saying.) I could understand films in all these languages, go to plays, overhear conversations, and read the newspapers wherever we went. There were museums to explore, monuments to visit—

*Bill being sworn in to the United States Senate in January 1979. He's holding Theresa Anne; Stephanie is between Vice President Mondale and me. (Paul A. Schmick/*Washington Star*)*

I had turned into the perfect tourist! On occasion, a group of crew members might rent bicycles. We had more than one picnic on the Via Appia, amid pine trees and barely recognizable ancient tombs. I was overcome by what I knew of Roman history and imagined that two thousand years ago, right on the spot where we were sitting, Roman soldiers in their combat gear and in strictest military formation might have marched; they might have drunk the same Italian wine we were drinking now. I had never slept under a ceiling fan until we stayed in Bangkok, and although I reveled in the temples and the fascinating water streets you navigated in little boats, the ceiling fan is what I remember best. I had read novels about the Pacific, and it seemed to me that ceiling fans always played prominent roles in them. The ceiling fan, and then the tailors, who showed us endless rows of silk fabric, raw silk and shantung silk, and took our measurements so that on our next trip we could pick up the finished clothes. Once, during a layover in Shannon, some of us went on a memorable hike along the west coast of Ireland in pouring rain. I remember standing on a precipitous cliff and looking down at the Atlantic pounding against the rocks. The Atlantic, the body of water I had been so afraid of! As I watched, fascinated, I was relieved to be standing well above it. The views on that hike were breathtaking, and the rain added a magical aura that made me imagine I saw Tristan and Iseult walking through the mist.

I flew before the advent of jet planes. We had to cook breakfast and make scrambled eggs for entire planeloads of passengers. There was always plenty of food left over (not so today, when the number of food packages on a plane is determined by the number of passengers). I had never had a Danish in my life before I started to fly. I loved them so much that after the passengers were fed I would eat half a dozen, until, one day, a flight supervisor told me that if I kept putting on weight I would be grounded. In the late 1950s, the airlines could still decide how their flight personnel would look and dress, and how much they could weigh. Hair had to be combed away from the face, neatly tied, not too long; no fancy combs or hairpins; jewelry could not be dangling, and costume jewelry was completely out of the question; no scarves or headbands, since they would compete with the neat, clean look of the Pan Am uniforms.

Customs, then as now, had its own set of stringent rules. Once, on a trip back from Frankfurt, I brought my then-favorite sausage, a long *Gelbwurst*, white meat sealed in yellow skin. The customs officer demanded that I throw the *Wurst* away, contending that it might carry contaminating germs. Throw food away—and such special food as that? Never! I therefore invited all the crew members and even the customs officer to a degustation of the most delicious white *Gelbwurst* to be had. We ate it in no time at all (although the customs officer had to decline and missed a great opportunity), and only then did I, highly pleased, proceed through the customs inspection. We all laughed.

It took me a while to get used to the American habit of "going out for dinner." After we arrived in London in the morning, for example, most of the crew members would go to sleep and then go out together for dinner. Why would you spend money on dinner when you could take leftover food from the plane, make a meal of it, and use the per diem to see a play or a show? It took me a while to understand that "dinner" was not just about food but about camaraderie, sharing, a little gossiping and fun.

We could request specific flight destinations, and whenever possible they were granted. Of course I wanted to go to the most distant places, to Bangkok and New Delhi and Karachi and Calcutta, but what was wrong with Rome or London or Shannon? Everything was new and incredibly exciting. One crew member requested nothing but flights to London, so he would have time to work at the British Museum on his dissertation. Eventually he received his Ph.D. from Princeton University.

That summer in America, I swam in the Atlantic Ocean for the first time in my life. On a hot day, I stood at Jones Beach, watching the white crests roll in, in an unending rhythm. There was the smell of suntan lotion mixed with that of hamburgers and hot dogs being grilled in the concession stands, all blended with the intoxicating saltiness of the ocean air. Radios were blaring the songs of that summer, and I learned them all. Andy Williams' "Love Letters in the Sand" was the first song I learned on American soil, and there was an advertising jingle—"Why don't you have iced tea more often? Why don't you have iced tea tonight?"—which also taught me the American concept of advertising. The radios, the wind, the crashing waves, the screeching seagulls . . . I had arrived, although I wasn't exactly sure where.

How many other immigrants and how many slaves had stood on the shores of the Atlantic looking back across the ocean to where they had come from, filled with hope or despair, longing or deep relief? How easy my own crossing had been! I did not have to worry about food for that first winter, or being put up on an auction block; I did not have to worry about finding a job, or about getting a green card—Pan Am saw to that. All I had to worry about—and I thought it was funny and "typically American"—was that I could not wear a bikini, as I had in Europe; at the time, only one-piece bathing suits were deemed appropriate for public beaches and pools. A lifeguard at Jones Beach tried to impress this rule on us; a group of young women out to explore America, we exaggerated, in heavily accented English, our total incomprehension of what he was telling us, exasperating and fascinating him by turns. We all flirted as much as we knew how to, and finally one of us walked away with a date!

A friend of one of my roommates had a convertible, and he would pick us up to go to the beach. For us, a trip on the Long

Island Expressway was an adventure, not a nightmare! And to drive across the George Washington Bridge, mesmerized by the strong steel cables that suspended it above the Hudson, on the way to Bear Mountain, and gaze upstream along the Palisades and downstream to the city, wanting to explore in both directions—all this was almost too much to stand. When I see young people in convertibles today, music blaring, bare feet on dashboards or seat backs, I am happy along with them, because I remember how happy I was then.

And New York! New York was then and still is today for me the capital of the world. In the late 1940s, as I was trying to chart my way to the United States via the Bering Strait, the son of friends of my parents won a scholarship to the United States, and they went to visit him. After they came back, I heard from them that in New York there was a restaurant on practically every block! Hard to imagine, when there were perhaps two restaurants in all of Ingolstadt—and those had to struggle as long as people lived on ration cards. And not only were there all those restaurants—there were skyscrapers, taller than the city's churches! For someone who had grown up in the shadow of cathedrals, with houses and the citizenry alike bowing before the majesty of the religious edifices, that was beyond imagining. Even today, when I see St. Patrick's Cathedral dwarfed by the Olympic Tower, I remember how affected I was when I finally saw the skyscrapers for myself.

On my first trip to Manhattan, I took the E-train from Queens, arbitrarily got off at 53rd Street and Fifth Avenue, and walked down Fifth Avenue all the way to Washington Square. I thought I was walking in a dream, though I knew that this dream was more real than anything else in my life. In the 1950s, Greenwich Village was still saturated with the existentialist atmosphere I had known in Paris. Eugene Ionesco's plays were a big hit at the Circle in the Square; jazz was indigenous, not imported, and the only concern was to find a knowledgeable jazz-loving escort. Rumor also had it that there were some exciting new American painters, later known as Abstract Expressionists. Where could one see their art, and might one find them hanging out in coffeehouses downtown?

It seemed almost as if I were too small a vessel to contain so much happiness. In the winter, I went ice-skating in the Wollman Rink in Central Park. The hotels and apartment buildings along Central Park South were little more than a magnificent backdrop for the exciting drama of my life. It never occurred to me that actual, real people might live in those buildings. Even less did I think that someday I would look down from one of those windows to watch new generations of skaters draw their circles of hope and aspiration on the ice of the Wollman Rink.

I never asked myself whether the joy in my life came from flying or from fleeing. Perhaps it was a combination of both. When I went to the foreign-language school on the other side of the Black Forest, was that fleeing? Yes, it was. I could have studied in Munich, but I wanted to get away from my family, become my own person. Yet the bonds to my mother held too tightly; I could not simply walk away and feel good about having grown up and become independent. I had to tear myself away—and that effort showed in the distance I sought. In America I was catapulted into the liberation I had always dreamed about. The exuberant strength that I had felt as a child roaming the streets of Passau, and that in Ingolstadt had metamorphosed into quiet perseverance, had re-emerged. The world seemed then—and still seems today—a wondrous place to me, fascinating, exhausting, challenging at every step, full of surprises, full of pain and miracles and chances, wide open and waiting for definition. I was boisterous, sometimes too loud, laughing a lot even when I did not understand all the jokes, loving the passengers and passersby and my roommates and my dates.

And then, on a blind date, I met a man I married soon afterward. He proposed on the first date, and I did not have the self-knowledge or the courage to say no. Was I still fleeing, waiting for the opportunity to make that flight permanent? Two of my roommates were beginning to be restless. One had transferred to the Western division of Pan Am and flew out of San Francisco; another one went back to Germany. Sooner or later I, too, would stop flying. For my roommates and me, flying did not translate into a career; it was a glamorous path to somewhere else. Would I fulfill my mother's hopes and go back to Germany? Would I fulfill my father's expectations and go back to the university, now that he had made peace with the egghead and thought a university education was all I was good for?

I was twenty-three years old. I had lived an unexamined life, and now I did not ask myself whether I really *wanted* to get married. I was too happy to think about the future as anything but a continuation of my current blissful state. I did not ask myself whether this marriage would mean giving up the most glorious time in my life. I did not ask myself why I agreed to the proposal so quickly—three months after our first date, after a year and a half of flying. I did not ask myself whether I was right to quit my job when I started to cry on my flights, knowing that they would soon come to an end. I did not ask myself any questions at all. Maybe I felt that I needed to be anchored and that I wanted to be anchored in the States. Maybe marriage appeared a safer and more stable commitment than a job. Maybe it seemed a natural progression on the road to ultimate fulfillment, even though I could not define what "ultimate fulfillment" meant to me. Maybe I felt, having witnessed the consuming marriage of my parents, that the absence of such romantic passion was the best guarantee for a stable relationship.

On one of my flights to Germany, I asked my parents to meet me in Frankfurt. I'm not sure even now whether I meant to ask their advice or merely to inform them of a decision I'd already made. Even now, as I try to excavate that scene from deep memory, there's a blank in my mind regarding their reactions when I told them I planned to get married. I see only the hotel room in Frankfurt, my mother sitting in the bed (her legs up), my father walking back and forth. I am hunched on the armrest of a sofa at the foot of the double bed. Gray curtains, beige carpet, a few pieces of blond wood furniture, a glass-topped coffee table. What if they had said, "No, you cannot do that"? What if they had said, "Fly a while longer, there is no hurry, and then see"? But they could not have said that; surely I would remember how I responded to any objections. They did not even say, "Let us first meet the young man." They did not try buying time. We must all have been too stunned to think clearly. My father seemed to have voiced less opposition to my marrying a man he had never met than he did to my completing the advanced high-school track. My mother did not bring up the question of *Heimweh*, did not ask what she had done wrong to cause me to escalate my travels into a permanent absence from "home." I wonder if they interpreted the resolve in my voice (was there resolve in my voice?) when I said I wanted to make a life in the States as a sign of my being in love. Were they willing to let me go forever after one conversation in a hotel room? Was I so little at home with myself that I needed my parents, with their strong opinions, to make my own life-shaping decision? Perhaps they deferred to the adult in me at the very moment when I wanted them to claim me as their child. And the child in me felt oddly betrayed, since they had spoken with conviction whenever they used to say that I ought to stay in Germany, with them.

I sometimes think this meeting in an anonymous hotel room in Frankfurt was the moment that determined the direction of the rest of my life. Even though I was riding high on my wave of happiness, I had not forgotten the traumas of my childhood and perhaps I wanted to heal that pain by seeking stability. The fact that my prospective husband, Bob Schlant, was a physician contributed to my longed-for sense of security. I had grown up seeing the wounded and mutilated soldiers, witnessed my mother with a belt around her head, with carbuncles on her arms, and heard her screams when her breast was being scraped; a part of me felt there was nothing in the world a physician could not protect me from.

Perhaps my parents knew that I would not follow whatever advice they might give me. None of us understood the powerful currents that dictated our behavior toward one another. After a brief courtship, Bob and I were married in September 1958.

Since I was still flying for Pan Am up to the last moment, my mother planned and executed the event all by herself. She even took care of the trousseau, which meant that I had lots of sheets and pillowcases that did not fit American beds, and tablecloths that did not fit American tables. Neither of her own two weddings had been very elaborate. Now she had the opportunity to make up for what she had missed and arrange the wedding she had never had. I know she took great pleasure in these preparations, like mothers everywhere. What could she have done to make me feel, in her busyness, less like a pretext for her enjoyment? Today, I would insist that we share the planning. But then I was unable to focus on the preparations. When I look at the photographs of that wedding, I am not even there. Of course I am there physically, but where are my emotions, my thoughts? I see a young woman with a slightly embarrassed expression trying to live up to the occasion by smiling shyly. As I search my memory, I see only what there is in those pictures.

The wedding ceremony took place in our Lutheran church in Ingolstadt. The church was filled with relatives and friends but also with many people who were curious to see "the American." Only relatives and a few special friends were invited for the lunch following the church ceremony. It was held at a hotel—a very extravagant event for the time. Nineteen fifty-eight was still only the beginning of Germany's "economic miracle," and the menu was fairly modest. But to show their approval of my marriage, my parents had executed as fine a wedding as could be had in Germany in those years.

Bob had accepted a position at a hospital in Atlanta, Georgia, and I joined him there in the fall of 1958. I had never lived in a Southern climate. I was not used to the uninhibited growth of these strange new plants, the imposing beauty of magnolia trees, the wispy fragility of mimosas, the jasmine with its intoxicating smell, the unremitting kudzu that suffocated trees and spread like a green carpet across the red Georgia soil. Atlanta appeared semitropical, at least during the spring and summer—lush and extravagant, both in its burgeoning vegetation and, as I came to realize, in its human emotions.

Very quickly I began to see the darker side of the American dream. I arrived in Atlanta at a time when the South was no longer a dormant society in which racial injustice was accepted without question. I witnessed the civil-rights movement without realizing what it was or why it was necessary. I did not participate in the demonstrations or marches; I lacked the visceral connection with that part of American history. Yet the seven years I spent in Atlanta are for me inextricably bound up with my exposure to a society in ferment and explosive unrest. The external rhythm of my life was punctuated by news of the Freedom Rides in 1961, the Mississippi riots in 1962, the Birmingham campaign in which Martin Luther King, Jr., was incarcerated and wrote the moving "Letter from a Birmingham Jail." In 1963, King delivered his "I Have a Dream" speech in Washington, D.C., with 250,000 people attending. In November of the same year, President Kennedy was assassinated. I witnessed these cataclysms, but I did not understand that they had built up over many decades, many generations. It was as if I were sitting on top of a volcano, but one so huge I could not distinguish it from an ordinary landscape. Where was I? I did not realize that in close proximity to me the volcano had started to erupt, and that these eruptions would irrevocably change the South and the entire United States.

On my first outing to downtown Atlanta, I was initiated into racism as it existed then. New to the city, I was not yet sure of the system of public transportation and decided to take a taxi back to our apartment. I flagged one down, but the driver explained that he could not take me, since he was black and I was white. I was shocked and dismayed, but it did not occur to me to think how humiliated he must have felt, explaining to an ignorant white woman a situation in which he was the victim, disguising his anger and shame (he must have felt anger and shame) beneath a veneer of courtesy. Only gradually, over the years, did I begin to understand the importance of nonviolence in the emerging civil-rights movement—that it prevented the individual and the community from exploding. When rage and hatred, no matter how justified and accumulated over generations, gain the upper hand and dominate a person or a group of people (as was the case in Watts in 1965 and in Washington, D.C., in 1968), self-destruction becomes a distinct possibility. But self-destruction was not the goal of the movement.

I became pregnant immediately, and our daughter, Stephanie, was born after we'd been married for nine months. Those were not happy months. I cried a lot and wrote interminable letters to my mother. I was lonely, without a support system of friends, in a part of the country I still had to get used to, and with a husband who studiously overlooked my depression. It was not long before I started to ask myself what I was doing in this marriage, what I was doing in Atlanta—and now we were expecting a child! My mother came a few weeks before the birth and stayed for six weeks afterward to help me "adjust" to what should have been a natural state. (My father stayed back in Ingolstadt and grew a beard. He wanted his friends to ask him why he was growing one, so that he could tell them that it was in honor of his first grandchild and that he was now an "old" grandfather. Then they would laugh and slap his shoulder and congratulate him.) I did not breastfeed my daughter, remembering my mother's agonies when she tried with Monika. While she was there, I rarely even diapered my daughter or bottle-fed her or held her or played with her. It was as if I had borne this child so that my mother could play with her. Sometimes I wanted to interfere—but, then, I knew my mother would soon leave and I could be with Stephanie uninterrupted after that.

When Bob came home at night, he and my mother would discuss Stephanie's daily progress; they were in agreement about child-rearing practices, feeding schedules, and how to handle matters before the baby began sleeping through the night. Not many young mothers had it as good as I. It was as if I were just another child who needed to be taken care of, humored, spoiled. And I let it be so, telling myself that Stephanie was in the best of hands. All I had to do was sit and watch her grow, day by day. How deeply underground had I gone emotionally, that I would not fight for hands-on access to my daughter? I should not even have had to fight: she was my child! But I was also the child of my mother. My mother had sacrificed herself to me, and so it seemed right to sacrifice a few weeks of my motherhood to her and make her happy. In Stephanie, she finally had a child under circumstances that had eluded her with her own children. This was a time of peace and plenty, not war; she was not ill; she was not driven to distraction by my father's busy life; she finally had a chance to enjoy what was the natural right of every mother— unimpeded access to a baby. She was only forty-three years old; Stephanie could have been her child. How could I, of all people, begrudge her such a simple pleasure? I could wait until she had gone back to Germany. Stephanie would always be my child, and nobody could ever break that bond.

During my pregnancy, I had fallen back on a support system I did not recognize as such: I went back to school, this time in earnest. I decided not to enter graduate school (for which I was qualified) right away, but to indulge myself by taking the last two years of undergraduate study. "Going back to school" addressed a long-suppressed desire. I felt I had never read enough and was never sufficiently prepared, because in high school studying had always been a privilege to be indulged in when all the other chores were done. My father took no interest in the brainy side of me, and my mother said that if I was not smart enough to make do with the time available after the chores, then perhaps I should not be on that school track. I managed, but I often muddled through, always with the feeling that there were vast areas left unexplored. It was not difficult for me to tell myself that circumstances prevented me from testing myself under the most favorable conditions, that, given my background, it was all right to be second best. To this day I feel I have never quite caught up.

Bob supported my decision to attend Emory University and helped me over the first few hurdles. I spoke French fairly fluently, but I had never heard of multiple-choice questions; I took a creative-writing course in English but misunderstood the instructions for submitting the final story; I prepared a paper on the Hellenistic period, but instead of presenting it to the class I dropped it off in the professor's mailbox and did not show up for class. But the reading and studying I did also functioned on a deeper level. They became a habit that in various phases of my life worked like a drug to shut out the rest of the world. I felt as if I were back in my grandfather's apple tree, reading in seclusion, blocking out my troubles. I had married for a sense of security and stability, and my husband's profession had suggested to me that I was "in good hands." My studies also made me think that I was now fulfilling what had been my mother's dearest wish—to gain a higher education. And I hoped that acquiring all this knowledge might help me build some ground of my own under my feet. But how could I, when I was crying every day, expect books to provide the soil that would allow roots to grow? I was still the mangrove tree with its roots in the air. Yet, as I was to find out, knowledge is the only possession you can take with you when you leave—knowledge and love.

I was not really interested in earning a degree in order to get a job quickly. I had no intention of getting a job. When it became clear that one day I would have to graduate, I would joke and say, "When I'm through, I'll take up studying the piano." Pan Am had allowed me to see the outside world. Now I had entered the world of the mind, and it was just as exciting. In art-history courses I discovered my European heritage; in American history I focused on the myth of the West; I took medieval Latin (why not, when all I was going to do was "take up the piano"?) and classical mythology, tried philosophy of science, ventured into creative writing. And always and again I took courses in Romance languages, until I had exhausted all the course offerings in French poetry and the novel and the theater and all the -isms from Romanticism to existentialism. With several languages at my command, I ultimately decided to focus on comparative literature. Today, after thirty years in the field, and after postmodernism decimated the working hypotheses of "master-narratives," I understand how limited my specialization was: there was no literature from Africa or Asia, very little from Latin America, and no "minor literatures," as Kafka called the literature of minorities written within a major culture, as we find it today, for example, in the texts of Asian Indians in America or Turks in Germany.

The first morning of my first semester is deeply etched in my memory. I thought I saw Scarlett O'Hara, the heroine of *Gone with the Wind*, walk across campus. I had seen the film when I was at the language school in the Black Forest and had been totally overwhelmed by the history and the story. And here was her modern version! She wore what I had never seen anyone wear on an ordinary weekday morning: a tight pair of silk-shantung pants, a matching top, Plexiglas high-heeled sandals, and a matching see-through plastic pocketbook. At nine o'clock in the morning she drank a bottle of Coca-Cola! She had the bluest eyes in the world and black hair. She was, to me, more beautiful than Vivian Leigh in *Gone with the Wind*. Though she was a student of theology, we eventually met in a class on French poetry. Since neither Bob nor any of the faculty I met were true Southerners, I had not much heard the Southern accent in all its lulling, drawn-out rhythms. I was enchanted. Now I knew I really was in the South. I loved to listen to her sprawling sentences, frequently interrupted by a surprising, raucous laughter. After we met in class, we quickly became friends. She was frisky and had the nervous energy of a racehorse about her. I did not see the fragility of her life. She went through a brief, disastrous marriage from which she never recovered.

But she was not alone in those years; it was as if the ferment of the larger society permeated private lives, too. Acquaintances committed suicide, and many of the marriages I knew broke apart. Ultimately, I, too, felt compelled to radically question the premises of my life, to confront my marital situation, and to muster up enough courage to draw the honest, extremely painful conclusion that I wanted to leave. In Atlanta I learned about friendship, but also about social injustice, and that the price for personal freedom can be heartbreak.

After Stephanie was born, and even with a full course schedule, I still cried a lot. My mother learned to type after she went back to Ingolstadt, so that she could respond more efficiently to my voluminous letters. (For many years afterward, she told me she had saved my letters, but I never wanted to see them. When, after her death, I opened the trunk, where she said she had kept them, it was empty.) Only much later did I understand the connection between crying and anger. Now I know that anger is often a mask for sorrow that cannot be expressed otherwise. When I was angry with my siblings back in Ingolstadt, would I rather have cried? Cried because I wanted someone to be there for me? My mother was a possessive person, viscerally devoted to her husband and her family, but she had not been nurturing. True, her letters at this stage in my life were an expression of empathy, a recognition that I needed support, but they also gave her the chance to impress upon me that I now had a family of my own and must therefore endure. She had had no choice and had sacrificed herself to give me a family to grow up in. I was in a situation of my own making. It took me several years to understand that I should never have agreed to get married so precipitately, and that if I ever found the courage to sever that bond I would inflict much pain. And so I cried; I cried for my current circumstances, and I cried for my past, and I cried when I did not even know what I was crying for. Today, I also think the "unforgettable forgotten" was struggling to the surface. But I was ignorant of the workings of all these processes and preferred to think this was just a case of prolonged postpartum depression.

When the crying eventually subsided, I thought I had grown out of the postpartum phase, and I ignored the fact that the anger returned. Clearly it is better to cry than to be angry: when you cry you solicit help, you call out for empathy; anger turns people away. But crying can be a veil just like anger, and, like anger, it shields you if you do not want to look at what is behind the veil. I did not want to look, because I was afraid of what I would see; and then I would have no excuse not to conclude that I must leave my marriage. It was easier to believe that I was settled. I was married. I had a child. I had a good life. I could indulge in studying just for the pleasure of it. What was wrong with me? Why could I not turn to my husband, tell him how miserable I was?

At the time, I excused my remoteness from him by deciding that he had "betrayed" me by becoming so close to my mother. Today, I think I refused to turn to him because I had no idea how to rely on a man; my father had come into my life so late, and under circumstances that did not allow us to establish a close relationship. Trust and confidence in a man—or in anybody, for that matter—was outside my experience and my imagination. Even today, I suffer a pang of jealousy when I see daughters take their fathers' presence and love for granted, see the casual intimacy of their relationships and the father's admiration, as if this were a daughter's birthright—and perhaps it is! Then I think of the many children today growing up without fathers and wonder how those absences shape their other relationships. I know that I was, nevertheless, privileged. From age ten on, I had a consistent male presence in my life, and if I could not learn from him how to relate to other men, I did learn from him what exuberance was, and commitment, and dedication to one's family under tough circumstances.

Until Atlanta, I had led life as it came. I had had my aspirations and preferences, dreamed about them, and when the opportunities arose, seized them, happily, joyfully. In Atlanta I developed the sideways glance; I did not look at myself directly. I took refuge in externals, and the externals looked good. I even adjusted to having a housekeeper and caretaker for the baby, once my mother had left and the semester started again. Were the comfort and assurance she gave Stephanie a license for me to focus on my books? Did she offer me a refuge from adult responsibility? Often I would come home from classes in the afternoon and learn that Stephanie had slept in her arms for hours. I thought of Tante Betty and how she used to rock me. Now this woman was comforting Stephanie by holding her—and she comforted me by showing me I did not have to be possessive in order to be a good mother.

When I received my master's degree in 1961, my father came from Germany. This was his first visit to Atlanta. We celebrated with barbecue, because I loved it so much. There were mountains of shredded pork and beef, and ribs and rolls, and big bowls with extra sauce. My father had tried to send a keg of beer over from Germany, hoping to bring a piece of Ingolstadt with him, but he had no luck: the alcohol content of German beer did not pass the import regulations. Poor Vati, he had to content himself with weak American beer, which he found drinkable provided it was so cold you could hardly taste it.

By the time I started to write my Ph.D. dissertation, Bob and I were separating. I no longer made jokes about one day taking piano lessons. I needed a job. Fortunately, I found a position as an instructor of French at Spelman College, a college for black women just west of downtown Atlanta. Across the street from Spelman was Morehouse College, where Martin Luther King, Jr., had studied, and at whose graduate school, Atlanta University, I taught during the summer months. By this time I had progressed far beyond my early ignorance of racial matters. Now I learned on a much broader scale how daily events flowed out of the history of black repression. One day, I experienced on a minuscule scale the harassments African Americans were constantly exposed to. I had moved into a garden apartment, and I invited several Spelman women for dinner. The next morning, I found my car tires slashed. I canvassed the neighborhood, furious, but of course nobody had seen anything. Everybody deplored my misfortune. Some neighbors suggested that because I came from a foreign country I perhaps did not understand the rules of the land. I felt as if I were trying to punch my way through a velvet curtain: no matter how hard I tried to get at the culprit behind it, the curtain would always give, smooth and soft.

One evening, I was invited to a party with faculty who were mostly from Atlanta University. We spoke French, we laughed, we reminisced about Paris. I did not see the open wounds or even the scars on my colleagues' souls and minds. I did not see their bravery and endurance. I did not see that they needed to work harder and be smarter than white people to arrive at what a white person could take for granted. I just felt we had a good time together, as it should be. Then I spoke with the Swiss wife of an African American colleague. She had met her husband in Europe and had only recently arrived in Atlanta. Naïvely, I asked how she liked it over here, expecting a positive answer. I will never forget what she said: "*Vous savez, je ne pense plus*"—"I am no longer thinking." It became a mantra for me when I found myself in situations that seemed nearly unbearable.

I was teaching at Spelman College the afternoon President Kennedy was assassinated. All our classes congregated in the library in front of the TV. There was much crying and disbelief and deep distress. Did I feel free enough within myself to cry over the death of a president who not long before had confessed, "*Ich bin ein Berliner*"? No. I was embarrassed to be witnessing the grief of people I did not know all that intimately. I was embarrassed that I could not cry with them. I was shocked and upset, but I had stepped so far outside of myself that the wall between my observations and my feelings had become insurmountable. In a moment of deep sorrow, I could not express my distress, and therefore felt I did not belong.

That night, there was an eerie feeling on Peachtree Street. It was dark. The streetlamps cast their small circles of light, leaving most of the street and sidewalks in obscurity. Yet the street was alive with the quiet noise of people wandering about, not heeding the cars, restless, in need of connecting, sharing, reaching out. And then, shockingly, I heard some of them rejoicing in the president's death. Only much later could I file this experience away as an education in America's darker side.

In 2000, during Bill's campaign, when I spoke at Spelman College, I met, to my great pleasure and surprise, two former students of mine, now professors there. One of them, Judy Tilman, introduced me and recalled that I had never spoken down to my students and had always expected the most from everyone in class. This was a compliment I did not really deserve. I was (and still am) a passionate teacher, who took it for granted that each student would give her best, and though I saw and felt the injustice of discrimination, I had not grown up with it, had not absorbed or rebelled against it, had not experienced the humiliations black Americans were exposed to daily, hourly. It did not occur to me that, in an ultimate act of discrimination and condescension, one might be tempted to counteract the injustices suffered by setting more lenient standards.

If I was not sensitized to the pains and wounds inflicted by slavery and discrimination, I was similarly oblivious—still oblivious in the early 1960s!—of the atrocities committed by Germans during the Holocaust. Atlanta seemed an unlikely place to be confronted for the first time by racism as it had been practiced in Germany in my own lifetime. Walter Strauss, one of my French professors at Emory, had managed to escape Germany with his family before the war, before the cattle cars to the killing centers in the East had become the only way for Jews in Europe to travel. Sometimes, after class, we would take walks, and Walter Strauss would gently but insistently tell me what our native country had done to some of its citizens. The burden of recent German history, of the Nazi period, descended slowly and piecemeal upon me, but it descended never to leave me again. I do not believe there are Germans of any generation, in Germany or elsewhere, who are unaffected by the knowledge of the Holocaust, whether they deny, repress, minimize, or think the time has come to move on. I have often thought of Walter Strauss as a kind and careful midwife, assisting me in the birth of monstrous knowledge and sheltering me from the devastation of the impact but not from hard, open-eyed confrontation. I was pregnant when we started our walks, and perhaps it was in deference to my condition, or because we were so involved in our conversations, that I see us stopping frequently on tree-lined sidewalks surrounding the campus, I nodding or shaking my head as, in a halting, slightly mocking voice, Walter quietly made his points.

What I also remember from these walks is that he did not seem angry about what had been done to him and his family. Did he not want to show me his true feelings? Did he repress out of self-protection? Here was the first person I knew who had escaped the Holocaust, and I did not ask him how he felt about Germans (me included). How must he and his family have felt when they were "lucky" enough to be able to leave their country, their homes, their professions? I tried to imagine the betrayal and defeat you must feel when your country, for which your father had fought, to which you had shown loyalty and given your best, does not want you anymore; when it vilifies you, harasses you, humiliates you, robs you of your sense of self-worth, your possessions, and ultimately of your life. Wasn't that an uprooting compared with which mine was trivial?

I suppose we discussed the fact that our chosen fields of study were French and Romance literature, not German. I had not even begun to grapple with the problem of how a people as educated and enlightened as the Germans—*das Volk der Dichter und Denker* ("the people of thinkers and poets"), which now, incontrovertibly, has become "the people of thinkers and poets and Auschwitz"—could descend into the abyss of utter barbarity, of an unspeakable inhumanity. I hid behind my infatuation with French. I avoided the question of whether I was fleeing the German language as I had fled Germany. When I eventually became a professor of German (and comparative) literature and began to write professionally, for academic publications, I decided to write in English. It seemed an appropriate decision, although many of my colleagues in German studies continue to publish in German without detriment to their careers. But saying, "I live in America, so I might as well write in English"—or, of greater import, "I want to be an American citizen, not a hyphenated one, and an American citizen writes in English"—was not the whole answer. It simply pushed the search for an answer a little deeper into the soft mush of the unconscious.

The sense of defeat I had experienced while watching the American soldiers on that dusty country road outside Passau was in some subliminal way associated with a belief that the defeat was deserved. Nobody spoke about it, but everybody seemed relieved that the war was over. On some level, I wondered at the time why we should be relieved, when what we had fought for was meant to be an honorable cause. I was confused when I heard we were now "liberated," since the liberators had not so long before been the enemy. From this crucial moment stemmed my deep conviction that defeat, even when it is deserved, is not an ultimate destruction and always carries within it the promise of betterment.

Isn't the success story of the United States precisely a triumph over adversity? Germany, as I was beginning to find out, raised a more disturbing question: can you triumph over a calamitous history? In the early 1960s, I did not think so. Today, I would submit that sustained acts of good will and a thorough acceptance of democracy bear witness to a profound change in the German understanding of human responsibilities. This understanding and the acts resulting from it can never undo the past, but they offer the promise of a better future.

In Germany, at the time of my departure, silence surrounded the Holocaust like an impenetrable wall. How strange that knowledge of it was brought home to me only when I was no longer living in Germany! After my walks with Walter, my visits to my parents inevitably turned into interrogations and vehement accusations on my part, and blatant refusals on theirs to give specific answers. Ultimately, my mother would conclude that America had made me into an unpleasant and negative person, different from the Wuschilein she had raised. I am relieved to have found that there were no murderers in my family, but I still come from a country that perpetrated the most heinous crimes on a scale that was previously unimaginable.

I have been living in the United States for the better part of my life, yet the Holocaust will always remind me where I came from. It has taken me many years of pain and soul-searching to realize that acceptance is my only option—acceptance combined with grief and a commitment to speak out openly, even as the burden of the facts and the trauma of coping with them threaten to paralyze you. Acceptance means that the events become part of your self-definition: This is who I am; this is part of my history; this is my heritage whether I like it or not.

When Bill was in the Senate, he was often asked to speak to Jewish groups, and sometimes I would go with him. When it became apparent that I came from Germany, there would be a shift in our hosts' attitudes from the socially polite toward a more personal interest. In such circumstances, I often thought of the German and Israeli scholar Dan Diner's term "negative symbiosis" to describe the relationship between Germans and Jews. In these political gatherings, there would be a sense, even if an illusory one, of familiarity. Then there would be questions like "When did you come to this country?"—and dates would tell entire histories. I met survivors from concentration camps, those who had barely escaped, and those with more foresight, who managed to leave Germany earlier. I met those who wanted to speak with me as a non-Jewish German and those who turned away as soon as they heard I was German. I met their children and grandchildren. And always there would be expressions of pain and sorrow and sadness on both sides. I felt mortified, overcome with sadness, and sometimes we would hug and cry, yet cry for reasons that were worlds apart. They would cry for the loss of family and futures and hopes, and I would cry for the pain that had been inflicted on them but also for myself, for being burdened with such a horrendous legacy and the shame and sorrow that came with it.

In the United States there are also many unresolved and silenced historical problems. The legacy of slavery and the treatment of the Native Americans are not addressed in appropriate and emotionally resonant ways. Would the burden of those legacies weigh on me more heavily if I had been born in this country? I often wonder what it must feel like to be born with a different national background. How would it feel to be born in a country without traumatic stigmas? What if I were Greek or Swedish and could be proud of the glories of my country's history? I cannot even begin to imagine what that must feel like. Younger generations of Germans now are involved in many different projects to overcome the feeling of shame. I poured the burden of having been born and raised in Germany into my academic work. And for that, Walter Strauss was the most fitting early guide.

He was my adviser when, for my master's thesis, I wrote on "The Labyrinth of Space and Time" as seen in three twentieth-century authors. Studying the work of Franz Kafka, the Prague Jew, brought me closer to an understanding of how it feels to be an outsider, a person not admitted (by others or himself) to a life everybody else enjoys unthinkingly. Samuel Beckett, the Irish Catholic expatriate who felt more at home in French than in English, reduced life almost to a standstill, its verbosity brought to the threshold of silence; he compressed the dynamics of existence like a densely packed atom into an ever diminishing ". . . it will be I, it will be the silence, where I am, I don't know, I'll never know, in the silence you don't know, you must go on, I can't go on, I'll go on." And the postexistentialist Alain Robbe-Grillet taught me that the apparent clarity of surfaces masked a world full of incomprehensible *chiffres*. Did Walter Strauss, who suggested that I write about these three, see that in my interpretation of them I presented him with a psychogram of my own soul and state of mind? If he did, he never let me know.

He was also my dissertation adviser when I worked my way from the alienation of Kafka, the minimalist reductionism of Beckett, and the enigma of the ordinary in Robbe-Grillet to Hermann Broch, the novelist and theorist of contemporary intellectual currents, philosopher of ethics, and interpreter of mass psychology in the wake of Nazi Germany. Broch was an Austrian Jew who, after Austria's *Anschluss* in March of 1938, barely managed to escape to America. He lived for years in the house of a friend in Princeton and was a fellow at Yale when he died, shortly before a planned return visit to Austria, in the spring of 1951. His writings gave me the background and foundation for an understanding of the late nineteenth and early twentieth centuries in Austria and Germany. His life story impressed on me from yet another point of view the problems of a refugee existence—the consuming desire and struggle to "matter" in a foreign culture— and transformed my theoretical awareness of anti-Semitism into a witnessing. In my career as a literary scholar, I focused increasingly on the ravages of the Holocaust and on its legacy as it was given voice in postwar German literature.

As did so many other refugees I met in later years, Walter Strauss had turned the "defeat" of expulsion from his home country into a triumph of personal achievement in the country that received him. When I knew him in Atlanta, I was not looking for role models; only in later years did I identify with his perseverance and his success.

Was my divorce inevitable? I'm sure there are legions of marriages that endure, plagued by the acknowledged or unacknowledged unhappiness of at least one of the partners, if not both. Perhaps it is commonplace to say that when children are involved the heartache increases, often beyond what seems bearable. Bob was well established in his profession. He enjoyed a comfortable income, and when our situation deteriorated his mother came to live with us, as if to demonstrate that her presence guaranteed loving child-care for Stephanie and an uninterrupted and smooth functioning of the household. I was still a graduate student, and I had as yet no career prospects. One day, in the midst of great inner turmoil and confusion, I took Stephanie and my pocketbook and we went to Germany. I had no plans for when I would come back; I needed distance and time to reflect. Where else would I go but to my parents?

My parents, and particularly my mother, were very upset by

my desire to leave my marriage. Apparently my mother cried for months after the visit. Settling into a respectable life had been her primary aspiration. When she married Baumeister Max, she made it clear that respectability was more important to her than happiness. And I was going to give that up! Did I want to condemn Stephanie to a life of misery? She would never have divorced Baumeister, she said, if she had had any children with him, or if she had not wanted me to be raised by my rightful father!

Bob and my mother had become friends, and for years after the divorce he would still visit my parents, taking Stephanie to see them. In those first years, I would not go back myself, precisely because I felt that my parents' sympathies were with their former son-in-law. When, on one of my infrequent visits to Ingolstadt, I asked my mother why he still visited, she explained that she simply wanted to see her granddaughter and he always brought Stephanie along. But that was not the whole truth. Both of my parents also wanted to keep up appearances. My mother in particular was ashamed that I was divorced. On one of my visits, perhaps five years after the divorce, I had dinner with my father and a friend, who remarked how strange it was that my husband and I took turns visiting Ingolstadt. "Last year your husband sat precisely where you are sitting now," he said. For a long time afterward I was angry at myself for not having answered, "My husband? But didn't my father tell you we have been divorced for years?" Perhaps I did not have the presence of mind, or perhaps I did not want to embarrass my father.

I knew that my mother liked Bob and loved being admired by him. He in turn loved things German, and sometimes I thought he had married me chiefly because I was German. I still see my mother's outstretched hands and hear her saying she could have at least one admirer for each of her ten fingers. I think he was one of them, an admirer of *Mutter Erde*, in all the symbolic associations of the phrase. I had disappointed her when I left for the States, had disappointed her when I did not come back, and now I was getting a divorce! She thought she no longer knew me; she did not realize that she had never known me. As far as she was concerned, America had changed me beyond recognition. Not long before she died, she told me, during one of our reminiscence marathons, that she had been surprised and disappointed when I did not come back to Germany after the divorce. She was certain that I would finally understand where I belonged and come back home.

My mother must have expressed that expectation to Bob during the divorce proceedings. She could not have realized the full import of what she was saying, perhaps genuinely driven by the desire to see me back. It should have been apparent to her that once she conveyed that hope to him, and even though he admired her, he would do his utmost to gain custody of his daughter; he could convince any judge that Stephanie, an American citizen, must be assured of growing up in this country. Perhaps my running off to Germany with Stephanie for a time convinced him that my mother's expectations were well founded.

And then there occurred a scene that is indelibly burned into my memory: I am on the front porch of our house in Atlanta, holding Stephanie by one hand, ready to go out. Perhaps her father thought I was trying to abscond with her again. In any event, he did not want me to leave with her. He grabbed Stephanie by the other hand. I did not let go, and so the two of us pulled our daughter in opposite directions. Stephanie screamed in a shrill, piercing voice and kicked the air with her feet in utter panic. We both kept on pulling. We both understood that this was a moment of far-reaching significance, way beyond its present horror. And then I let her go. I let her go physically. I could not bear to keep pulling on her arm, literally pulling her apart. From that moment on, I knew she would stay in Atlanta with her father.

As the divorce proceeded, I was swallowed up by an overwhelming sense of helplessness and guilt. I engaged a lawyer, but

I don't know whether my case was so hopeless—since it could be alleged that I would take Stephanie away to grow up in Germany—that the loss of Stephanie was foreordained. There was also a part of me, tiny but very loud, that said I did not deserve to have Stephanie with me. I felt tremendously guilty for not following my mother's example of sacrificing herself to her child to give me (and herself) a legitimate existence in society. Here I was, condemning my own child to a painful life because I was selfish enough to believe I should not stay in a marriage that had been a mistake to begin with and in which I was miserable. Stephanie would grow up in the house of her father and her paternal grandmother, who came to preside over the household, and she would be surrounded by the love of all of us, but I would be only an intermittent presence in her life. I was swirling in a maelstrom. But what had I expected? Wasn't it only fair that her father fight for his daughter in any conceivable way?

Once it had been agreed upon that Stephanie's father would have custody, all other arrangements were amicable. We promised—and kept the promise—that neither of us would ever use the child to hurt the other or inflict more pain on her than she had already had to endure. I let go of her, but I never lost her. Today, Stephanie and I are best friends.

I became acquainted with many kinds of pain. Sometimes the pain was acute, piercing, sometimes throbbing and steady; sometimes I did not even think of the pain but was aware only that something awful had happened. A depression settled on me that lasted for years. I knew that Stephanie, in her gentle way, was also suffering enormously. Often I thought my heart would break, but of course it never did.

In 1965, I received my Ph.D. in comparative literature and left Atlanta. Like a homing pigeon, I returned to New York. I had found a job at the State University of New York at Stony Brook.

I was no longer the wide-eyed and exhilarated new arrival, but a divorced woman with a cracked heart, without her child, and prone to depression. Anonymous New York seemed the only place where I could rest and recover. Questioning myself, analyzing what I had done to others, done to myself, and what had happened to me became obsessive occupations. I was consumed with the attempt to come to an understanding. Financially, I could not afford a lengthy commitment to therapy; but remembering, juxtaposing events, looking for patterns on my own and with occasional help, became my life's preoccupation. I read and I read. Psychology, philosophy, religion—fields that are supposed to give answers to the why and how of existence. Reading and teaching provided me with a structure and with a focus away from myself. Reading and teaching were not only a refuge and solace but a narcotic.

I went to see Stephanie in Atlanta as often as I could, and as she grew older, she would come and be with me in New York City. During the summer months, we established a tradition of traveling, a tradition that I am now reviving with my grandchildren. I still see her riding down the trails by the Magdalena River in Colombia, her blond hair streaming behind her, and people in the Andes gathering around us, marveling at her blue eyes. We were in Portugal in 1968 when we learned that Bobby Kennedy had been shot, and we were in Marbella, Spain, in 1972, when the person I was dating in New York, Bill Bradley, came for a two-day surprise visit. (Did that visit tell me anything about the state of our relationship? You bet!) Stephanie had injured her foot when she stepped on a sea urchin, which had released the poison of its quills into the sole of her foot. A doctor attended to the foot, but for a few days she could not walk. And so Bill lugged Stephanie on his back through the Casbah of Tangier.

Eventually I began to ask myself whether I was going to be a teacher for the rest of my life. I had come to this profession by accident, just as I had become a stewardess by accident. The underlying drive of my life had been to get out, but I did not have any clear idea what I intended to do with the freedom after I had it. I had entered precipitately into a marriage as if afraid of the freedom I had so longed for, and when I had achieved the security of a supposedly stable relationship, I found it unbearable. In those early years in New York, I was more alone than I had ever been in my life. I needed to find out what my life was about. While I taught, I began to take weekend courses in filmmaking at New York University. I felt I could become the definitive cinematic Kafka-interpreter. As a class project I produced my version of Kafka's "The Judgment." It was badly out of sync and incomprehensible. Would this be the end of my aspirations?

Then I saw Eugene O'Neill's *The Iceman Cometh* at the Circle in the Square, in the Village. The play turned my life around. Was I going to be like O'Neill's characters, forever making excuses for their miserable lives, hiding in pipe dreams, afraid to confront the reality of their hopes? Walking out of the theater, I knew I had a choice: either regret for the rest of my life not having tested my dream, or follow it, whatever the obstacles. I quit my teaching job and found work as an assistant producer in a small film company in the city.

To ascend to the heights of interpreting Kafka's work on film, I had to begin by working on educational films. The company wanted to produce interviews with great artists to inspire young students and give them a sense of what art might mean to an individual. I was asked to contact a basketball player by the name of Bill Bradley, who, I was told, lived in the same building I did. Would he be willing to interview the poet Marianne Moore?

I had grown up with soccer and knew the rules of that game. I had watched American football, mostly on TV, and considered it a kind of fascinating ballet, the players in their exaggerated costumes performing savage rituals. But even now, by the fall of 1970, my Americanization had not progressed far enough for me to know what basketball was—or baseball, for that matter. Basketball I subsequently learned about; baseball is still an enigma.

I asked the superintendent of our building to which apartment number I should address the letter to Bill Bradley proposing that he participate in the project. One day, as I stepped out of the elevator, there was a tall young man leaning against the wall, waiting for the elevator. We looked at each other and nodded a tentative, slight hello. Was that Bill Bradley? Had he read the letter yet? After I came to know Bill's habits, it seemed a miracle to me that he actually answered it: there were times when he was without a telephone or electricity because he had forgotten to open the mail and pay the bills. But he answered my letter, and we discussed the project. I tried to stay focused and sell him the idea. He, a lanky young athlete with a superb education, would interview the tiny, elderly intellectual with an admiration for athletes and sports, particularly the Brooklyn Dodgers. A wonderful and camera-friendly constrast! Bill was interested enough to want to see a script. Unfortunately, by that time Marianne Moore had suffered a stroke, and the project could never be realized. But I had met Bill.

In retrospect, I often thought of Bill as my reward for the lonely years of soul-searching and for having dared to follow my dream. The dream of a career in filmmaking did not come true, but something much more important, much larger than any dream I could ever have had about filmmaking, did: I met the man of my life. Almost peripherally, and very quickly, I found the limits to my talents as a filmmaker. I stumbled even at the first step: I could not hustle; I could not sell my cinematic ideas. But I had given it a try, and the iceman could no longer threaten me. I went back to academics, wiser but by no means sadder.

Not having Stephanie with me was a continuous source of pain; it was the *basso continuo* that accompanied my life. But we saw each other regularly and were deeply attached to each other, and I was comforted by the knowledge that she was rooted in a stable and loving environment. Should I have felt that only I was the key to her happiness, as my mother had seen herself in a colossal miscalculation in relation to me? Isn't this precisely what had driven me away? There were many things I wanted to do differently from my mother, and having open and honest communication with my daughter was the most important one. As Stephanie grew older, her questions became deeper and more encompassing, and I hope that I never betrayed her with self-serving answers and partial truths, or manipulated her to bring her over to my point of view. How easy to bend someone who loves you to your own purposes! How easy to fill the open and vulnerable heart of a child who trusts with the phantasmagoria of self-justification! We both needed courage and strength to cope with our situation, and as we supported each other, our mutual love grew in ways for which an ordinary mother-daughter relationship sees no need or has no room. Slowly and tentatively, I began to heal. It was during this healing process that I met Bill.

Bill and I have been together for more than thirty years. By now, we have established half a lifetime of memories together, have built on the affinities that drew us together in the first place. Can the memories of our life together have as profound an impact on our hearts and souls as the memories of our childhoods? I think so, if they are not mere surface enumerations of what we experienced together but also connect, in each of us, deep down in ourselves, with traces of an unforgettable forgotten. Perhaps it is not even memories that shape people, but events that are no longer accessible to them. Why, out of the endless stream of life, do I remember precisely what I do remember, and not something else? I, for whom rootedness has always been problematic, feel connected to Bill in ways that are inaccessible to rational inspection. I think of the story of Philemon and Baucis, who after their death were transformed into trees, so that their branches could forever be intertwined.

We met when both of us were already shaped to a large extent by our earlier lives and by the values that had gone into our upbringing. Coming from an exhausting family circus, I found peace and refuge in his unassuming, quiet gentleness, and I felt accepted when I saw that he felt at home with my enthusiasm and exuberance. But he was not all calmness. I was fascinated by the passion with which he played basketball. This passion came to be symbolized for me in his elbows. When I met Bill, he struck me as a soft-spoken, gentle person, and I would never have thought him capable of being rough. Only as I watched him play did I find out that there was another side to him. I saw that he knew very well how to take care of a situation and of himself, and I was infinitely comforted by his uninhibited strength and spontaneity. With abrupt, hidden moves that had to escape the quick eye of a referee, his elbows would throw an opponent off balance, or he'd block a pass that seemed inevitable. It took me a long time to learn to see these moves, but I immediately identified with the energy, and I learned that you do not need words to make your point. Indeed, in our life together, a number of Bill's most important statements have been nonverbal.

I remember the first time he invited me to a game. This was a few months after we had started to see each other—casually at first and, because of his travel schedule, intermittently. Did I want to come to a game? Yes, of course, I wanted to see him play. I did not know who the Knicks were, I had no idea how basketball was played, and frankly I did not care. I came to see Bill. I had become used to his height; I no longer felt it was overwhelming but, rather, fun to walk alongside this man who towered above me. Now I saw him for the first time surrounded by other giants, and he appeared fragile to me. When the team lined up before the game while the national anthem was sung, some of them looked over to where their wives or dates were sitting. With Bill it was never that obvious. He would seem completely absorbed, head bent forward, feet fidgeting, yet with a sideways glimpse he would check to see whether I was watching him. I was enchanted that he wanted my attention.

After a game, and if the team had to take a bus to the airport, there was often time to meet friends for a few minutes in a bar called the Iron Horse, under Madison Square Garden. The first time this happened, Bill told me how to get there and find his friends before he arrived, showered and dressed and ready to board the bus. I found them, and we all ended up around a little table, waiting for Bill, his friends curiously eyeing Bill's latest date. When he arrived, he ignored completely the empty chair that had been reserved for him and squeezed in next to me. To this day I feel the happiness I felt then welling up in me at this non-verbal but intimate gesture, an unmistakable announcement to his friends that we belonged together. He would never have said it to me in words.

Bill and I had talked about the film project in the fall of 1970. I fell in love with him then, but was not ready to admit it. I was as circumspect as he was. I had a history. From New Year's Eve on, however, there was no further doubt. He had invited me to a friend's New Year's Eve party, and that was that. Only later did I begin to ask why I fell in love with a person who was at the height of his celebrity status, who was known by half of New York, who was a public performer, cheered and booed by crowds. On the most accessible level, and before I knew very much about his public life, I was moved by this modest, humble person who shielded his delicate sensitivities in a strong, powerful body. As I became introduced to the "other" Bill, I was fascinated by the contrast between the private person and the public personality. Competition, with its ups and downs, victories and losses, was the lifeblood of Bill's public existence. I watched, mesmerized. He was not tossed up and thrown down by these events; he was a low-key, stable person who charted his own course in the midst of the public noise.

I often marveled at how easily he coped with his celebrity status. From him I learned the difference between anonymity and privacy. I had come back to New York because I wanted its anonymity, which allows you to disappear as a person, whereas privacy means protecting yourself as a person from general consumption. Anonymity does not need protection; it *is* protection. Being with Bill, I learned how you guard your privacy without giving offense: you need to be quick-witted and have a sense of humor. Once, in Morocco, some tourists wanted to lionize him; he answered them in French, so they thought he was somebody else. Once, I heard a cab driver ask, "Aren't you Bill Bradley?" and he answered, "A lot of people say that." Another time, in a restaurant, a lady who had had one too many drinks asked him, "Aren't you Willis Reed?" "Aren't you Elizabeth Taylor?" he replied. The woman was elated by what she thought was a compliment, and I was pleased that I understood the joke.

Bill's desire for privacy and my need for anonymity meshed; neither of us cared for a public life. I had never belonged to any club or group while growing up, because I always felt I had a "secret" associated with my birth that should not surface. Later in my life, my German background may also have made me wary of joining groups; the devastating consequences of crowd behavior had left indelible marks on the German people. In college, when I was invited to become a member of Phi Beta Kappa, I said, on impulse and in complete ignorance of the academic system, "No, thank you, I don't join clubs." Walter Strauss was amused, but he insisted that I join, saying acceptance would not entail any obligations.

I was deeply stirred by Bill. He was tender and protective in ways so subtle as to be barely perceptible. It was as if you had to decipher the tiniest and most difficult handwriting, but, oh, the messages it contained! I felt at home in him emotionally, felt I could trust him, could rely on him. Would he become the soil in which I could spread my roots? Atlanta could never be relegated to the past, because Stephanie was there, but the pain became manageable.

Bill and I discovered many common interests. If he was in town, we would follow a Saturday-morning ritual of going to art galleries. On a day without a game, we would sometimes see three movies in a row and even squeeze in a quick dinner. He invested in a Broadway play and promptly lost his investment. We went to concerts to hear Bob Dylan, the Rolling Stones, the Band, Bruce Springsteen, and, later, Bruce Hornsby. Bill loved Joni Mitchell and Carly Simon; I preferred Leonard Cohen and Richie Havens. But both of us were humming along all the time. (I found out that Bill could not carry a tune.) I wanted him to see *Ariadne auf Naxos,* because I had laughed out loud over the clever use made in the libretto of the German and English languages and I wanted to share that with him, but it was not a great success.

We had the summer months to travel. When we met, Bill had just come back from Afghanistan, where he hiked the Hindu Kush in search of the descendants of Alexander the Great. He liked Maine and Canada and thought the best way to get to know a piece of land or a stretch of coast was to contact a real-estate agent. We did that. In Machias, Maine, we found a particularly eager real-estate agent who showed us miles and miles of waterfront property in Maine and New Brunswick. We walked the coasts of Penobscot Bay, Mount Desert Island, the Bay of Fundy. We drove across Prince Edward Island and along the Cabot Trail of Cape Breton Island in Nova Scotia. With my German background I was under the influence of *The Tyranny of Greece over Germany,* as an important scholarly study by E. M. Butler called the German preoccupation with Greece in the nineteenth and twentieth centuries. I wanted to go to Greece. We did that, too. We walked Euboea and Monemvasia and the coasts and towns of the Aegean Islands. Bill and some friends bought a property on one of the islands and later built three houses there. Once, Bill leased a small boat and, together with my sister (what was I thinking, inviting Monika along on such a romantic trip!), we cruised the Greek islands. I had visions of suntanning in my bikini on deck. We did not know that in August the Meltemi, a strong wind that sweeps across the Aegean from the north, blows so fiercely that sometimes we could not leave the harbor and once out in the open sea we would huddle behind protective oilcloth, wet and freezing, in yellow rain-gear. Bill and I returned to Athens on the big ferry. Monika braved it out. But no matter what happened, we were on top of the world.

In my mind, Greece was "classical." I had not counted on its being so alive, so passionate, so in the present. I had read the *Odyssey* and now saw that the customs of almost three thousand years ago still held: the rituals of hospitality, the easy conviviality, the appreciation of clear water, lovely beaches, hidden coves, the courtly politeness harnessing lively tempers. In the Aegean, to this day I feel I am at the beginning of the world, and that world consists of the four elements only: the water, turquoise green and sapphire blue, capped with white foam; the rocks, harsh, with barely any vegetation on them, allowing no shelter; the sun, blazing, merciless, giving no reprieve; and the wind, the breath of the universe, incessant. This is a formidable, elemental universe that makes no allowance for weakness and gives no expectation of ease. Here in this primordial world I feel at home. Not rooted, but one with it.

In 1973, the year before we were married, Bill and I went to Germany. I wanted to introduce him to my parents and to show him where I had grown up. We went to Passau. The old town had not changed significantly since I had left, a quarter-century before. I wanted Bill to see the tourist Passau, impressive and beautiful with its majestic cathedral and the Oberhaus, a fortress above the confluence of the Danube and the Ilz where, rumor had it, Hitler Youth had re-enacted Germanic rituals of tribal justice. But what mattered more to me was "my" Passau, the Altstadt of passages so narrow no car could pass through them, of hidden shortcuts through tunnels and inconspicuous alleys, of steep stairs chiseled into walls and rocks, with unexpected turns that made you lose your sense of direction, of inner courtyards with multiple exits into divergent streets, with cavernous ground floors in buildings showing the marks of the periodic floods from back into the last century. I was surprised to find that my world of those years was actually very small. Sizes and distances had shrunk. Perhaps my mother never understood the extent of my efforts, like the epic journey to the milk store before school, because she had measured everything with adult eyes.

In showing Bill around, I discovered that my excitement was not the excitement of coming home but the excitement of reviving, for the person I loved, the outlines of my childhood paradise. Against the background of an indifferent reality, I made Bill see the church where my Catholic classmates, all dressed in white, had received their first Holy Communion while I, a Lutheran (in Luther's Germany, almost all Protestants were Lutherans), stood in the back of the church, watching and feeling excluded, although I, too, had put on a white dress. I showed him where, one summer evening, I had fallen and ripped my knee open (I still have the scar) when I ran out into the street to join my friends with a rolled German pancake in my hand. A dog saw me, pursued me, and jumped up on me, hungry, wanting my pancake, and I tried to run away and fell. I showed Bill the movie houses I had sneaked into (still there after twenty-five years), and we stood on the promenade along the Inn River, where a baby carriage with a baby in it had been seized by the raging current and carried far downstream. As we stood there, my memories were the only reality left of that time, even while we were creating another layer of memories, this time of our being there together.

On that trip, Bill and I went to the opera with my father, the great opera-lover. How often had I seen him kneeling in front of my mother, singing to her the love arias of *Carmen* or *Aida* or *La Bohème,* the passionate arias that always occurred on the threshold of death. Like good tourists, Bill, my father, and I went to Bayreuth and to Salzburg for the music festival. In Salzburg, Herbert von Karajan was conducting Mozart. I had never been to the Salzburg Opera Festival, all dressed up. Some of the women wore taffeta and brocade versions of Bavarian *Dirndl* dresses; the men expensive *Trachtenjanker.* I had long forgotten that these indigenous costumes, symbols of a deep conservatism, were still popular. The most fascinating memory of that evening for me was Bill's comment on the movement of von Karajan's arms and hands as he was conducting. A supreme artist of movement, Bill was attracted to the moves of this other artist as with subtle gestures he controlled his "team," the orchestra.

On this trip, I was alone with the two most important men in my life. I compared them. My father was funny, eager to entertain Bill across the abyss of a foreign language. Bill was receptive and appreciative and went along, smiling. My father, president of a sports club, liked the athlete in Bill and could not understand how Bill had fallen for an egghead. Watching them side by side, I realized that my father created attention, whereas Bill commanded attention. My father had to work at it. So often, particularly in an environment where people did not know him, he needed to whip up a whirlpool of excitement—always pleasant, funny, laughing, people understanding his good spirits and responding—but he made a huge investment of effort and energy. Bill did not need the circus. He was like the quiet center in a storm.

Bill and my mother did not hit it off quite so well. My mother wanted to be courted, taken on as an ally in his growing relationship with me. She had always thought, from my tentative high-school "admirers" to my first marriage, that I needed to be "presented," explained, because otherwise I was incomprehensible. She also wanted to enlist Bill as one of the men on each of her ten fingers. Bill was polite, but he would not be one of them, and he made it clear that he did not need an interpreter to understand me. He was the first person to stand by me, to take me just as I was. And, amazingly, he sent my mother these signals without a deliberate word. The scene in the Iron Horse when he sat down next to me was repeated here, on an immensely magnified scale.

In subsequent years, my mother would visit us in New Jersey and, after Bill had been elected to the Senate, in Washington. But she never felt as comfortable as she had been in Atlanta. There she had been without question the ruler, a benign ruler to be sure, but firmly establishing in the household the rhythm of her priorities. When she visited after I was married to Bill, I knew she felt like a guest. It was an ambivalent situation. I tried to tell her, in Washington, that she should consider herself part of the family, that she was in her own house, and that when she wanted a cup of coffee or a snack she should feel free to help herself. She was upset that I did not fix the coffee or sandwich for her. Should I have treated her like a guest who needs to be served, who in her own mind is not free to open the refrigerator and take what she wants? I knew that she wanted to be courted, served, fussed over. I could not bring myself to do that. I used the mask of familiarity to let her fend for herself, to make her understand that this was my territory, that this was how I did things. She was a good fighter; she did not wilt. She told me that living in the United States was easy. If she, as a young woman, had had a chance to come here, she said, she would by now have a successful hair salon, because she knew how to relate to people, how to understand their wishes, how to get along with them. I was miserable. I could not have fixed her a sandwich even if I had wanted to.

Bill saw my misery. With his light touch, he suggested one evening after dinner that we all take a ride and get some ice cream. When we were at home, my mother wore housecoats—colorful, happy housecoats with lots of flowers and prints. After my father's death, she had begun to put on weight, and these housecoats were very comfortable. (I was so happy my mother liked them; I never had to worry about what to give her when the time for presents came. Over the years I sent her so many that she gave some of them, as a great privilege, to her best girlfriends and neighbors.) Now she felt she should change before we drove to the ice-cream parlor, but Bill insisted that she looked fine, was actually overdressed for where we were going. She gave in and classified the event as an "American experience." But once we were at the little shop and sat down with huge cones and dishes of ice cream with sprinkles and hot chocolate sauce and butterscotch, she felt she had made a real discovery—indeed, a conquest. America was so casual, so lacking in stress and strife, so steeped in abundance, so unassuming when it had the best to offer! You did not have to dress up for the best ice cream in the world! Bill's excursion to the ice-cream parlor did more for my mother than all my efforts to show her what "casualness" could mean. As so often, Bill had mediated in a nonverbal way, by his actions. I was so caught up in my grievances that, I am sure, there were many times when I did not even notice his efforts. We had often talked about our parents. I was confident that he understood me, understood the ocean of resentment within me that was directed at my mother. Was it difficult to live with me? How much healing had I really accomplished?

On one of our outings in Washington, we went to Roosevelt Island, which sits in the middle of the Potomac River. We walked along the gravel paths and stood before the giant statues. The inscriptions on the monuments to President Theodore Roosevelt were phrased in the language of idealism and high-mindedness. They conveyed the hope that politics can make the world a better place. My mother started to cry. I had seen her so upset only once, when my friend Rita was visiting us in Ingolstadt. Now she gave voice to a feeling of shame she had never before expressed in my presence. She explained to Bill how terrible it was when you could not be proud of the country you came from. She accused Hitler and described him as the Pied Piper of the German nation. How naïve was I, even then? Why did I think that the only thing people had to do was choose not to follow him and the tune he was piping? Today's dictatorships, with their routine tortures and killings and the disappearances of thousands of citizens, demonstrate clearly how difficult it is to oppose a system from within. Hitler's early supporters and implementers had been thugs, people with criminal records, who enjoyed threatening and beating up others, and who could demolish and vandalize with impunity, since the society saw them as fighting communism and, once Hitler was in power, there was no recourse to the law. They were intent on "creating order"—the order of a madman propelled by a vision of violence that allowed them to do as they pleased. And so I listened to my mother, from a distance, as she bared her soul to Bill. Bill knows how to listen, but my heart remained closed.

Perhaps I could not forgive her for the fact that I saw no reason to be proud of her. (Wasn't it enough for me that she married a man she did not love? Now I also wanted her to have fought Nazism from within.) I had not yet begun to realize that, ultimately, peace comes from acceptance, not from wishing that circumstances and events had been more to your liking.

After we first became "serious," Bill had invited me to Crystal City, Missouri, his hometown, where I discovered that he, an only child, was the perfect blend of his parents. His mother showed in the way he played; his father showed in the way he lived. His mother, Susie, was energetic, lively, full of zest and an enterprising spirit. His father, Warren, was the wise man—calm, considerate, reflective. He suffered from calcified arthritis of the lower spine, could not bend or move about a lot. When I knew him, he would let his feet shuffle over the floor rather than walk because he could not raise his legs high enough. Susie's energy was akin to that of my father, although it showed in a different way. In later years, when her granddaughter, our daughter, Theresa Anne, would spend vacation time in Crystal City, Susie would do for her what she had done for her son, Bill, as a boy: she would organize swimming-pool parties, take entire crews of children to the golf course, to the zoo, drive them to St. Louis to show them the sights, to visit the St. Louis Art Museum, to take them to the top of the Gateway Arch. She always made sure that Theresa Anne had enough companions to play with and learn "social skills" from. I was more drawn to the quiet solidity of Bill's father. On a deep, nonverbal level, we liked each other very much. As a banker, he was also pleased that I was frugal; at least, that's what I imagined he liked in me, and I was anxious for him to like me.

As I had shown Bill "my" Passau, so Bill showed me "his" Crystal City: the quadrangle of his early life, bounded by home, church, bank, all of them flanking a beautiful park; there were the railroad tracks, forever symbolizing an open world, and, eight blocks away, the elementary and high schools; and then, most important, "his" river, the Mississippi. I knew about the Mississippi from the geography lessons in high school. The Mississippi-Missouri, the Amazon, the Nile. You can see them, like the Wall of China, from outer space. I was very moved when we went out on the river. Downstream I saw, on the Missouri side, the high bluffs whose silica sand gave Crystal City its name and, for many years, a flourishing glass industry. Bill showed me the cotton-wood trees and explained the levee system, and we retraced the walks he had taken as a young boy with his grandfather, an immigrant from Germany, hunting for animals among the backwater undergrowth of the river. I was moved because Bill wanted me to see this part of the country, this stretch of the mighty river that had helped shape his life and his imagination and was so meaningful to him. And I was moved because here, at the very spot where we were standing, the past and the present fused. I was again the high-school kid who had wanted to come to this country. I had studied its geography, had imagined what the Mississippi would be like. And here I was, Bill's girlfriend, introduced to his parents, to the river, to what was dearest to his heart.

In January 1974, we were married, not in Crystal City or New York but in Palm Beach, Florida, during the three-day All-Star break of the 1974 NBA season. Our wedding night we spent around the dining-room table in the apartment of Bill's parents, addressing the envelopes of our wedding announcements. Bill had not wanted the press to know about our wedding and create a fuss, and even his teammates found out only after the fact.

I think our wedding must have been a terrible disappointment for Bill's mother. Over the years, when Susie would speak of her own wedding—coming down the wide stairs in their huge old house, dressed in a beautiful gown with a long train, and hearing the organ played by one of her sisters in the music room—I slowly realized that such moments could be the highlights of a lifetime. Only over the years did I understand that this is how she would have liked her only child's wedding to be. Indeed, years later, Bill's cousin Susan, the daughter of Susie's sister, had just such a wedding in the family church in Crystal City. At that event, our daughter, then five years old, was supposed to be a flower girl and walk down the aisle by herself, strewing flowers before the bride. At the last minute she balked. I remember how impressed I was when, in the midst of all the excitement, Susan, decked out in a beautiful and cumbersome wedding gown, took the time to reassure her, quietly and convincingly. Susan wanted her wedding ceremony to be perfect, and if it took a few extra minutes to persuade Theresa Anne of the significance of her role, Susan was willing to take the time.

When Bill and I married, I did not want to be reminded of my first wedding. I wanted to show that I had broken with the past, that Bill and I were our own, independent persons. My parents were not even invited. This wedding was not for my mother's pleasure, it was for us—for Bill and me. I wanted Bill for myself on this big, first day of our lives together; I did not want to share, or make polite conversation, or have to translate so that our in-laws would get to know each other. I bore my mother a grudge that I knew would surface if she were present. And so we celebrated our wedding as an anti-wedding. The only person attending, in addition to Bill's parents, was Stephanie. Little did I realize then that by doing the opposite of something you are still in chains to the original. To be truly free you would have to become a different person.

As a four- and then a five-year-old, I repeatedly dreamed the same dream. This dream is still so alive in me that I could have dreamed it last night. I stand in front of a large meadow that is divided into green squares, like a chessboard. Each shade of green signals a different footing—some of the greens are solid ground, some are swamps, some are spongy soil, or a slime-covered pond—which you discover only when you step on it, and by then it is too late to retreat. I have to cross the checkered meadow to the other side, where my mother is waiting. I never make it. Inevitably, I step on a wrong square and sink. As I go under, my eyes are level with the horizon, and I see my mother on the other side, arms and legs spread wide apart, jumping up and down in triumph, like a fan cheering at a sporting event. In later life, I interpreted this dream as expressing my feeling that I was a hindrance to her, that on an unconscious level my mother, then in her early twenties, wanted me gone. Now, with Bill's support, with his unshakable, anchored presence, I had the courage—inauthentic, since I was leaning on Bill rather than relying on my own strength—to show that the pain from early injuries was still alive in me. Now it was my turn to reject. Bill gave me license to do that. His presence protected me, so I could feel free to do as I saw fit.

Would Bill have preferred a different kind of wedding? Didn't he want to please his parents with a wedding ceremony they would have liked better? No. He had his own needs, came with his own issues: he was so much in the public eye that he instinctively veered toward the private, the secluded. Although for different reasons, we meshed completely as we planned our wedding. We drove along parts of the coastline around Palm Beach, looking for an ideal spot where we could be married in a by-the-sea ceremony. This was the early 1970s, and unconventional wedding sites were growing in popularity, and the idea seemed natural to us. Finally, we decided on a small ceremony in the chapel Bill's parents regularly attended; after the ceremony, presided over by a ninety-two-year-old Scottish Presbyterian minister, we had a festive lunch outdoors in a lovely restaurant garden.

We did not even get wedding rings. Bill was averse to wearing jewelry. When I tried to persuade him that a wedding ring was the sign of a bond, not mere decoration, he shifted to a different excuse: it would interfere with his handling of the basketball. In the spirit of equality of which we were so proud, I then insisted that I would not wear a ring, either. Instead, we bought a painting, which to this day we call "the wedding ring." Over the years I came to regret that I did not have a wedding ring, and on our twentieth anniversary I broke down. Bill still does not want to wear a ring, even though he no longer plays basketball, but he bought me a lovely sapphire-and-diamond ring—blue, the color of loyalty and continued love.

A week after our marriage, my father was diagnosed with cancer of the throat. He, who had barely ever smoked and then only as a young man, had contracted a smoker's disease. We tried to "explain" to ourselves and to each other how this could have happened—not because we believed an answer, any answer, could point to a course of treatment, but because we wished in vain to impose some reason on a disease that eludes reason. My father used to say, "As you eat, so you work," while he poured boiling soup down his throat or gulped his food, piping hot, to show how lazy the rest of us were, and perhaps this habit over many years had had a disastrous effect. Perhaps all his screaming over a lifetime had affected his throat. Or perhaps it was the dust from the wood shavings that he inhaled every day in his *Werkstatt*.

I could not allow myself to think that, by not inviting my parents to the wedding, I had perhaps deprived him of the concluding highlight of his life. I needed to tell myself that his concluding highlights had occurred two years earlier, and that I had not been part of them. In 1972, at age sixty, my father officially retired from public life. My mother had finally persuaded him that they were entitled to a private life; he had agreed not to run for re-election as *Bürgermeister,* and my brother had joined the company and relieved him of many of his business obligations. The concluding highlights were the many farewell celebrations and official dinners given by every organization he had ever belonged to. There were private dinners with bands, and trips with the bowling club to restaurants and hotels in familiar, well-recognized spas. In the Bavarian tradition, *G'stanzl* singers committed the story of his life to syncopated melodies and performed them in front of the house. He saw this period as "harvest time," conjuring images of horse-drawn wagons, filled with wheat and barley and oats, driving home from the fields to the barns and the threshing floors. He had accomplished what he had set out to do in this life. Now he would dedicate himself wholeheartedly to my mother.

Perhaps he could not adjust to the thought that from now on he would have unlimited days of leisure. Or perhaps he retired because he knew how deeply, irredeemably exhausted he was. He put his house in order, and then he let go.

Before my father was diagnosed with cancer, my parents had decided to buy a smaller, bungalow-style house for their "golden years." In her panic over my father's rapidly deteriorating condition, my mother insisted that they move there quickly. In the new house, my father did not have to climb stairs, since all the rooms were on the same floor. But for the few months he lived there, he never felt quite at home. Soon after they moved in, Bill and I visited for a few weeks. My father had undergone a debilitating operation, from which he tried to recuperate by exercising each morning, lifting weights and trotting in place. He was subjected to cobalt-radiation treatments that made the hair of his beard grow inward, into his mouth cavity. He thought he could defeat the cancer with willpower. That summer, the final game of the World Cup in soccer was played in Munich. It was a point of honor for my father to attend, but there were no more tickets to be had. He asked Bill, who had contacts through the Italian basketball team Simmenthal, for which he had played when he was at Oxford. The price for the tickets was that Bill should play in a few exhibition games in Italy. Which he did. When the day of the World Cup final arrived, my father could no longer go. We all pretended that the game was not going to be all that interesting, and he smiled, knowing we told him a pious lie. (It would have been one of the more exciting games of his life: West Germany beat the Netherlands 2 to 1; Johan Cruyff of the Netherlands played a fantastic game, but more important, Franz Beckenbauer, a brilliant player on the German side, was a native of Munich!)

My father's overinvestment of energy, which was so typical for him throughout his life, is caught for me in a short scene from that summer before he died. Late one afternoon, he was driving with my brother and me to the post office. A letter had to be on its way that evening, and he wanted to see that it was posted. At a red traffic light, we stopped right next to a mail truck. My father, with his neck wrapped in soft cloth to protect the raw skin, worked himself out of the car, waving the letter in one hand as he supported himself with the other hand on the hood of our car, and then made his way to the driver of the truck. We saw the driver shake his head; he did not want to take the letter. The traffic light changed, and the cars behind us started to honk. Perhaps the driver took pity on my father, whose speech was an inarticulate forced gargle, perhaps he was nervous because of all the cars behind us—he finally took the letter. My father got back into the car, totally exhausted but triumphant. Was the letter worth the effort invested in sending it on its way? He did not care. He was infinitely pleased and proud of himself that he had seen the opportunity and prevailed.

I went back to see my father over Thanksgiving of that year, on the pretext that I needed to see a publisher in Munich. I knew it might be the last time I would see him, and he knew I had come to say goodbye. We sat and watched TV, and since he could no longer speak, we simply held hands. His hands were still as warm and dry and fleshy as on that day when he had held my hand on the way to register me for school in Ingolstadt and said that I was a Misslbeck, and they still spelled comfort for me. As so often, I screened out my emotions: I analyzed and criticized the TV program. I pretended I wanted to spare my father the knowledge that soon he would die. But he knew. I was trying to spare myself.

Death was violent to him, and his agony lasted almost the whole year. My brother came every day and gave him the pain-killing injections that he needed in ever-increasing intervals. Once, my brother was stuck in traffic because of an accident and arrived twenty minutes late. In order not to let my mother know how excruciatingly he suffered, my father made his way into the garden and bit into the earth to muffle his crying. This is how my brother found him.

During all that time, my mother rarely left his side and almost never slept, since my father did not want "strangers" (i.e., nurses) in the house and would not consider staying in a hospital. After all the years he had spent caring for her, it was now her turn to care for him, and she did. To keep herself busy and awake as she watched over him, she did needlepoint embroidery. I have a piano bench for which she embroidered the seat cover during that year. As she often said, every stitch in this tapestry was done thinking of him in love, in prayer for his health, in tears over his deterioration, in gratefulness for the life they had had together, and for the children that had sprung from it. They were married for thirty years. In subsequent years, several men wanted to marry her, but she would never contemplate a successor to her unique love and remained "faithful" (as she called it) to my father throughout the rest of her life, for almost as many years as they had been married.

As Bill and I built our lives together, new rhythms and patterns were established. He was now a married man and no longer a roving bachelor immersed in "life on the run" (the title of his basketball memoirs). For many years there had not been proper Christmases, because there were always games to be played somewhere. Our daughter was born during his last season as a player, in 1976. From then on, we spent all our Christmases with Bill's parents in Florida, establishing a tradition that has outlived both of his parents. Ironically, their apartment in Florida, where we spend the least amount of time in the course of a year, has become the most stable point of reference in our peripatetic life. In January 1974, as we were getting married, we acquired our first home together, in Denville, New Jersey, and in the thirty years since, we have moved twice in the state. In Washington, where Bill represented New Jersey in the Senate for eighteen years, we also moved twice. Perhaps, by the standards of a mobile society, that is not much. But only Florida is imbued for us with a sense of continuity from generation to generation: as a little boy, Bill would spend part of the winter in Palm Beach with his parents; he and I were married there; our daughter was baptized there; both of Bill's parents died there, although they are buried in Crystal City.

I remember the first time Bill invited me to Palm Beach, at the end of the basketball season in May 1972. Florida meant palm trees looking into our windows; it meant seeking shelter from a humidity I was not used to, walking on Bermuda grass, watching the abrupt movements of small lizards flitting across hot sidewalks, and swimming in a warm, powerful, but nonthreatening Atlantic. Again, reality outstripped my wildest dreams—or, rather, I did not have any dreams at all beyond being there with Bill, happy, loose, in love. I lived for the present moment; I did not think about the future. I could not imagine that one day we would be married, would have a child, would spend every Christmas in Florida.

In the early years of our marriage, those Christmases were very difficult for me. It was not because of Bill's parents. On the contrary. Seeing Bill's mother happy, having prepared jar-fulls of his favorite chocolate-chip cookies in advance of our arrival, and busy fixing Bill's favorite food (pompano, which was not always easy to get, and for which she would drive to the most out-of-the-way seafood markets), I came to see how a mother can show love to her child in a casual, nondramatic way. And I could see his father beam when he sat with Bill and they talked about Bill's life and career. But Christmas in Florida was like summer for me. People were on vacation, visiting, just as we were, walking around in pastel-clad clans of three generations. On Christmas Day, I could go swimming. If I had been a tourist, this would have been an adventure. But now, to my great surprise, I started missing the white Christmases I had grown up with in Germany. I remembered how the dry snow on the side streets muffled all noise, and cars made sloshing sounds on the main roads as they plowed through wet snow. Windows and doors and front yards in Passau and Ingolstadt were not decorated with blinking lights; only the streetlamps cast small islands of illumination along semidark sidewalks. The excitement of Christmas was interior: it resided in the contrast between the dark, cold, quiet outside, and the warm glow of candles and bright lights once you entered the house; between the clear, freezing air saturated with the smell of snow, and the smell of baked apples, *Zimtsterne* (star-shaped cinnamon cookies), and *Glühwein* (mulled red wine). When the front door opened, there would be a sudden whiff of freezing-cold air, a glimpse out into the darkness, and a renewed sense of comfort at being inside, sheltered, protected, warm. This contrast was all the keener because the major celebration occurred on Christmas Eve, when it was dark, not during Christmas Day. Gifts were opened on Christmas Eve, and the Christmas story was read under a tree decorated with blazing candles. We children would recite poems as the smell of sauerkraut and sausages—at least in Bavaria, where the proverbial Christmas goose was reserved for Christmas Day—wafted into the living room from the kitchen. In those days, Christmas Eve was the only night of the year when young children were out late in the street, holding the hands of their parents, going to Midnight Mass—where the music of the trumpets seemed to come directly from heaven. The summer atmosphere of Florida, with its gaily blinking outdoor lights and the opening of the gifts in broad daylight, for many years seemed perverse to me. I did not dislike it. It just was not Christmas.

When our daughter, Theresa Anne, was born in 1976, Lamaze, the preparation and method for natural childbirth, was in high fashion, and Bill and I decided we would prefer to have our child delivered this way. My obstetrician was less sanguine about it. "If you want to," he said, "grin and bear it!" I grinned and I bore it, and I never regretted it. I was lucky that there were no complications that would have necessitated other medical procedures. Bill was anxious to contribute his Lamaze share to the birth process. A major aspect of the method focused on correct breathing and on not becoming dehydrated. Sucking on hard candy was considered helpful. It was about 6:30 a.m. when Bill discovered, at the hospital, that he had not brought any Life Savers. The little stores in the neighborhood of the hospital that would most likely sell Life Savers were not open yet. Bill was nervous and upset. After finding each little store closed, he would come back to tell me of his misfortune and then run off again, reassured by the nurses and the doctor that I would not give birth during his absence. The Life Savers assumed a major function: they absorbed Bill's anxiety and gave him the sense of being a vital participant in an all-important process. When he finally and triumphantly brought back several rolls of them, I was too distracted by what was going on to thank him appropriately. He popped a Life Saver into my mouth, but instead of sucking it I chewed it to bits.

A few weeks later, Bill and I invited some friends to a party at our house in Denville. Of course they all wanted to see the new baby. Bill was hesitant. Finally, he decided they could tiptoe into the room where she was sleeping but they would have to wear face masks, so that no one would breathe a germ on her. Our friends had no idea he was serious; when they saw that Bill had a supply of masks, they went along with the gag. But I knew better: to Bill, this was no gag!

That summer, we rented a house on the Jersey Shore, at Barnegat Light. We would return there every summer for over a decade, until our daughter's teenage schedule left me alone in the house during the week. Without her, the reasons for being at the shore were gone. Those summers were good times. For most of them, Bill was in the Senate. This is when he established, for a week every summer, his annual beach walks, which helped him to stay in political and handshaking contact with his constituents. He walked stretches of the shore from Cape May to Sandy Hook, returning at night to Barnegat Light. Sometimes we would accompany him along stretches of the road. Here I found the American version of the family circus. His young summer interns would carry a huge banner, alerting the bathers that Senator Bill Bradley was among them. One intern had a bullhorn, and those bathers who did not see the banner certainly heard the bullhorn, blasting over the crashing noise of the waves. People would run up to Bill.

They would shake hands, talk a lot, wave to their friends and kids, want pictures taken. Nervous husbands wondered out loud why in tarnation it took so long for the wife or the kid to bring the camera. Didn't they see Bill was moving? More yelling, more gesticulating! Many people had compliments; a few had complaints. A group of interns would write down the names and addresses of the constituents with a gripe, along with the nature of their objections. Around Cape May and Atlantic City, most beachgoers were from Philadelphia. I often wondered why Bill would waste his time shaking hands with people from a neighboring state. But he was interested in all opinions and comments and found some of them helpful. Seen from a distance, Bill was the calm but forward-moving center of a swirling commotion. And he kept moving, whereas, when I spoke with people, I did not know how to end a conversation in the middle of a sentence. Mostly, women wanted to know what it was like to be married to Bill, and I was happy to say it was wonderful.

During these summers, I would invite friends to come to the shore for a visit. From the deck of our rented house, we could see the beach. Little kids ran like puppies, jumped into the water and out again, giggling and screeching because they thought the waves were chasing them; parents threw Frisbees or played paddleball with them and built elaborate sand castles. Bodies of the most disparate age groups were broiling in the sun, united in their desire to look healthier, more beautiful, only a few of them sheltered by colorful sun umbrellas. I was no longer quite afraid of the Atlantic, although swimming through the breakers remained a *Mutprobe* ("test of courage").

At the shore I was probably my most "American." We were relaxed and casual. Every day we bought enormous amounts of fresh fish, tomatoes, and the famous New Jersey white corn. We had cookouts. Guests brought their favorite recipes to share. I learned new ways to prepare coleslaw and acquired a reputation for my German potato salad. There was no need to be on time for anything, and no need to plan days in advance. We would go on late-night rides for some frozen yogurt. Friends challenged Bill to some midnight basketball shoot-outs at a nearby playground. No one could even see the rim of the basket, but we made up for it by commenting and yelling and shining the car lights on the black-top. My habitual anger melted away. I lived without pressure, surrounded by family, friends, at a congenial place, at a wonderful time of the year. This was the right moment for time to stand still. But it did not.

Athletes acknowledge earlier and with greater clarity than the rest of us that inevitably there will be an end to the glory days. Bill and I were married in 1974, the season after the Knicks had won the World Championship for the second time. Old team-mates left, new ones arrived, the stiffness in his joints became noticeable, and Bill began to think about a future beyond basketball. While in college at Princeton, he had put down roots in New Jersey. After my experiment in filmmaking, I had, in 1971, started to teach at Montclair State College, now Montclair State University, in New Jersey (and would continue to teach there until 1999, when I left to participate full-time in Bill's presidential bid). We had both become New Jerseyans. After much soul-searching, Bill decided to run for the United States Senate, and was elected in 1978.

efore Bill decided to run for the Senate, we had long discussions. These discussions have become a ritual in today's political landscape, but I wonder whether they are not rather like those of blind people talking about color. How does one know in advance what one's tolerance for stress will be, how great one's willingness for continued sacrifices, where the limits between private and public can be drawn once one is a public official, what will happen to family time? The Senate reminded me of academia, only more so: you are never done with your work, there are always more papers to read, more issues to study, more briefings to attend, more frameworks to elaborate, more ideas and concepts to formulate. But none of this did we know in advance.

How could I not support Bill as he arrived at that momentous decision? Of course I supported him fully, and I learned to campaign for him. I was determined to do it well, but I had not expected to enjoy it as much as I did. In a sense, I come from a political family and grew up with my mother's complaints about the demanding schedule and the theatrics over my father's Sunday-morning phone calls. (Fortunately, unlike my parents, Bill never had a problem answering the phone, and he either engaged in a conversation or said that he would have to call back, that right now was not a good time to talk.) I had been disgusted with the family circus and my role in it and had promised myself that I would never be a burden on the professional aspirations of a husband. Now I was put to the test. I was determined not to follow in my mother's footsteps, was determined never to complain. My mother thought she was showing her love for her husband by fighting for every minute to be with him, and though my father would pursue his own agenda, he acknowledged her complaints. On a Sunday, for example, he might come back from an engagement with a big bouquet of flowers. To get flowers in Germany on a Sunday evening is difficult. My father would prevail on the owner of the shop to open the back door for him and bind up a bouquet—all of which was complicated and time-consuming, so that he would arrive home even later. But he would sing to her, fall on his knees as he handed her the flowers, and then, in mock-seriousness, ask her forgiveness. Of course my mother was charmed, and the hours of waiting were forgotten!

When Bill won the Senate seat, we entered a world different from anything we could have anticipated or discussed. The Senate is a demanding workplace, and the Senate schedule is an enigma. While Bill was playing basketball, people often asked whether his schedule was not a drain on our relationship. Compared with the Senate schedule, it was easy. At the beginning of each season, the games were fixed, and you would know where your partner was to be on any given day. You could plan dinners months in advance if you wanted to. My initiation into the Senate schedule occurred soon after Bill was elected and we were invited to a dinner. It turned out that only the spouses attended the dinner, since the senators were voting all evening long. They did not arrive until it was time to go home. Bill once explained to me that it was a strategic move to leave the end of the day open as a negotiable item, so that colleagues who had further appointments could be pressured or cajoled to cast their vote a certain way in exchange for the freedom to leave for these other engagements. When I was preparing dinner while the Senate was in session, Bill would often not know at 7:00 p.m. when he could be home to eat.

At least one thing was certain: Bill had to live in Washington. My position was more complicated. I was reluctant to give up my job at Montclair State, where I was a full professor with tenure.

Nobody in Washington was willing to offer me a similar position, and I did not want to settle for an adjunct slot. I had worked myself up the professional ladder, paying my dues with enormous teaching loads and a respectable list of publications, if not as long a list as those of colleagues at more research-oriented universities, who had significantly smaller teaching loads. Feeling I deserved to be where I was, I simply could not throw it all away. It would never have occurred to me to ask Bill not to run for office. I would not have been able to live with the thought that I had stood in the way of even greater personal fulfillment for him than basketball had offered. But what about me? Over time, living with Bill had made me confident enough to consider my own wishes as being as legitimate as his. I did not ask him to refrain from running for office; could he ask me to give up my job? He did not.

Bill and I decided that I would stay in Denville with our young daughter and that he would commute, since he had to be in the state frequently anyway. New Jersey is not far from Washington, so people expected him to show up for lunches and brunches and dinners and speeches and parades and dedications and town meetings and handshakings. Once, he made the round trip three times in one day, trying to accommodate senatorial business in New Jersey and maintain his excellent voting record in the Senate. When I had a sabbatical, we spent it together in Washington, and on several occasions I took leaves of absence. We put a great deal of energy into making this arrangement work, but it was far from ideal. How did other couples manage? I took a good look at those in the Senate and in the House of Representatives who had school-age children. Their lives were easier if the spouse found a position in Washington, as often happened when the spouse was a lawyer or could work for a lobbying firm. A number of political spouses became real-estate agents. This is a lucrative and potentially interesting business, particularly when you know who is arriving or leaving with each change of administration and you have good listings to offer. But I found I was not flexible enough to drop my academic credentials and start something totally new. If a couple had many children, the family often stayed in the home state so the children would not be uprooted. The six-year election cycle of the Senate is of course easier on families than the two-year cycle for House members, who are practically always campaigning; they are in their home state much of the time, always working.

Another reason not to pull up stakes and move to Washington was our house in Denville, which both of us loved, and which Bill thought provided a center of stability for us all. It had a high cathedral ceiling and a big living room, whose vast expanse had initially given me a sense of being almost lost; one wall was all glass and looked out on a deck. Since the house was built on a hillside, the deck jutted out above the slope and made us feel as if we were sitting in the treetops. On clear days we could see the Manhattan skyline. When the sun set at a certain angle, the windows of the World Trade Center towers blazed like pink and orange candles across the distance and made me feel close to the city I loved. I filled every empty space in the house with plants. One of them, a *Dracaena marginata*, has survived and prospered all these years. It is as old as our marriage, having weathered all our moves, and has become its symbolic incarnation. Bill gets upset when even one leaf turns brown, and I do my best to take good care of it, feeding it seasonally with coffee grounds, which also help to keep the bugs away.

I loved the summers, when we hung the wet beach towels over the railing of the deck after a day spent at the bottom of the hill at Cedar Lake. When our daughter was still a toddler, barely strong enough to lug a watering can, she would giggle and laugh as she splashed herself, watering the impatiens I had planted. I loved early August, when we came back from Barnegat Light, and the rose-of-Sharon bushes were in bloom. I loved Thanksgiving, when the big table would accommodate lots of friends and our daughter designed the most adorable place cards (which I still have) of Pilgrims and Indians and animals that even bore a resemblance to turkeys. And I loved winter, when it was warm inside and the indoor plants provided a contrast with the white snow on the deck. But most of all, I loved it when there were thunderstorms, and I would sit with Theresa Anne out on the deck, under the deep overhang, holding her and making her feel how wonderful it was to be so close to the elements, to feel the wind and the spray of the rain, and to hear the thunder and see the lightning and count the seconds between them and simultaneously feel safe and dry and part of it.

In these moments, I would tell her about Schambach, the rustic cabin my father bought in 1948, in a picturesque mountain valley not too far from Ingolstadt. Today, my brother's family has turned it into a comfortable and beautiful country house, with all the amenities one could wish for—running water, electricity, telephone, oil heat. When I was growing up, we children, during summer thunderstorms, would run around in the rain in our bathing suits and stand under the rainspouts to wash the soap off our bodies. We had kerosene lamps and a wood-burning stove and an occasional, frightened mouse under one of the beds. We had to carry our drinking and cooking water in buckets up the mountain from a spring that we shared with frogs, and where, shivering in the early morning, we brushed our teeth, with fog rising from the creek that gave the valley its name.

And I told her how I considered Schambach the curse of my adolescence, since all my classmates were in town on weekends, promenading with dates along the major streets of downtown, while I had to be in the mountains! For several years, until my father was able to buy his first car, he and I bicycled each weekend the fifteen miles from Ingolstadt to Schambach on gravel roads, because during the week I had to go to school (in Germany, summer vacation does not start until the middle of July and lasts only six weeks) and he had to attend to his business. In her later years, as a widow, my mother would occasionally go up to the house, making frequent stops on the narrow switchback path, gasping and struggling for breath, because she was so overweight. The last time I remember, she needed strong assistance: she leaned against Bill's back and he pulled her forward while my brother pushed her from behind. She was so pleased when she finally sat down, wheezing and unable to speak, ready for a strong cup of coffee and a slice of *Torte,* which I, as ever the stern taskmaster, denied her because she was by now diabetic. In hindsight, I now know she should have enjoyed her *Torte* and compensated with a bigger insulin injection. When we went to Schambach in these last years of her life, I was struck by the smooth and quick ride on wide, well-asphalted roads, while I still lived with the memory of the dirt roads, the torn bicycle tires, and the provisions my father and I had to lug out there every weekend.

As we sat on the deck in Denville, comfortable in the midst of a storm, I did not want to think of the problems associated with our house: the difficulty of access up a narrow, one-lane road that became icy in winter; the problems of finding handymen or yardmen; the deer that ate all the plants, including the rhododendron blossoms and the azaleas; the high utility bills that come with this type of open-plan architecture; the commute to Montclair, which, though only twenty miles, was always nerve-racking, with trucks surrounding my small car on all sides and traffic accidents a daily occurrence.

Although Washington was not our home base, we were there frequently enough that Bill thought we should look for a house there, too. Perhaps he hoped that a house would entice Theresa Anne and me to spend more time there; perhaps he did not want to live permanently in an apartment in D.C., particularly when the two of us joined him. We looked together and found a wonderful, rambling house with three stories and a full basement in Cleveland Park, a child-friendly neighborhood in the District. When we moved in, in 1981, it was much too large for us, but it had been filled, wall to wall, by the time we moved out. The house had been built before World War I, before the advent of air conditioning, and its layout indicated a great concern for air flow. But it needed a lot of work. For years I had dreamed of "doing" a house. This was my opportunity. We started by installing central air conditioning, and every year another major project—new bathrooms, a new kitchen, a new basement, a new roof, a reconfigured backyard—was completed. Until late in the spring and the onset of suffocating Washington humidity, I kept all the windows open to let the breeze blow through. I had sheer curtains installed on all the windows, and the wind made them billow and wave, and I felt as if I were living in a nineteenth-century East European novel. It was a good house, and perhaps because I had invested so much effort and imagination in it, I came to love it better than the house in Denville. It, too, had a deck, which in summer looked out into a lush greenery that reminded me of Atlanta. Here, too, I could sit with Theresa Anne under a protective roof in open space and watch and feel the thunderstorms go by, the trees bowing in the rough winds and driving rains. As in Denville, I had a clothesline installed so I could smell the freshness and greenery in the laundry when I brought it in from drying in the sun.

The house in Washington did not have a grand view. It was embedded in a neighborhood that suggested the suburbs, as much as that was possible within the District, fifteen minutes from the Capitol and twenty from the airport. Close by was a thoughtfully laid-out playground that was always teeming with children and dogs, and there were front yards full of flowers and shrubs that took turns blooming throughout the year. Mothers were forever driving their youngsters to school- and sports-related activities, car doors were slammed, kids were yelling, the older ones forever going from house to house collecting signatures or money for some worthy cause or school fund-raiser, and on Saturday mornings you woke up to the noise of basketballs being dribbled on the concrete surface of the playground.

The house came with a cat named Muschie. The previous owners had two cats, and they had moved only a few blocks away. One cat settled in with them in their new house; the other one was bound to what became our house. She was a beautiful calico. For a while, I thought we had a stray cat hanging around, until one day, when a door was left open, the cat streaked in and ran upstairs, where, apparently, her litter box had been in the old days. We could tell she knew the house as she stalked through the rooms, assessing the changes we had made. We talked to the previous owners, who were at a loss, since every time they opened their door she ran back to the old house. So, if we wanted to feed her . . . This is how Bill acquired a companion for his lonely nights. Muschie would jump on his lap when he came home late at night, and he would pet her while we had our nightly telephone conversations. But Bill was frequently in New Jersey. On those occasions, who would take care of her? Should she stay in the house, all alone, or be left outside, since she was used to it? Neighbors fed her while Bill was gone, but I always felt bad knowing she was alone. Perhaps I identified with Muschie's uprootedness. She didn't suffer from *Heimweh*, because *Heimweh* had driven her back to where she came from; at least she knew where she wanted to belong, but it was not a welcoming environment; she was often lonesome. To me, her presence epitomized *Ausweglosigkeit,* a situation that cannot be brought to a good end. And then, inevitably, she got sick. It was sad to see her fur all matted and clinging in patches, to see the bones on her back sticking out under the pitiful fur, to see the fur fall out in clusters while her belly swelled. The veterinarian said she died of cancer; I felt she died of disorientation and loneliness. Her burial was a family affair. Bill dug the grave under the front porch, and Theresa Anne and I marked it with stones and flowers. I wondered about the other cat, which had adjusted to the new circumstances, to the new house. Isn't it the same with people? Some make the transition, like my Grandfather Keller, and some, like my grandmother, do not. For all her apparent toughness, Muschie seems to have been the more vulnerable one.

Bill was thriving, what with the constant challenges of the Senate and a wife who did not object to his being a workaholic. The wrinkle in our life was the commuting, but we felt we were masters of our own arrangements and with good will and mutual respect we could manage. I was often, in the most unexpected moments—such as preparing dinner, or hanging laundry out to dry, or planting a few peonies (remembering my grandfather's garden)—overcome by the distance I had traveled in my life. I had traveled without clear design or specific goal and had arrived somewhere, guided by good fortune. I was filled with gratitude and marveled that all this had come to pass. I led a life that was way beyond the horizon of whatever expectations I could have had, that was outside the periphery of my wildest imaginations. With Bill's life swirling about me, I sensed that I would be destroyed as a person if I devoted myself exclusively to his advancement. I needed a firm grounding in my own accomplishments.

Hanging on to my own identity did not, of course, prevent me from being interested in Bill's activities in the Senate, or in the issues he worked on. When I sat in the visitors' gallery and looked down into the Senate Chamber, I felt as if I were entering the white areas on the maps of ancient explorers. To watch the senators, adorned in the full regalia of their own importance, walk around in that pit, was like witnessing the unfathomable rituals of a strange tribe. As they cast their votes, they seemed to be performing an elaborate dance to the inaudible music of internalized rules. I don't think I understood the magnitude of Bill's achievement when the Tax Reform Act of 1986 was passed. (With time I learned that laws are there to be dismantled: there is not much left of what at the time was called his Fair Tax.) As a member of the Finance Committee, Bill had worked on this legislation for four years. He was a Democrat in a Republican administration, and he succeeded where everyone had predicted failure. Bill understood that the absence of flamboyance and a subtle sense of humor could soften a recalcitrant opponent. He won over President Reagan by reminding him of his past: "Mr. President, both you and I support tax reform—you because as an actor you paid a 90 percent tax rate; me, because as a basketball player I was a depreciable asset." On another occasion, someone pointed out to Bill that, actually, his ideas had been appropriated by "the other side of the aisle," whereupon he answered, "To succeed in a Republican Senate is to have a good idea and then let them steal it."

I was extremely moved when, after the disintegration of the Soviet Union, he shepherded the Freedom Exchange Act into law. Under it, high-school juniors from the Newly Independent Republics apply annually in vast numbers and undergo intense competition to spend a year living with an American family. By the program's tenth anniversary, in 2003, fourteen thousand awardees had come here out of over half a million applicants. Similar programs had allowed generations of young

Germans after World War II to come to the United States and, after their return to Germany, grow into positions of leadership in politics and industry. I believe there cannot be too much personal contact between old enemies, particularly when you begin with the next generation, and I strongly believe that we should lead the world by the power of our democratic example. To build these bridges from culture to culture, with consequences reaching far into the future, is more constructive and life-affirming than confrontation. Bill's efforts made a difference not only in the lives of these young people but, through them, in the future of their countries. Out of this conviction, I served on the board of a youth-exchange foundation, called Youth for Understanding.

But with victories came defeats. When Bill and others passed catastrophic health insurance for the elderly and asked only the well-to-do senior citizens to pay for some part of it, these wealthier citizens organized opposition and succeeded in repealing the legislation. And, more than ten years after the passage of a law dealing with federal water allocation in California, many of the provisions have still not been implemented. These setbacks over time made me realize I could never be a legislator. I would become too angry, depressed, and cynical; legislation is so often motivated not by devotion to the common good but by commitment to a narrow special interest or even to personal advantage. Legislative achievements are like sand castles at the edge of the ocean, exposed to the constantly nibbling wavelets, waiting for the inevitable big wave to wash them away.

In small ways, Bill and I participated in the Washington social circuit. On occasion he would say, but without reproach, that perhaps we did not do enough entertaining and should "show up" at events more often, but overall we were doing fine. Did I enjoy meeting "interesting" people—ambassadors, diplomats, politicians, artists, journalists, tycoons? Yes, of course I did; how could I not? But what does "meeting" mean? A handshake? A polite sentence? A shared dinner? And at the next event, you have forgotten the names of the people you met at the last one, because too many other "meetings" are interfering. There is rarely any time to cultivate an incipient affinity. I began to divide my friends into two groups—those who thought I had a glamorous time in Washington, and those who knew how hectic my life really was. The latter I considered my true friends.

In the beginning, I had felt like an outsider in Washington, since I was so unfamiliar with the political rituals Americans have grown up with. For example, I had to learn to hold my right hand over my heart when I pledged allegiance to the flag. But I cherished the collegiality among the Senate spouses. We all knew that private time with our husbands had to be arranged through the office; it did not come spontaneously, it had to be scheduled. Dinners could never be counted on until you sat down, and then they could be interrupted by votes or emergency phone calls. Vacation time could be invaded. In our family, this meant vacations were rarely long enough for us to go to our favorite place in the Greek islands. Friendships developed that withstood separation even after Bill had left the Senate, and bloomed in fresh colors when he started to campaign across the country for the presidential nomination.

Trips abroad on which spouses could accompany the senators were considered a kind of compensation for the many sacrifices incurred on a daily basis. (The spouses did not cost the taxpayers anything, since the plane would fly whether all seats were occupied or not.) In the eighteen years that Bill was in the Senate, I remember only five trips on which I went with him: one was to Saudi Arabia; one to the former Soviet Union; one to China; one to Afghanistan, India, Pakistan, and Thailand; and one to Argentina, Brazil, Venezuela, and Mexico. Bill thought the taxpayers weren't getting their money's worth unless meetings went from early morning until late at night, so the spouses would be provided with guides to direct them to the sights. Only in China did Bill and I and the entire delegation go sightseeing together, to the Great Wall and the Forbidden City. Visiting all these places was like leafing through a beautiful photo album. You saw only what was in the picture, and the pictures you were shown were carefully edited.

Not so on a memorable trip to Egypt, in which only spouses and a few friends participated. This time we paid our own way and were without the burden of an official schedule, but nevertheless privileged: the wife of the Egyptian ambassador chaperoned us through all the marvels of this ancient civilization and the travails of a contemporary country struggling with the tremendous problems of modernization. We got up early to see the sun rise behind the pyramids of Giza; we went to Luxor and the temples at Karnak; we visited some of the tombs in the Valley of the Kings, and spent many hours (but not enough) at the Egyptian Museum in Cairo. We took an almost empty boat down the Nile, and from its upper deck we saw the fragility of the Nile Valley, the narrow strips of green on either side of a river that was less imposing and yet spoke more to my soul than I had anticipated. I was deeply moved, more than impressed, that out of this river and the slim margins of riverbanks had risen one of the most enduring and powerful civilizations on earth. The breeze blew as it had blown for millennia, a breeze that had contributed powerfully to making the Nile easily navigable: the Nile flows north while the breeze blows south, helping the boats go upstream. We floated past small villages and mud houses and children tending goats, and I imagined them having been there for thousands of years. Some of us were restless, and those of us who worked out regularly at home did sit-ups and push-ups in the rear of the deck. It was at this moment, when we were drifting through an ancient landscape and indulging in the exercises of "liberated" modern women, that I experienced an overwhelming sense of oneness—the uniting of a distant past and the present. We had also brought books, and we read them out loud to one another: the Old Testament, which told the story of Joseph in Egypt; Herodotus, as he understood the Egyptians twenty-five hundred years ago. And I had brought the last volume of Thomas Mann's *Joseph* tetralogy, *Joseph the Provider*, which Mann completed in 1943, as the barbarities of the Nazi regime engulfed the world, and in which he used Franklin D. Roosevelt as the model of a wise leader.

Bill was not happy with our living and commuting arrangements, and I agreed with him. Usually he did not come home to Denville on weekends just to spend time with his family. There were all the political obligations, and although the wife could tag along, it was often inappropriate to bring a child, who would in any case be bored, and Bill did not want her to be drawn into the political circus. What could we do? We knew that, out of respect and love for each other, we had to make allowances. But our daughter was a different matter. Only two years old when Bill was elected to the Senate, she was growing up, every day a little bit, and Bill felt he was not playing an active enough part in her life. She and I had it good together in New Jersey. I would sit her on the counter of the post office when I mailed letters, and she developed intricate communications with the post-office employees even before she could speak. One of the bank tellers showed her a little kitten she kept in a side room, and Theresa Anne was heartbroken when the kitten found a better home. Before she started school, we had regular Wednesday lunches of grilled-cheese sandwiches at the Arrow Head Diner in Mountain Lakes, and I think the name of the diner was even more alluring to her than our fare. We took walks around Bald Hill, and fancied that we saw traces of bear claws on the tree trunks and in the muddy soil.

Above all, we had a wonderful housekeeper, who included our daughter in her family. May and "Pap-Pap" became Theresa Anne's second set of parents—the "normal" ones, with a normal schedule, who found little chores for her when they worked in their house or yard, and who had a car seat installed in their car so they could take her along when they did their errands or watched their own daughter compete as an ice skater. Once, they even took her in their trailer on a tour through southern New Jersey that lasted several days! When May had cancer and was too sick to work any longer, we found a college student who lived with us while she studied for a B.A. in philosophy. Philosophy can be exciting for a five- or six-year-old if the conversations do not get lost in esoterics. She and Theresa Anne built a puppet theater with an ever-expanding set of characters and gave regular performances, for which they wrote the scripts. Up the narrow gravel road from us lived an elderly gentleman who was a composer and such a Wagner fan that he had the walls of his house decorated with scenes from *Der Ring des Nibelungen*. For a little girl, that was fascinating. He gave our daughter her first piano lessons. Eventually we realized that she looked forward to going to his house because of his murals and his cats, not because of his music, and decided that his instruction was perhaps a bit too rigorous.

Our daughter started first grade in Washington since I had a sabbatical, but after a year we were back in Denville. I was again teaching at Montclair, Bill was still commuting, and our daughter was growing. We had to make changes. After prolonged discussions, we decided that our daughter would live in Washington and that Bill, the fussy and protective father, would find the right kind of child care and be there when I was not.

I started looking again for a position in the Washington area, but I still could not conceive of taking just anything to keep busy. I wanted to continue in my career. Today's women are no longer so adamant about women's rights and their own careers as my generation was. I had translated Kate Millet's *Sexual Politics*, the bible of my generation, into German; I knew every word of the new gospel; I expected my husband to be part of my journey as much as I was part of his. Job promises were extended by various universities around D.C.—not for permanent positions but as replacements for colleagues on sabbatical. I could have taken unpaid leave from Montclair and filled any of these slots. I did not have to worry about academic qualifications; I had those. But the field of German studies is fairly small; to find a senior position in a narrowly circumscribed geographic area is nearly impossible. There were lunches and friendly conversations, and one department head concluded with the encouraging comment "I will let you know as soon as this colleague decides to go on sabbatical; you don't need to call me." I invested all my hope in this offer. When I finally did call, I found out that the slot had been filled for personal reasons with someone from another nearby university. It did not help to be dejected. Over time, I met other highly qualified and widely published colleagues in other disciplines who could not find the right positions in Washington, either.

Now I would be the serious commuter. In contrast to Bill's schedule, mine was firmly fixed by Montclair State. And so I would, for nine years, take the Metroliner every Thursday afternoon to Washington and arrive there at 6:00 p.m., when Bill would meet me in our old battered Buick Skylark at the train station. We would then either drive home for the rest of the evening, or, if there was an impending vote, go to the Senate, or he would drop me off at home and then return to the Senate. On Monday mornings, I would return to New Jersey, and again Bill would be the family driver. He would drop Theresa Anne off at school, and then his wife at Union Station, before he arrived at the Senate.

I rationalized that this was not too great a sacrifice for the members of our family. After all, the semesters each consisted of only thirteen weeks, so that the commuting arrangement applied to only twenty-six weeks, exactly half a year. And in each of these twenty-six weeks, I would be away from Washington "only" three nights a week. On Monday, Tuesday, and Wednesday nights, father and daughter were on their own; on Thursdays, I would arrive and interfere with their arrangements. These "arrangements" were based on breaking a lot of rules, like having dinner whenever it was convenient, usually featuring take-out food. Theresa Anne had a little desk set up in a corner of Bill's office, and on occasion she would do her homework there, spoiled by the entire staff. I adored the statement made by that little desk in Bill's office. As always, he was, in his nonverbal way, right on target. From now on, when Bill spoke at gatherings about the need for appropriate child-care for working parents, he could speak with true authority. He knew from firsthand experience the conflicts a parent had to face when a child was sick, when there was no care-taker available and work could not be postponed.

Even though many of his constituents (his wife included) admired him for being such a committed husband and father, I could not help thinking that both he and my daughter still enjoyed a privileged position. How many working mothers or fathers can bring their children after school to their offices? How many of them can take off for a few hours during the day without losing any of their salary, if not their job altogether? How many have the time deducted from their vacation if they need to take their child to a doctor or watch the child compete in an event? Later, during the presidential campaign, I had a discussion with telephone operators and women who work for credit-card companies, and I was devastated to hear under what conditions and pressures they must work; mothers are often forced to work overtime while they know their children are home from school, waiting for them. Bill was in a much better position, even though appointments had to be honored and votes had to be cast.

During the times we were apart, nightly telephone conversations became a routine, and I looked forward to them every day. For me, these calls had a single-mindedness that our face-to-face conversations often lacked; on the phone we were not distracted by externals. My days became accumulations of thoughts and scenes that we then shared every evening. In these conversations, each day found its completion. I voiced my love and my anger, my concerns and plans, Bill provided samples of his overcrowded days, and we discussed our schedules—always our schedules. I saw the schedules as bringing order into the turbulence of our lives. The telephone line became the umbilical cord that connected and nourished Bill and me when we were not together—or Ariadne's thread, which brought Theseus safely back from his battle with the Minotaur.

This was the second time in my life when I agreed that my child's primary residence should be with her father. This time, of course, I did not really leave, and over the course of a week I was absent only three nights. Nevertheless, I was not the mother who could always be taken for granted when a kid needed to be driven to after-school activities, to be picked up from a friend's house, when some school material or equipment was urgently demanded, when there was no milk in the refrigerator and no toilet paper in the bathroom. I could agree to that arrangement only because I had Bill's promise that there would always be adequate help, that he would be there when I was not, that we would share in this situation as in everything else.

I was (and still am) firmly convinced that children respond to necessity, that they not only adjust but contribute their share when they understand the need for their help. After all, hadn't I done that? But my help to my family when I was a child came at a time when the society saw nothing wrong in demanding such things of children. Our daughter grew up in an affluent neighborhood where it was expected that parents would sacrifice themselves to realize the aspirations they had for their children. When I expressed my confidence in the resilience of children, in their adaptability to specific situations, Bill would pinpoint the source of my attitude and say, "Stop fighting that war!"

We also live in a society in which women's struggles for autonomy are finally—if still only peripherally—recognized. Shouldn't children be proud of their working mothers, feel for them, help them out? Shouldn't children take their mothers, as much as their fathers, as role models, emulate their aspirations, participate with interest in the many-sided aspects of their lives? Did I project these hopes onto my daughter only as a way of making excuses for a decision that emphasized my own needs? But it was not only my decision; I had arrived at it with my husband! Before Bill ran for the Senate, we had discussed his options together and at length. He made no excuses for wanting to be in the Senate, nor did I or anyone else expect him to feel guilty about his choice. On the contrary: when he was seen, a lonesome shopper, buying milk and cereal in the local supermarket around midnight, many people felt for him and admired him even more. He was a "total" person, not a one-sided company man. Yet I felt the need to make excuses for my choice. I felt guilty for clinging to the career I had created for myself, rather than finding fulfillment in motherhood alone and relying on the satisfaction I would get from dedicating my life to my child. (Woe to the child who has to carry such a burden!)

Perhaps because my father came into my life fairly late, I felt that my daughters should not be similarly deprived, and that, if they needed to be even temporarily with only one parent, it should be the father. I had a vague sense of wanting to give to them what I thought I had never really had—indeed, could not even imagine having—namely, a deep emotional bond with the first and most important man in their lives. I had never quite outgrown the feeling that I had ruined my mother's life. I therefore did not want my daughters to be burdened with the guilt of feeling that they were demanding sacrifices of me. I know I did not want them to resent me later for having obliged them to feel grateful. I did not want them to feel as conflicted about what I had given up for them as I felt in relation to my mother. Did I decide that Theresa Anne would be fine with her father because I trusted Bill so much, or because I thought so little of myself? Perhaps I thought too much of myself: I took a mother-daughter relationship for granted as something deeply rooted, indestructible, and therefore less in need of tending, while I believed that the relationship with a father had to be more carefully cultivated.

Finally, I fear I needed my professional position as validation; after all, I was married to a towering, powerful man—the kind of man around whom people had a tendency to overlook the wife. Yet, in the course of the eighteen years Bill served in the Senate, women would often come up to me and ask whether I was still teaching at Montclair State. When I said that I was, they seemed genuinely pleased that I had "hung in there," "did not give up on myself," was "my own person." I was always heartened by their encouragement. I may not have wanted to admit that my job gave me a sense of identity I could not derive from being a mother. How many contradictory answers were there to these questions? I didn't know then, and I'm still not sure today.

Bill was unable to find the right kind of child care. It had seemed natural to us that he would engage in the search, since he lived in Washington and had his own punctilious standards. Theresa Anne once counted and found that in a period of eight years she had seven different women trying their hands on her! For some reason, it was practically impossible to find a good and loving person to take care of our good and loving daughter. We had a wonderful housekeeper, who stayed with us through all the years Bill was in the Senate, but she had children of her own and had to be with them after school, at the very time we needed somebody for our daughter. We did not want a full-time nanny; our daughter was too old for that. We did not want an illegal immigrant, though many were available. For a while, we had a kind and gentle grandmother whose time schedule was flexible, but she became ill and could no longer work for us. For one year, we had a young woman from New Jersey, but she had to go back there to finish college. We had a series of unsatisfactory au pairs from Europe and from other parts of this country. Our daughter navigated these rapids more gracefully than we, her parents.

These were the hard years. Between not finding appropriate child-care and not finding an appropriate job, I felt more than merely disappointed. A person without my history might have been equally discouraged, even upset, and then moved on to other alternatives. But I felt betrayed and abandoned by the very person in whose promise I had invested all my trust and confidence—my husband. Bill's inability to find the right caretaker became for me his inability to take care of us in general; the more I hoped he would step in and act decisively, the more I felt he withdrew, hiding behind ever-mounting Senate obligations. He seemed not to be there when he was most needed, and I had to compensate for that lack. Like a whirling dervish, I danced myself into a trance of ever more work, spinning faster and faster. There was the commuting, there were the two houses, the two full schedules in both places: in New Jersey my profession was scholarly, in Washington were my husband, my daughter, and our so-called social life. I had to buy groceries in both places, had to cook, pay the bills, call the handyman, the plumbers, the successive contractors involved in redoing the Washington house—and always the schedule was complicated, since I had to insist on inconvenient appointments with a "Remember, I am here Fridays only!"

Bill tried to get me to "Relax!"—which frustrated me even more, since it demonstrated how little he understood the pressures building up in me. He wore socks with holes in them to show how well *he* could relax, but that was no consolation for me. I began to admire women whose kitchens were messy, whose yards were littered with their children's toys, whose beds were never really made, whose bathroom soap dishes were grimy. It seemed to matter to nobody but me whether my daughter's drawers were immaculately arranged, whether the inside of our car looked like a dump truck, whether our frying pans were scoured to look like new, whether we had run out of toothpaste or shampoo. I still wanted to hang the laundry out to dry in the sun, take care of my plants, pick up my daughter from school at least on Fridays, and sit with her on the deck when it rained.

In order to ward off any thought that I should, under these circumstances, give up my career, I met even the slightest chores with a force way beyond what was necessary. I was once again the good Wuschilein, *die Grosse,* who worked and worked and in the process became a machine, well functioning and efficient but aggrieved, and not really there. I gained a sense of inner satisfaction and accomplishment from being able to do it all. Was I also trying to create order in a chaotic life in the best and most familiar way I knew? I think I fell back on the emotional habits of my adolescence because those early wounds had never properly healed, they had merely been forgotten. I had learned nothing about myself in the intervening years.

I knew that under the surface of Bill's and my mutual understanding and support festered disappointment and anger. Like a volcano in the deep sea, the source of my anger was hidden. The crust of the earth, deep down under miles and miles of water, kept breaking open and caused the surface of the ocean to heave. Occasionally the force of the eruptions catapulted huge liquid rocks through tons of water into the air. I remember I slammed doors, I yelled, and once I smashed dinner plates on the floor. These eruptions of my anger were random and without logical provocation, thus totally confusing for those around me. From my perspective, though, I was frustrated, disappointed, and on permanent overload. I was difficult to live with. It was during this period that a friend coined the sentence: *"Ernestine est toujours en rage."* I thought it was a compliment and laughed.

When I met other career women, I would ask them how they juggled their lives and their families. They always made it sound easy. Or they had a terrific support system. Or the husband had a job that allowed him to participate more fully in the daily activities. Sometimes a hurried tone betrayed their inner tension, sometimes an impatient gesture gave them away, sometimes they were too preoccupied even to listen carefully. To me it seems that someone or something in these arrangements always suffered and that the suffering was simply not noticed, just as I was oblivious of the tensions in my own life.

It gives me great pleasure to see Stephanie happy as a suburban mom with a busy lawyer husband and four active young children. Having grown up as an only child with much love but only partial family structures, she gave up her prospering career as a clinical psychologist when the first child was born. She is, in her adult married life, making up for the deficiencies she felt in her childhood. When I sit in the car with her as we pick up one or several of her children from sports events or after-school programs, I see her waving to other mothers who are picking up their children, filling the cars with lively chatter, and hustling. I hear the dog in the back of her car greeting each of her kids with a special bark. Her identity is invested in being a suburban mom; she does not need a professional job to be fulfilled, even though she holds a Ph.D. in psychology; she does not ask whether what she does is "rewarding," because it is rewarding beyond question. Being a mother and a wife and a homemaker gives her more satisfaction than a profession ever could. Perhaps I was asked to be a mother to my siblings too early; perhaps I was exhausted even before I started.

I held fast to the promise I had made to myself as a teenager—namely, that I would never complain about my husband's dedication to his work—and I continued to believe that this refusal to complain about Bill's devotion to his public life was the most convincing proof of my love. It never occurred to me that he might have been as much a prisoner of his obsessions as I was of mine—that he would have liked me to claim him, once in while, for me, for us. I know I should have insisted that we take days, weekends off, even if that meant he would have to rely more on his staff when the next vote was cast, or that I would not return student papers on the dates promised. Instead of being angry because he was absentminded, I should have canceled the contractor and packed the car for a weekend in the Blue Ridge Mountains. Perhaps I lacked the self-assuredness of women who state their demands and find that men, more or less, bow to them. To this day, I am amazed when I see women insist, in the face of opposition from their husbands, on something they want, be it a small thing like going to a specific movie, or a big thing like moving to a different part of the country. I had created a bind for myself that I could not break: I should have been concerned about the source of my anger, about feeling that I was left to fend for myself, not having the support I had hoped for, even as I admired Bill, his clear analyses of convoluted issues in the Senate, his startlingly adept conceptualizations "outside the box." I could not even admit that I was angry (although I acted my anger out), because I did not like women who complained and because I was too convinced of the importance of the work Bill was doing. We continued to be profoundly committed to a partnership that allowed both of us to find fulfillment in what we were doing. Though we understood that our daughter was always at the center of our concerns, we did not understand that we should also take care of ourselves in order to be the best, most sparkling, for each other and for her. We did not understand that we should slow down each other's all-consuming work habits. Instead, we sat together at night, he at his desk, I on the sofa next to him—the perfect image of a couple in harmony. I saw us scaling the mountains of difficulties around us, hand in hand, and identified completely with the French philosopher Michel de Montaigne when he said, of his friendship with the poet Étienne de la Boétie, that it was possible "*parce que c'était lui, parce que c'était moi.*" Intermingled in these tough years were love and endurance, pressures, tensions, and rewards. It was a time to prove that we had meant what we had said about being helpmates. We were also very proud of each other.

TOWARD HOME

Then, in the spring of 1992, I felt a lump in my breast. I can't remember whether I noticed it for weeks or for months, whether I pretended the lump was not there, whether I thought it was just a bruise, whether I waited to see if it would go away on its own. Stephanie was getting married that May, and I certainly did not want anything to interfere with such a glorious time. Besides, it seemed to me that the lump was getting smaller. So why panic?

But the lump did not go away, and finally, after Stephanie's wedding, I decided to see a doctor, who performed a biopsy. I should have known that she did not have good news when she called me back so quickly. Yes, I had cancer, and after further tests it became clear that I needed a mastectomy. I was too traumatized to hear what the doctors were saying. Bill took over. I just sat there, stunned. I once had a conversation with a woman cancer patient who was single, and I asked her how she remembered what the doctors told her. She said she went with a tape recorder, and once she was at home, she would listen to the tape over and over. How sad that she had to rely on a tape recorder instead of a loving partner, but how admirable that she took care of herself!

For a short while, I pretended that this was not happening to me. At night, at home, bits and pieces of the doctors' pronouncements would flash into my mind. New words led to a frightening new world. What did "in situ" mean, or "multifocal"? What was

On the lecture circuit.

"adjuvant therapy"? I guessed what "metastatic" meant and did not want to hear more about it. If I woke up in the middle of the night searching for a word, for an explanation, Bill would be at my side. He would always know, and tell me, wide awake; he would draw pictures for me, comfort me, comfort both of us. I was never alone.

Perhaps I was guided by my instincts, or by a sense of self-preservation; perhaps the feisty child in me just did not want to see me as a victim. I managed to stay away from the shattering, dead-end question "Why me?" I wanted and needed to believe that I did not have to succumb to fate, that I could influence my lot even while I had a blooming malignancy. Perhaps my body was trying to tell me that I had not taken good care of myself—it had intervened on my behalf. I had worked too hard; I had lost sight of the pleasures of life. Bill and I had become workaholics. Cancer put a stop to all that, forced me to focus on myself; suddenly all the pressures I had invoked so I could labor under them fell away. I needed to believe that in some way I had caused my cancer. I know there are many people who vehemently object to that view—but then their only alternative is to see themselves as the victims of a cruel and blind fate. I needed to believe that my body was sending me warning signals (too late?) that I had done something wrong, and that what I had done wrong could perhaps still be righted. The exact causes of cancer are still unknown. Heredity, nutrition, and the environment are factors, and perhaps also stress. I thought stress was a possible explanation for my case, and it was also the most easily remedied if I should ever get out of this situation.

I wanted to assume responsibility for the calamity, since (however wrongheaded I might be) I needed to use this idea to my advantage. If my body had thrown me into this horrible state to teach me a lesson, then I could perhaps amend the situation—be more careful and attentive and promise my body and myself that

I would no longer lead such a stressful and self-abusive life. In this way, I could imagine myself in control, if ever so slightly. I wanted to bend this cancer, without knowing whether I would succeed or not, into a life force. I knew I could not "battle" cancer with a façade of bravery and determination. My father had done that and died a most miserable death. I wanted "my" cancer to give me insights into my life, time to reflect on what I had done wrong. I hoped for a second chance, a chance to put this new knowledge to work.

Amazingly, while I had cancer I was never angry. Perhaps the shock of what was happening to me absorbed all my emotional energy; perhaps the sense of gratitude for still being alive washed away all the minutiae that would so often frustrate me; perhaps, because I let go, there were no sources of tension left. I underwent a considerable transformation of values, and that transformation has held up. Many of my compulsions were cauterized away. I now divide my life into BC (before cancer) and AC (after cancer). AC life is infinitely richer and deeper; friendships are more meaningful, time is more precious. The smallest things count more: the brief conversation a cashier and I have at the checkout counter; the way I wave ahead another car that tries to cut me off; the way the smallest, dullest objects catch the light. Instead of rushing, instead of tensing up, I take a deep breath and try to feel grateful for every moment of my AC existence. I have learned to ignore the half-empty refrigerator, the unmade beds, the unwashed car, the shoes in need of repair. Sometimes, when the old pressures threaten to inundate me, I remind myself of the privileged position of still being here, on this beautiful earth, with my family, loving and being loved.

Yet, paradoxically, even as I struggled to believe that I had some control over what was happening to me, I felt infinite relief in simply letting go as I went through chemotherapy. I was excused from any responsibilities; nothing more was demanded of me than just to be, to be there and get well. The cancer that had stricken me was no longer an unknown, dreaded fate. I made it into "my" cancer (or at least I thought I did). My body and I talked to each other. I was sad that my body, so brave in telling me that I must stop leading this stressful life, had been punished, like a messenger in classical drama, for bringing unwelcome news. I was devastated by the threatening subtext of the message, which told me that I might die, yet I also believed that the messenger meant well. I apologized to my body and tried to explain to it (and to myself) why it had to be subjected to the cruel treatment of chemo. Perhaps I was out of my mind at that time, and this was my way of coping. But I still think it was a good way. It saved me from despair.

For most women and men in our culture (is there any culture where this is not the case?), breasts are a symbol of sexuality. If you do not have the right kind of breasts, you are not considered a complete woman. I now had to let go of this part of my body, which up to then had been an outward symbol of my womanliness. The night before the mastectomy, I said farewell to my breast. I cried as I thanked it for having been such a good part of me. I cry even now as I write these words.

I hope I don't sound insensitive to cancer patients who have had very different experiences, but I learned that cancer doles out not only sorrow and pain but also great gifts. Cancer brought Bill and me together in unanticipated ways—ways that we had not known existed. I am sure he was afraid of losing me (although he would never admit that there was even the slimmest chance). To combat this fear, he became an expert on the various types of breast cancer, on state-of-the-art research, on the treatments preferred by one oncologist or one hospital over those of another. I am convinced that his immersion in the subject helped him cope with his own anxieties. In contrast to me, who would turn to him with all my questions all the time, he did not want to express his concerns and worries to me. In a marriage founded on equality and sharing, there occurred a significant shift of power. As I grew weaker, he grew stronger. As I found reason to let go, he found an "excuse" to take care of me. What does it say about me, about the mask of bravery and can-do postures that I had worn with so much anger, that I needed cancer to be able to let go, to be vulnerable and in need, to accept gratefully and with a good conscience all the help and comfort that was offered with a full heart? I felt that Bill was my guardian angel, his hand resting lightly on my shoulder as he steered me through the devastating confrontations with the disease. This is how I saw us walking through the days.

I now understand more clearly that my cancer allowed Bill's protective instincts to emerge. I no longer asked whether his schedule permitted him to take me to yet another medical appointment, or whether it might cause him to miss a vote. Everything became simple and easy; I could finally accept all the large and small gestures of love with which he enveloped me. (To this day, he makes a better cup of coffee for me than I could ever make for myself.) I entered into a blissful state of obliviousness to the world at large, and from within that state, and with the conviction of the ignorant, I told Bill not to worry—I had discovered the transforming power of cancer!

As Bill became an expert on the disease, friends turned to him for advice. He became a reference center, a consultant, and a careful appraiser of the emotional states of those with whom he talked. In the process he, too, learned that cancer not only takes but also gives. The very act of giving advice and comfort to friends lent him strength and courage. In all of us, love and support grew out of fear and the attempts to cope with it; good will and hope took the place of blind faith and fatalism; energy and the joy of being alive kept us from looking down the long road toward an uncertain future.

Cancer can truly become the watershed in a relationship. Particularly where partners are concerned, it reveals the foundations on which their relationship is built. In the best of cases, closeness arises as imminent loss threatens the humdrum, daily existence. I have seen husbands or partners cry more than the afflicted women, and I have seen them grow under the impact of this new reality. Here, as in so many other instances, defeat—or potential defeat—is the stimulant that brings out the best or the worst in us. Faced with this calamity, we find out who we truly are. Cancer never leaves us indifferent.

I also know that there are men who turn away from their spouses or partners when they are stricken with breast cancer. These men are either afraid of being reminded of their own mortality or don't want to invest any more of themselves in a relationship that now requires extra caring and supporting, never mind loving. Others simply don't want "damaged goods." I wonder whether a relationship that is so negatively influenced by a mastectomy was a deep and stable relationship to begin with. But, then, it is distressing to see that many women, too, gauge themselves with the value-assessing eyes of a male-dominated culture and, after a mastectomy, feel less like a woman. For them, cancer delivers a double blow.

One of the immediate positive side effects of my cancer was that the treatments kept me in Washington. No more commuting! What a bonus! I was lucky. I did not have to go to work, and could give in to being ill with total abandon. I have met women who continued to work while they underwent chemotherapy, to which they subjected themselves during extended lunch hours. Some of them needed the money, others did not want their bosses and co-workers to know they had cancer, fearing they would be treated as if they were already dead, might conceivably lose their jobs, would certainly be overlooked when the time came for promotions. In her eye-opening essay *Illness as Metaphor*, Susan Sontag militates poignantly against the metaphoric and distorting uses we make of the disease, confounding the fears and "mythologies" we have spun out of it with the disease itself. As in so many other respects, the "victims" of an illness also fall victim to the superstitions that have been built around the illness.

Secretiveness about cancer even when there are no work-related threats is almost universal. On one level, there is probably magical thinking at work: if you do not talk about something, it doesn't exist. On another level, there is a stigma associated with cancer: you are an outcast, singled out to die. If you don't mention it, nobody will know the threat under which you labor, and people will treat you the way you want to be treated, as a "normal" human being. I also found that many people, particularly those not afflicted, do not want to talk about your illness because they do not know what attitude to adopt. Clearly, they see you as already half dead and don't know whether to give you their condolences and sympathy, or to be cheerful and pretend they know nothing, or to be cheerful and assure you that you have nothing to worry about. Yet they betray themselves by their slightly dishonest voices. If the afflicted person speaks first, they will take their cue from that person's tone and then commiserate, encourage, repress, deny, or say whatever they sense is appropriate. Only the truly intimate friends dare to speak from the heart. It may sound paradoxical, but it is the afflicted person who must offer them the chance to extend themselves beyond their embarrassment and fear, into the realm of compassion and humanity, where we should all nestle.

In our family, communication took many forms. With Bill, there was little need to elaborate, since, on the deepest level, it was "our" situation and we both knew we were in it together. As so often, he showed his concern in nonverbal ways. One day he arrived home with a gigantic carrot-juicer. From then on, we all had to drink huge quantities of carrot juice every day, since beta-carotene, derived from carrots, might help fight cancer. (It was good for all of us to drink so much carrot juice, but it had to be cut with juiced apples to make it palatable.)

With my daughters, things were different. My older daughter, by now in her early thirties, was newly married, and my younger daughter was a sophomore in high school, when they both had to accept the fact that their mother was mortal. Stephanie tried to comfort me, enumerated over and over the cases of people she knew who had survived cancer, and in comforting me comforted herself. Theresa Anne witnessed the effects of chemotherapy on a day-by-day basis. She took refuge in the assurance that I did not really look sick, in the sense that I was not unable to get dressed or to walk, and that I did not have to lie in bed, all bandaged up or with tubes sticking out of various parts of my body. Yes, I lost my hair, that was expected, but my appearance was not threatening and my nausea did not show. I wanted both of them to see that I was "OK," that my inner strength kept growing, and that the foundation of this strength was love. With Stephanie, away in New Jersey, I talked on the phone. With Theresa Anne, I acted out my strength and confidence, using Bill as my model. I did not use words to convince her that I was fine: I simply attended her school and sports events.

My mother offered to come from Germany to be with me. I did not want her to come; I was afraid that her anxieties would over-whelm me. After all, she had been with my father during his year of excruciating agonies, and she knew what it meant to die from cancer. I promised her that we would celebrate together once the "ordeal" (no more than that!) was over. If my condition deterio-rated, there was always time for her to come. She seemed con-soled by my good spirits and, I sensed, relieved that she did not have to witness my illness as she had my father's.

As I became more acquainted with the various aspects of life as a cancer patient, I began wanting to speak out publicly on the disease, and Bill's position as a public official offered me many forums. Keeping silent would have been, for me, tantamount to betraying this life-transforming experience; I needed to speak out on a calamity that touched so many lives, and I hoped that sharing could provide consolation and help. Whether one is afflicted with cancer or trying to relate to someone stricken with it, the situation is always so new, so without precedent, that it is difficult to find the right tone of voice, even the right body language. When I went to my fifth chemotherapy session, I was so near the end of my strength that I started to cry even before the nurse inserted the needle. She suggested that I see a counselor, someone who would help me. Help me with what? Help me not to cry? But crying was natural under the circumstances, and I was glad not to be repressing the grief I felt. Perhaps I wanted someone simply to understand that I had to cry and to assure me it was natural. Did my crying disturb her? I knew she could not afford to become invested in her patients, since she had a very tough and demanding job. (What if the needle had touched the walls of the vein and the chemo cocktail burned them?) And I knew she meant well, even though I felt she wanted me "off her hands," wanted me to function according to impersonal standards.

In time, I discovered the many support groups that want to break the silence surrounding cancer, to destigmatize and humanize a disease from which none of us may be exempt. But it was not just speaking out that mattered, although that mattered a great deal. The hugging, crying, laughing together mattered even more. When partners embraced in tears yet laughed through their tears, when mothers and daughters huddled with their children or grandchildren and made each moment special, when granddaughters drove their grandmothers to chemotherapy or grandmothers drove their granddaughters, the emotions poured out without fear or constraint. It was and is all right to show the people you love, on either side of the disease's great divide, how much you care for them, that you suffer with them and for them but also on your own. And when you meet strangers laboring under the same calamity, it is all right to hug them and comfort them and share your own experiences and emotions and thoughts.

If my body and I were going to cooperate, we had to contemplate the worst together—death. It did not help to tell myself that eventually we all must die. We always think that we are not ready to die yet, that there is still much more living that needs to be done. Under normal circumstances, death is mercifully shrouded in haze and inattention. But cancer or any other life-threatening illness tears away the veil of a self-serving postponement and confronts us directly with the thought of our final day. I wanted to be clear-eyed about death; I wanted to think about it; I did not want to die in fear of dying and deprive myself of the dignity that can come only from accepting and transforming a mindless disease into a personal journey.

I was scared of dying. I was scared of the incredible, intolerable pain that is in store for so many of us and that I had seen in the tormented dying of my father. But I was also scared of death. I did not want to look at death as the black hole that extinguishes all of us, our bodies, our minds, our energies, our everything. I wanted—and still want—death to fulfill the promise all of us invest in a life fully lived, a life that assures our survival in our children, in the work we have created and leave behind, in the memories others keep of us. I wanted to, and did, focus on the wonderful life I had had, on the good luck and the many miracles that had brought me to where I was. I worked on having the strength and single-mindedness to be full of gratitude for the riches, for the love and caring that life had bestowed on me.

I saw that, even if I should die, I had been given a chance to get ready for death. I could show those dearest to me how much I loved them; I could accept their outpourings of love with gratitude, not be afraid of their fears, and in consoling them console myself. If my time had come, I wanted to die in peace and be assured in the knowledge that those left behind would also be in peace. I wanted no one to feel remorse over missed opportunities to show the love we all had for each other. My father and I had held hands the last time I saw him, before he died. That was not much, and yet it was sufficient. If this was my time to go, I wanted my family to remember that I had had a full life, and draw comfort from that.

But I also knew that I was privileged, even as I visualized my dying. How many women are the mainstays of their households and have no certainty that they can rely on other members in their family to take care of their children once they are gone? At a support-group meeting, I once met a single mother who had no other relatives at all; as she was dying, she tried to find loving foster parents for her two small children and prepare them for a life without her. I cannot imagine the agony of such a dying.

Another one of the gifts cancer bestowed on me was new friendships. Our neighbors in Cleveland Park had been casual friends: we had said "Hello" to each other and "How are you?" and "How are your children (parents, dogs, cats, flowers) doing?" Now intimate friendships sprang up. One such new friend and I developed a Wednesday late-afternoon ritual of going to the Goethe Institute to see films from the former German Democratic Republic. We would walk and take the subway (no taxis for us!) to show that life went on as usual, that I was not an invalid, and we looked forward to our discussions along the way about what we had seen, how the old communist part of Germany saw itself, what the problems of integrating the two parts of Germany might turn out to be. Life "out there" did not stop because my life was on hold, because I had cancer.

I also found the way my friends cared for me typically American. Our family was consistently provided with elaborate dishes, often with entire meals, so I would not have to cook, particularly when I was nauseated and dizzy from chemo. Friends came from as far away as New York just to see how I was doing, and again they brought food, and news, and said, in one way or another, "Get well, we need you, we have all these projects, and you are indispensable to them and to us." It is not surprising to me that some people put on weight during chemotherapy. The desire to provide the body with additional resources, to make it stronger and more resilient when it ails, is universal, and recourse to the proverbial chicken soup is its most popular expression. I associate this elaborate culinary generosity in times of need with the American frontier, when offering food to a neighbor was a thoughtful and even necessary gesture in a shared and potentially hostile environment. It is part of the image and the myth of America as a land of plenty that food is so often and so freely given away. I had been a recipient of that generosity in the early postwar years, when the United States sponsored a huge school-lunch program in Germany, the *Quaker-Speisung*. We heard that in some American families the wives went to work for extra income so the family could send CARE packages to starving Germans.

For mastectomy patients, there is an initial and far-reaching question even before the removal of your breast. The question is: do you want breast reconstruction or not? Before cancer, I had never had a sick day in my life. I was scared enough of having my breast removed; I certainly did not want another operation in addition to the mastectomy. Furthermore, the surgery for reconstruction sounded even more formidable than the mastectomy itself. A silicone implant? Injecting solutions into the breast before surgery, so that the skin around the breast could stretch? Skin to be grafted from other parts of the body to replace the lost breast skin? I was incapable of focusing on a decision, since I was totally concerned with how far the cancer had spread, whether all of the cancerous tissue could be removed, how many lymph nodes would be involved; and Bill saw no reason to urge such a decision on me. As a palliative for my rising panic, I was told that I could have reconstruction at a later time if I chose. This gave me an easy way out. I chose that option, although I knew I would never avail myself of it. I now wear a prosthesis. It is a good thing. Every day, as I dress, I am reminded of the fragility of life and stay away from the danger of taking anything for granted.

Whenever I felt sad about my mastectomy, particularly in the early years after the surgery, I had to remember that breasts are external parts of the body, not essential for a fully functioning life, not even a fulfilled sexual life. They were needed before the advent of baby food and have outlived their biological necessity. The market has co-opted breasts as aesthetic objects, as luxury items, and has developed an extremely lucrative business with them, forever enhancing their display value. At least a mastectomy is not invasive in the way an operation for lung cancer is, or for a stomach ulcer, or a heart transplant. Losing a breast is not so great an inconvenience as losing an arm or a foot. I am lucky. For a while, I began to identify so strongly with my scar that I wanted to find a topless beach and go there—though I knew that ultimately I would not have the courage to pull off such a revolutionary gesture. . . . I still think I ought to!

Scars. Physical, emotional, psychological scars. Is there anyone among us who does not carry scars? All scars are in one way or another visible; some take a bit longer than others to see. Scars (as opposed to open wounds) are a sign of triumph, not of defeat. When those of us who have gone through cancer laugh and cry more easily, this is not a sign of emotional distress, but of emotional liberation. We have learned that the fullness of life encompasses sorrow and joy both, distress as well as peace, and that out of defeat comes triumph.

But scars can be threatening. They display the threat of what has been overcome, and remind others of their own fragility. If I walked on a topless beach, would people admire my courage or resent the threat implicit in my scar? During the summer months in the early postwar years, we children would go swimming at the municipal outdoor swimming pool in Ingolstadt. On certain days of the week, we had to get out of the pool at 6:00 p.m. That was when the crippled and mutilated war veterans were allowed to swim there. Was the *Bademeister* afraid that the general population might be traumatized by the wiggling stumps of arms or legs as they tried to keep bodies afloat, by the enormous scars crisscrossing their bodies, by faces that were no longer faces but smooth masks with openings for seeing, breathing, introducing food? Fascinated and scared in equal parts, we would watch them from a distance as they splashed in the water, until the *Bademeister* chased us away. I still admire the courage of those mutilated men, although I don't think I was ever able to fathom the depth of their humiliation.

Fashion designers are starting to realize that we are a sizable market, and they, as well as some alert department-store buyers, have begun to make concessions to us. There are summer dresses with high-cut armholes; bathing suits with pockets in which to insert a prosthesis; necklines that descend close to but never below the confines of a well-supporting bra. It has taken me many years to find the right kind of bra, and only in the last few years have I dared to wear dresses and suit jackets that show some cleavage.

Not so long ago, I went shopping for a suit and found one I liked, except that the jacket buttons started below my critical cleavage point. Should I have a hidden hook placed a little above the buttons to disguise the onset of my scar? Should I wear a camisole that would distract from the beautiful line of the jacket? Should I have a bra with lace across the cleavage part? The real gift was the woman who sold me the suit. I explained to her why I could not wear the jacket without some sort of covering. What a relief to mention my mastectomy not as a trauma but simply as something that needed to be considered when I bought a suit! As I tried on the jacket one more time, she told me that she, too, had had cancer and had opted for reconstruction. The outline of her breasts looked so natural that I was amazed. She asked whether I wanted to see her reconstruction. Of course I wanted to! So here we were, two women who a few minutes before were complete strangers, standing together in the dressing room of a department store showing our bare breasts to each other. I was tremendously impressed with the beautiful result of the reconstruction, after the sheer tortures she had subjected herself to. We both started to cry, for no apparent reason, except that we were bonded by the knowledge of what it meant to us to be alive.

(These individual encounters personalize larger events. One of the happiest big events in which I participated showed concretely the strength and vitality of women who had gone through cancer. The event was a fund-raiser for a cancer support group and took place in a big gym. For each year after the conclusion of her treatments, each woman made a loop of colorful construction paper. Then the women interlocked and glued all the loops together into the longest chain I ever saw! Multicolored, joyful, this chain of life waved around the gym, upheld and swirled by dancing women, some of whom had tears rolling down their cheeks.)

During chemotherapy, there were other fashion decisions to be made. What to do as you lose all your hair? I know women who shaved their hair off, right at the beginning of chemo, so that they did not have to cope with the gradual loss. I went the slow way. Every time I took a shower, I tugged at my hair and it would come out, easily and in fistfuls. What was I going to do about being bald? I was surprised to find how cold it is "up there" without hair. How do bald men manage? Ever since I lost my hair, I look at them with some curiosity, especially in winter. Some women prefer to wear wigs, others wear baseball caps. Bill went with me to buy two wigs. We went to several stores specializing in them. I was tense, nervous, and constantly on the verge of tears, which I tried to cover up with an uncalled-for impatience. I wanted to get out of the store as quickly as possible. Bill tried to be supportive, and as I looked into the mirror, horrified to see a totally strange face staring back at me, he would suggest that I looked "interesting." We came home without having bought a wig. I could not accept that strange face that was supposed to be me. Then I tried some exotic fabrics for turbans, which Monika had sent me, but I could not deal with them. The strips of fabric were very long, and winding them around my head required too much patience. In fact, and particularly during the early phases of chemo, I did not want to be confronted with my baldness. It made me sad, and then I tried to cover the sadness by pretending to be frustrated, and it was all the turban's fault! Eventually I settled on scarves, big attractive silk scarves for every occasion. They were not so difficult to tie as turbans, I could recognized myself in them, and they were colorful. I began to like the fact that a "new look" had been forced on me, and started to experiment. I became free enough to wear clothes I would not ordinarily have worn. They might have been perfectly normal on others, but I had always felt too conservative to flaunt, for example, wide-brimmed hats. Now I would wrap a feather boa around my neck and let one end dangle down in front, the other down my back. I found skirts of delicate fabric cascading to the floor, and heavily embroidered jackets; I wore costume jewelry galore, earrings jingling from under my scarf. I was not trying to dress up like a Gypsy. I just used the freedom cancer gave me to explore aspects of my personality I had thus far repressed.

Sometimes I have had second thoughts about the inconvenience of the prosthesis. Sometimes, in my more frivolous moods, I wonder whether I should have a second mastectomy, pretending I want it for prophylactic reasons. It is inconvenient to have only one breast; to be flat-chested seems simpler. I have spoken with women who needed double mastectomies, frequently because of a high risk of recurrence or genetic predisposition. But to have a mastectomy out of "convenience"? Mostly we laugh about it, with tears in our eyes. Once, in a magazine, I saw the photograph of a Swiss woman who had undergone a double mastectomy. She had beautiful flowers tattooed over her scars. I was enchanted by this idea, infinitely preferring those delicate flowers to the Gothic lettering and snakes and dragons that men adorn their bodies with.

The arrangement of the seat belts in cars is another daily reminder of the inconvenience of a prosthesis. The seat belt cuts right across it. I am not complaining; I made my choice. But sometimes I wonder whether, if one had a completely flat chest and did not have to worry about having the prosthesis squashed or pushed out of place, car travel would be somewhat easier. When I sit in the passenger seat, I often pull my right knee up and place it between my chest and the seat belt. I have been told that this renders the seat belt useless, but what are the acceptable alternatives? By now, pulling my right knee up has become an automatic gesture.

I have been granted the extraordinarily good luck of living beyond cancer. It is in this spirit that I refuse to use the word "survivor," as in "breast-cancer survivor." Perhaps because of my German background, the word "survivor" has been pre-empted for me by its most singular use, in the phrase "Holocaust survivor." I have seen photographs of cancer "survivors" made to look like the inmates of camps. True, they have no hair, but they are not starving skeletons, and they do not have the staring, far-away look of the inmates, who have seen what no human being should ever have to see. Cancer is a dreadful disease, but even the threat of death, or death itself, does not compare to the horror of the camps. The sufferings of cancer are human sufferings, and even the most horrendous treatments are still in the service of life, whereas the camps erased all vestiges of humanity and death for all was the supreme goal. Going through cancer has changed my life in the most profound and unexpected ways, all of them positive, enriching, loving. You cannot say that if you have survived a concentration camp. I like to think, not that I "survived" cancer, but that I was allowed to triumph over it.

In 1996, Bill decided not to seek re-election for a fourth term in the U.S. Senate. Over the next few years, he had professorships and associations in various parts of the country—at Stanford, at Notre Dame, at the University of Maryland—he wrote a book about values in basketball, did TV commentaries on America, traveled widely to give speeches, and continued to think about issues such as the economy, health care, and America's role in the world. This was a period in which he took counsel with himself and searched his soul as to whether he was prepared to run for the most important office not only in this country but in the world. Our daughter had graduated from high school and was in college, a young adult on her own way. I was again teaching at Montclair State, standing by for whatever decision he might make.

Once the campaign started, I, too, was traveling the country—with a wonderful assistant, Anna Ponder, who kept my sense of humor alive when flight schedules did not work out, when a stalker made me furious, when the press did not report an event the way I felt it had taken place. On occasion Anna would become angry (for example, when we were bumped off a plane because the seats had been overbooked), and I made a discovery: I did not have to become angry if someone else did it for me. I could be the one consoling, laughing, showing an unaccustomed patience. Perhaps, if Bill had been more explosive during our tough years in Washington, I could have relaxed more. I had apparently been in need of my parents' tantrums, which had always told me that after the storm everything would be all right. Anna and I developed a habit that we practice to this day whenever we see each other: When we were stuck in an airport, we repaired to the bar for a margarita.

I loved speaking to groups of people, speaking to reporters. For me, the art of teaching consists in communicating to people with clarity and conciseness. I had been a teacher all my adult life, and now my forum was as big as the country itself. Bill's campaign staff provided me with briefings of his position on issues—but for me, these briefings could never be brief enough. I was not interested in becoming a quick expert on issues Bill had studied for eighteen years and longer. I was not the politician—Bill was. Nor did I see my role as that of a surrogate speaker. I had a mission that only I could accomplish: I was and wanted to be the wife who could speak with deep conviction about the best candidate this country had to offer, her husband. Often, when Bill had told me about votes in the Senate, I had admired his ability to conceptualize issues in new and far-ranging ways, to have a vision for the future of our country that was broad-minded, fair, and generous, and to get things done—not flamboyantly, not by courting the limelight, but by working behind the scenes with quiet persistence. This I could explain to my listeners. I did not have to criticize what was wrong with our political establishment (although I did that, too, as often as I had a chance), but I could focus on what was good about America, our restless democracy, forever in need of reinterpretation, an unending experiment that demanded openness and flexibility even as it guaranteed frustration and constant combativeness.

I campaigned on the idea—culled from Bill's speeches—that we should lead the world by the power of our example. That left plenty of room for self-criticism, which is one of our democracy's strong points: it opened the door to talking about how much more work needed to be done on issues that touch people's lives, such as jobs, health care, education, the environment, immigration (an issue of personal import for me). Being part of the campaign was a wonderful way for me to pay this country back for its open-armed generosity.

Bill made one crucial mistake in planning the campaign. He thought he could bring enough new people, often idealistic or disenchanted, into the primaries to allow him to win. But the primary was dominated by hard-knuckled party politics. Since his opponent was a sitting vice-president who had the full resources of the White House at his disposal, everyone from the Democratic National Committee to organized labor sided with Bill's opponent. Bill had hoped that his vision for the future, his grasp of the problems and how to solve them, his record, his accomplishments, his life would persuade voters that he was the best candidate. The political establishment and the Democratic interest groups that stood to gain favors from the existing White House refused to risk supporting someone who had nothing to offer them but his ideas and ability. And so they nominated someone who couldn't appeal to a broad enough electorate to win the general election. Although Bill had the considered promise of some organizations that they would support him, when it was time to stand up and be counted they went with his opponent.

This was brought home to me with devastating clarity when NARAL (the National Abortion and Reproductive Rights Action League) invited the wives of both candidates to speak at a fund-raising dinner in Washington. It was understood that NARAL would then endorse the candidate with the best approval rating for their interests. Bill had a lifetime approval rating of 95 percent, the vice-president 66 percent. NARAL endorsed the vice-president.

I think back to the campaign for the presidential nomination with great fondness and still savor its excitement. There was never a question of being too exhausted to keep going; the adrenaline supplied ever new bursts of energy. Not being the candidate, I had it easy: Anna watched with iron determination over a schedule that only in exceptional cases (like being with Bill during his debates) broke the rule of twelve hours on, twelve hours off.

When the campaign was over, I walked away with a profound and
enduring respect for many of the people I had met on the trail. I
had witnessed, had been part of, democracy at work. The fund-
raisers for Bill were impressive, but so was the grassroots movement of moms in neighborhoods, of workingmen taking time out
from their schedules to help Bill organize in various parts of the
country, of entire families canvassing districts, of people using
their vacation time to help set up offices wherever needed, of
young idealists organizing on campuses, of senior citizens who
opened their homes, inviting neighbors and strangers alike in to
hear what Bill had to say, and who housed and fed exhausted campaign workers and labeled and mailed tons of letters. I was again
and again overcome by the generosity of people all over the
country, by their willingness to make personal sacrifices to support their candidate, by their faith and active participation in the
democratic process, by their pride and commitment to the best
political system in the world. Despite the daily hassles and con-
tretemps—in St. Louis, Bill's chartered plane had to make an
emergency landing, with fire trucks and ambulances awaiting the
touchdown, because the plane was literally close to falling apart
in midair—the time of the campaign was glorious and deeply
stirring. Bill had always regarded it as a privilege to serve the people of New Jersey as their elected representative, while I, observing from close range the sacrifices and amount of work invested
in that privilege, had always thought that it was the people of
New Jersey who were privileged to have such a worthy representative. During the presidential campaign, I came to accept his
point of view: it is a tremendous and unique privilege to offer
one's services to one's country. Even if the campaign did not end
in victory, for me it was a triumph. Bill's presence had raised the
level of discourse, highlighted issues, brought people into the
political process. There are many young people now who will not
desist in their efforts to make this country a better place, and who

understand that our democracy, as sturdy as it appears to be, is a fragile system forever in need of being tended. Bill could walk away from the campaign with his head held high, even if for years a sadness filled his spirit. He had given his best and set an example of an idealistic, dedicated contribution to our working democracy. Even in losing, he was not defeated.

Before Bill's presidential campaign started, my mother had a severe stroke and then a series of mini-strokes. For a while, my brother organized nursing care at her house, but eventually she had to move into a nursing home outside of Ingolstadt, in the Donautal, under constant care. It was during this time, and while the campaign was going full-force, that the Passau town archivist found it important to improve on the information I had given the press about my family background. After our campaign was over, in the spring of 2000, while I was visiting my mother in her nursing home, I asked her where my adoption papers were. I still see her sitting in bed, looking like one of those overweight women in a Botero painting, her white hair surrounding like a halo her pink, smooth-skinned face. She flicked both her wrists in an offhand manner, laughed, and said, "Vati and I tore them up, threw them away. We know you are our child. We did not need papers to tell us that." I should have been suspicious, but at that moment I was her child and I trusted her. I remember how impressed and tickled I was at the way she flicked her wrists, totally alert (which now she often wasn't), throwing her head back on the pillows, laughing. This impression changed to seething anger, mixed with grudging admiration, when I found out that at the moment of the flick of her wrists she had lied to me, had lied to perfection, had handed me her last and ultimate betrayal, and I had fallen for it.

In July 2000, a friendly colleague of the Passau archivist who had never responded to my inquiries sent the papers Bill and I could not obtain during our visit over the feast of Corpus Christi. I looked at them perfunctorily. They recorded the date of my birth, the dates when my mother was married and then divorced from Baumeister Max, the date of her marriage to my father, even the date when I started first grade in Ulm with my Tante Emma, address included. Several of the papers also contained references to the effect that, "according to the determination of the government of Upper Bavaria in Munich on January 10, 1955, and due to a change of name on January 4, 1955, she now bears the family name 'Misslbeck.' " In January 1955, I had been all of nineteen years old, and a Misslbeck for years! I was stunned and chose not to think about it any further. I put the papers aside as if they were of no concern to me.

My mother's condition deteriorated markedly after Bill dropped out of the presidential race. Without a campaign schedule to follow, I was free to see her frequently. Every time I went to the nursing home during the summer and fall of 2000, I asked the nurses to lift her into a wheelchair so we could go on long walks across the open country, see the hops being harvested and the wheat brought in (*eingebracht*, as they say in Bavaria). When my mother fought the nurses who tried to get her ready for our outings, I became angry. "Fresh air is good for you! You cannot simply let go! You have an obligation to stay in good condition." I did not say, "Stay alive for us," because I knew that was no longer an argument that would mean anything to her. In this last period of her life, she wanted nothing anymore but to be with her Bebs. She was ready to go, whether we were ready for that or not. Monika spoke to me more openly than did my brother, but both thought I was in denial about her true condition. I did not want to realize that my mother was too ill to be lifted and dressed and wrapped in blankets and pushed down bumpy country roads.

She had disappointed me after my father's death, by not making good on the opportunity to take adult-education courses and catch up on the education she had always, as she insisted so often, missed. She had said she was too tired. And perhaps she was. As she aged, the circumference of her life and of her interests shrank. When my father was still alive and travel had again become possible for Germans, they had traveled in Europe and come to see us in America. But these were family visits; my parents never traveled anywhere else in this country. Likewise, when I went to Ingolstadt, I rarely had a chance to go anywhere else; this means that, outside of Bavaria, I do not know Germany very well. After my father's death, my mother did go on trips with her women friends from the *Kaffeekranzl*, mostly to Italy. As one after another of them became too ill to travel, Ingolstadt became the exclusive focus of her life. She volunteered at an orphanage for a number of years, but in Germany volunteerism is not appreciated, and the social workers did not want her to "meddle." She went for walks within an ever-diminishing circumference; then it was only her house and her garden; finally, only her bed, and outings in a wheelchair.

But even now, as I pushed her over roads built two millennia before by the Romans, I wanted to look up to her, see her as a role model, be justified in the outrage I had felt as a teenager when she talked about the education she had so craved and been denied. I was judging her now by my standards, and I judged her harshly. It did not help to tell myself, over and over, that she was living out her own mother's life, a life of withdrawal and resignation to which she was, in my opinion, not entitled.

Sometime in late fall of 2000, while Bill was on a trip, Monika came from New York to spend the night with me in New Jersey. After dinner we indulged in "family mythology." I pulled out the genealogical documents I had started to collect about our parents and grandparents, including the documents I had received from Passau. Only in Monika's presence did I finally have the courage to absorb what the text said, and Monika was there to comfort me in my crying and my rage. How could I, for months, not have focused on the wording of this document? How could I ignore the significance of "change of name" and not realize that it meant I had not been adopted at all? I was beside myself, no longer coherent. To think that my father had never adopted me! Perhaps I had waited for my sister to be with me when the blow struck, needed her as part of the family, so that she could assure me that I continued to be "one of them," that I belonged, even as I realized in a flash of lightning that legally I was not part of the Misslbecks. I groped for excuses. An adoption involves a lot of checkups and interviews. Perhaps my parents wanted to avoid such investigations or thought they were not necessary. They knew I was their natural daughter, and perhaps they assumed it was nobody's business how they dealt with helping me adjust to my new life. They must have had an arrangement with Baumeister Max; he had been more than noble to my mother in her turbulent life. Perhaps they had all agreed that once we moved to Ingolstadt there would be no further contact. Certainly Baumeister could not have had any interest in staying in touch with a child who was not his own. If it had not been for the town archivist, I would never have found out that I had not been adopted.

During that fall and into the winter of 2001, I was mostly out of my mind. Pain leads an independent life and is not accessible to reason. I could not sleep; I lost weight. I was agitated enough to think I wanted a DNA test done on my father's bones to prove that he was my father. Bill believed I should just "turn the page." It was not so much that my identity was at stake—I will never believe that I am not my father's daughter—as that my trust in the people dearest to me, and therefore in life as a whole, was once again shattered. Some of my friends tried to reason with me. Clearly, it made sense that even a biological father cannot adopt his own child if, in effect, there is a legal father—in my case Baumeister—and perhaps he, like my parents, preferred not to get involved in legal procedures and trusted the strength of their mutual self-interest. Their agreement held for fifty-five years, from the time we left Passau in 1945 until Bill's presidential bid.

In the course of further inquiries, I found out that, in Germany, in second marriages the last names of children from first marriages are frequently changed so as to avoid "undue psychological hardship" on the children, who would otherwise not feel part of the new family. Was that the scenario my parents had arranged for me instead of adoption?

I have since wondered whether the town archivist wanted credit for having exposed an American presidential candidate's wife as a liar. Was he suggesting that I had tried to hide the fact that my "father," the "hairdresser," was a Nazi, and the air-force officer was not? I decided that I needed to know about Baumeister's possible party affiliation, even though it was now long after the end of the campaign, when it no longer mattered from a political point of view. Upon my request, the Bundesarchiv informed me that he had joined the Nazi Party in 1937 but was never actively engaged in any party business. A *Mitläufer* (fellow traveler).

At the beginning of the campaign, before the archivist intervened, I had talked with my mother about my mottled birth and had mentioned that the press might well ask her about me. How would she deal with that possibility? Would she tell them her life story and explain why she had to enter into that first marriage? Again I see her sitting in bed, flicking her wrists in her typical manner. Again she laughed. "Oh, I will just tell them that you were my love child," she said. I was stunned and hurt, and could not believe how flippantly she dismissed the trauma she had inflicted on me when I was a child and she had demanded that I not tell anybody about my true identity. I had labored under that burden and the emotional consequences of that enforced secrecy throughout my childhood and adolescence. And now I learned that my father had not even adopted me!

I wrote to the government of Upper Bavaria's Division of Name Changes to find out the reasons my mother had given them when she had my name changed. (I assume my father could not request the change, since he was "only" my mother's husband and had no legal rights over me.) An official responded courteously and promptly, saying that the documents had long ago been forwarded to Ingolstadt. In Ingolstadt, I had enough leisure to visit every official in every pertinent government branch that had to do with name changes and adoptions. Since I had been known in Ingolstadt as a Misslbeck the whole time I lived there, some people must have been surprised at the inquiry, but they were professional enough not to show it. Ultimately, I was informed that documents of this nature were not kept beyond a certain number of years, and that my request had come too late. There were no longer any documents to do with me.

But I could not let go. If I could no longer examine the name-changing documents, I could take issue with the archivist's meddling. And so I wrote, shortly before my mother died, to the Data Protection Agency in Munich to find out whether the archivist had had a right to post this personal information on the Internet. I also wanted to confront my mother and ask her why she had lied to me when she said the adoption papers had been torn up, whereas in truth there were no adoption papers. She was failing rapidly now. Could I, should I, bring this battle to her deathbed? Now she was lying in bed, her heavy body immobile, her blood flowing thick and slow through her veins (as I imagined it), semi-comatose or in a state of constant drugged sleepiness; there was her howling, bellowing, barking, stuttering voice, but no speech. Should I have persisted, waited for a lucid moment? I did not, and to this day I think I made the right decision. Next to her dying, my question was trivial. The papers were the facts, undeniable, the motives always subject to manipulative, exonerating explanations; the "truth" was inaccessible. This was the time to "turn the page," as Bill had said. I needed to let go, find peace with my mother and with my past, and do that while she was still alive. I needed to let her go in peace.

My last two visits with my mother were particularly sad—full of a lifetime of love that was so often inadequately expressed and had been bent in so many different directions. Monika and I took turns flying in from the United States to be with her, and of course my brother was in Ingolstadt anyway. I saw her between Thanksgiving and Christmas of 2000, and then for almost two weeks from the end of January to early February 2001. I was not with her when she died, on Valentine's Day.

Farewells are always emotional. They bring all our love and our regrets, our joyful moments together and our missed opportunities, into such clear focus, into an unbearable brightness. I remember, as I left in December, it tore my heart apart when she cried as we said goodbye. I cried, too, and promised to be back within a few weeks; I tried to console her by saying that, with me gone, she would have Monika and Seppi all to herself. And then, at my suggestion, she wrote a birthday card to Theresa Anne. She could hardly hold the pen but was concerned about her handwriting, upset that the lines were not completely straight, and she wrote much more than I had expected or hoped for. Her fingers were so stiff that it took her the entire afternoon to write the card, but she was pleased with the result. I could bear it when she was judgmental, opinionated; I had developed defense mechanisms to deal with that. But I fell apart when I saw the loving and giving side of her. I had blocked her giving so often, because I always felt that it was a kind of devouring. Now she no longer wanted to possess, to rule; she simply wanted to write the nicest birthday card she could, to her granddaughter, to the next generation. To be remembered by. I went into the bathroom and cried tears I had held back for I don't know how long.

My mother was eighty-five when she died. I had not expected that her death, which in its finality closed all doors for further questions, would also set me free. I had to accept the facts, make them my own, make them part of my life story. I needed no DNA tests to affirm who I was then, or who I am now. I am who I am, and what I made of what I was handed defines me more clearly than any test.

For a long time after my mother's death, I was overcome with a kind of grief I had not known before. Nor had I anticipated that her absence would be such a constant and overwhelming presence. Amazing also that I am not angry at her anymore. How could a lifelong grievance vanish so quickly and so undramatically?

In early 2001, I received an answer from the Data Protection Agency in Munich. A *Ministerialrat* (this is the title of a high-ranking civil servant) informed me that it would take some time to investigate whether my right to privacy had been violated; he would get back to me *unaufgefordert* (the German equivalent of "Don't call us, we'll call you").

My brother telephoned during this time to tell me that the Passau town archivist had asked him to speak with a reporter who had interviewed the archivist and now wanted a contact with the family in Ingolstadt. What aggrandizing role was this archivist envisioning for himself?! At the same time, there was a leak to the German press that I had contacted the Data Protection Agency. The press (*Die Süddeutsche Zeitung, Die Welt, AZ, Bild-Zeitung*) agreed with the town archivist that I had tried to "upgrade" my father and had invented a more prominent one. Where did that leak come from? The Data Protection Agency wrote to me and apologized, saying that they could not find out where the leak had originated, but since only the "town of Passau" had knowledge of my request, they assumed that somebody in the town administration was behind it. In May, the DPA informed me that indeed my rights to privacy had been violated when the information was posted on the Internet, and that a censure was in order. However, since the archivist had acted as an employee of the town of Passau and not as a private person, it was the town of Passau that was censured, not the archivist. This result was not much of a triumph, but it was more than a defeat.

In subsequent months, Monika and I went back to Germany repeatedly to settle my mother's estate. We were very much in agreement on everything. Both of us were surprised and impressed with how orderly *Mutti*'s affairs were, how neatly and carefully she had filed her bills, her taxes, her memos, and preserved our letters and photographs. I brought a lot of them home with me, to start comprehensive albums for my daughters. Many of the photographs are dated and inscribed on the back in my mother's handwriting, and I cried over personal, trivial comments like "Don't I have the best-looking husband?" or "What a happy family we are!" because I could hear the timbre of her voice as she said the words, laughing and proud. The pain of going through all her belongings was part of taking leave from her. My mother loved beautiful things, and over the years I had given her a number of exquisite handbags. These I would now bring back for myself. And I cried again when I discovered, in the mirror compartment of each of them, tiny photographs, carefully shielded in protective, see-through plastic covers, of my father and herself. All these years, she had carried her husband with her wherever she went. She had never shown us these photos or mentioned where she kept them; they were too private even for her children to know about.

Monika and I were aware that once the house sold (as it did, quickly) we would no longer have a home in Germany. I don't particularly miss the house itself—I am sad because there is no longer a place I can go back to and put my legs up and feel at home. The bathrooms in that house were too small, my bedroom was in the basement, and the washing machine a cumbersome monster, but it was a place where I could fix myself a cup of coffee or anything else I wanted without having to ask for it or waiting to be served because I am a guest. There is no longer a house in Ingolstadt where I feel as naturally at ease when I walk through the door as I do here, when I walk into my own home. I may never have had roots there, but now even the umbilical cord was cut. Only in remembrance can I now, stubborn and blind, push my mother in a wheelchair across bumpy country lanes and feel my father's fleshy hand, dry and warm, in mine.

When I think of Germany, certainly, the *Schrebergarten* are still there, and there may be young children sitting in apple trees reading, or invited by their grandfathers to have a glass of Malaga. But for me, there will never again be such an apple tree anywhere in the world, nor my grandfather with his rabbits and chicken and flowers and vegetable garden. Even if I stood in front of the apple tree, I could go back there no more than I can go back to the beer gardens as a way of summer life, although beer gardens exist aplenty. When I go to Germany, there is a long-bred familiarity. I still fit in. But fitting in is not the same as belonging, as being rooted there. I want to believe that I am rooted in my family, in my American family.

In April 2003, I celebrated the tenth anniversary of my final release from cancer treatments. It was a day of great jubilation, but even more so of enormous gratitude. Only now do I understand the most important message of all: defeat is never permanent, nor triumph everlasting. Only memory seals these moments in unending glory.

A NOTE ON THE TYPE

This book was set in Fournier, a typeface named for Pierre Simon Fournier *fils* (1712–1768), a celebrated French type designer. He was the author of the important *Manuel typographique* (1764–1766), in which he attempted to work out a system standardizing type measurement in points, a system that is still in use internationally.

Composed by North Market Street Graphics,
Lancaster, Pennsylvania
Printed by Berryville Graphics,
Berryville, Virginia
Map by Jeffrey L. Ward
Designed by M. Kristen Bearse